THE BEST OF family handyman®

Pierce
Pierce

THE BEST OF
family handyman®

by The Editors of *Family Handyman* magazine

Content Director Mark Hagen
Creative Director Raeann Thompson
Senior Editor Julie Kuczynski
Editor Sara Strauss
Associate Creative Director Kristen Stecklein
Senior Print Publication Designer Sanjeev Dhiman
Deputy Editor, Copy Desk Ann M. Walter
Copy Editor Rayan Naqash

A FAMILY HANDYMAN BOOK

1610 N. 2nd St., Suite 102
Milwaukee, WI 53212-3906

ISBNs
978-1-62145-955-2 (dated)
978-1-62145-956-9 (undated)

Component Numbers
118300118H (dated)
118300120H (undated)

We are committed to both the quality of our products and the service we provide to our customers. We value your comments, so please feel free to contact us at *TMBBookTeam@TrustedMediaBrands.com*.

For more *Family Handyman* products and information, visit our website: *www.familyhandyman.com*

Printed in China
10 9 8 7 6 5 4 3 2 1

Text, photography and illustrations for *The Best of Family Handyman 2024* are based on articles previously published in *Family Handyman* magazine (*familyhandyman.com*).

WARNING
All do-it-yourself activities involve a degree of risk. Skills, materials, tools and site conditions vary widely. Although the editors have made every effort to ensure accuracy, the reader remains responsible for the selection and use of tools, materials and methods. Always obey local codes and laws, follow manufacturer's operating instructions and observe safety precautions.

Photo Credits
p. 26, main: Anatoli Igolkin/Shutterstock; p. 27, main and 3 circles: LL Flooring; p. 28, FLOR (4); p. 29, main and top circle: LL Flooring; p. 29, bottom two circles: Mannington; p. 30, LL Flooring (4); p. 31, main and black circle: courtesy of Greatmats.com; p. 31, gray circle and brown square: We Sell Mats; p. 38-39, PM Images/Getty Images; p. 40, flooded basement: Helioscribe/Shutterstock; p. 40, phone: Issarawat Tattong/Getty Images; p. 41, wet rug: Catherine McQueen/Getty Images; p. 44, sump pump: Jason Kolenda/Shutterstock; p. 50, top: Abbie Miller; p. 50, bottom: courtesy of Jessie Cannizzaro; p. 51, top: GeorgePeters/Getty Images; p. 51, bottom: courtesy of Jessie Cannizzaro; p. 52, top left: Supersmario/Getty Images; p. 52, top right: A stockphoto/Getty Images; p. 52, bottom: courtesy of Jessie Cannizzaro; p. 53, top: IcemanJ/Getty Images; p. 53, monitor bundle: Moen; p. 53, Cannizzaro: courtesy of Jessie Cannizzaro; p. 60, isitsharp/Getty Images; p. 76, spoon pattern: Charlie Eiler; p. 126-128, all images: Ally Childress; p. 129, top: cmannphoto/Getty Images; p. 136, Gorica Poturak/Getty Images; p. 137, dog: Shutterstock/Pixel-Shot; p. 137, foil: Douglas Sacha/Getty Images; p. 137, lint roller: Camilla Svensk; p. 138, dryer: owngarden/Getty Images; p. 138, rug: Shutterstock/3dmitruk; p. 138, brush: image c/o Goodee; p. 138-139, dryer balls: Food52.com; p. 139, glove: JoKMedia/Getty Images; p. 139, humidifier: tashka2000/Getty Images; p. 152-153, JamesBrey/Getty Images; p. 154, top: Johnrob/Getty Images; p. 154, gray collar w/phone: SpotOn GPS Fence; p. 155, blue collar w/phone: via Amazon; p. 155, cat: Ivan Kukin/Getty Images; p. 155, dog w/pool: FOTOGRAFIA INC./Getty Images; p. 165, saws: photos courtesy of STIHL Inc.; p. 178, Westend61/Getty Images; p. 179, outlet: Thinkstock Images/Getty Images; p. 180, plants: Maureen P Sullivan/Getty Images; p. 180, water filter: Venus Angel/Shutterstock; p. 181, toilet: Sinisa Kukic/Getty Images; p. 182-183, blueprints w/tree: Guy45/Getty Images; p. 183, top left: DonNichols/Getty Images; p. 183, top right: michalPuchala/Getty Images; p. 183, MemBrain: via Amazon; p. 185, cedar decking w/saw: SimplyCreativePhotography/Getty Images; p. 188, background: Nomadsoul1/Getty Images; p. 223, main: Comstock/Getty Images; p. 224, weed preventer: The Espoma Company; p. 224, weed control: via Herbanatur .com; p. 225, top: groveb/Getty Images; p. 225, weed killer: via greengobbler.com; p. 231, All-America Selections/Pot-a-peno; p. 232, All-America Selections/Katarina; p. 233, NOVA PHOTO GRAPHIK; p. 234, yellow tomato: All-America Selections/Patio Choice; p. 234, red tomato: All-America Selections/Little Napoli Tomato; p. 235, eggplant: All-America Selections/Patio Baby; p. 235, peas: W. Atlee Burpee Company; p. 264, main: courtesy of Greenfiber; p. 264, cork: PeterHermesFurian/Getty Images; p. 264, sheep's wool: Havelock Wool; p. 264, denim: BanksPhotos/Getty Images; p. 265, cellulose: courtesy of Greenfiber; p. 266, bottom: BanksPhotos/Getty Images; p. 267, top: Havelock Wool; p. 267, cork rolls: VIKTOR FEDORENKO/Getty Images; p. 268, top: Oppdowngalon/Getty Images; p. 270, top: Fuse/Getty Images; all cartoon illustrations throughout book: Steve Björkman

SAFETY FIRST—ALWAYS!

Tackling home improvement projects and repairs can be endlessly rewarding. But as most of us know, with the rewards come risks. DIYers use chain saws, climb ladders and tear into walls that can contain big and hazardous surprises.

The good news is that armed with knowledge and the right tools and procedures, homeowners can minimize the risks. As you go about your projects and repairs, stay alert for these hazards:

Aluminum wiring

Aluminum wiring, installed in about 7 million homes between 1965 and 1973, requires special techniques and materials to make safe connections. This wiring is dull gray, not the dull orange characteristic of copper. Hire a licensed electrician certified to work with it. For more information, go to *cpsc.gov* and search for "aluminum wiring."

Spontaneous combustion

Rags saturated with oil-based paints and stains, or oil finishes like Danish and linseed oil, can spontaneously combust if left bunched up. Always dry them outdoors, spread out loosely. When the oil has thoroughly dried, you can safely throw them in the trash.

Vision and hearing risks

Safety glasses or goggles should be worn whenever you're working on DIY projects that involve chemicals, dust and anything that could shatter or chip off and hit your eyes. Sounds louder than 80 decibels (dB) are considered potentially dangerous. Sound levels from a lawn mower can be 90 dB, and shop tools and chain saws can be 90 to 100 dB.

Lead paint

If your home was built before 1979, it may contain lead paint, which is a serious health hazard, especially for children 6 and under. Take precautions when you scrape or remove it. Contact your public health department for detailed safety information or call (800) 424-LEAD (5323) to receive an information pamphlet. Or visit *epa.gov/lead*.

Buried utilities

A few days before you dig in your yard, have your underground water, gas and electrical lines marked. Just call 811 or go to *call811.com*.

Smoke and carbon monoxide (CO)

The risk of dying in reported home structure fires is cut in half in homes with working smoke alarms. Test your smoke alarms every month, replace batteries as necessary and replace units that are more than 10 years old. As you make your home more energy-efficient and airtight, existing ducts and chimneys can't always successfully vent combustion gases, including potentially deadly carbon monoxide (CO). Install a UL-listed CO detector, and test your CO and smoke alarms at the same time.

Five-gallon buckets and window covering cords

Anywhere from 10 to 40 children a year drown in 5-gal. buckets, according to the U.S. Consumer Products Safety Commission. Always store these buckets upside down, and store ones containing liquid with their covers securely snapped.

According to Parents for Window Blind Safety, hundreds of children in the United States are injured every year after becoming entangled in looped window treatment cords. For more information, visit *pfwbs.org* or *cpsc.gov*.

Working up high

If you have to get up on your roof to do a repair or installation, always install roof brackets and wear a roof harness.

Asbestos

Texture sprayed on ceilings before 1978, adhesives and tiles for vinyl and asphalt floors before 1980, and vermiculite insulation (with gray granules) may contain asbestos. Other building materials made between 1940 and 1980 could also contain asbestos. If you suspect that materials you're removing or working around contain asbestos, contact your health department or visit *epa.gov/asbestos* for information.

CONTENTS

1. Interior Projects, Repairs & Remodeling

2. Plumbing & Appliances

3. Woodworking & Workshop Projects & Tips

4. Pet Owner Projects & Ideas

5. Exterior Repairs & Improvements

Special Section: ENHANCE SUSTAINABILITY

6. Outdoor Structures, Landscaping & Gardening

7. Miscellaneous Odds & Ends

1 INTERIOR PROJECTS, REPAIRS & REMODELING

STAIRCASE BONUS SPACE

USE THIS DORMANT AREA IN FIVE CREATIVE WAYS

BY JAY CORK

In most multistory houses, space under the stairs is enclosed and unused. But with a little time and creativity, you can turn that wasted space into something special. Here are five ideas to inspire you.

WINE STORAGE

If you have a wet bar in the basement (or one on the way), consider building wine storage into your staircase. It is a beautiful project and frees up space in your bar or, depending on the size of your collection, maybe even an entire room.

1 START WITH THE CASEWORK

Build this wine rack as you would a fixed shelving unit, using ¾-in. plywood for the casework and shelves. Assemble and install only the casework—it will be much lighter to handle. Trim it to match your style and apply the finish.

2 MAKE THE RACKS

It's easiest to attach the dividers before the shelves are installed. With a 2½-in.-wide piece of scrap wood to space the dividers evenly, use a brad nailer to attach them to the shelves. Install the shelves with pocket hole screws.

3 TRIM IT OUT

Trim the wine rack with a style that matches your space. Frame it with a wide base trim to create a bold look. For jobs such as this, you could use chair rail for a unique look.

MEET THE EXPERT

JAY CORK USED TO LIVE UNDER THE STAIRS IN HIS PARENTS' HOUSE—WHICH MIGHT EXPLAIN A LOT.

SIMPLE SHELVING

This easy upgrade to an under-stair space adds both function and style. Recessed shelves don't require any structural changes to the wall or staircase. You can trim each shelf or just paint them to blend into the drywall as shown.

1 USE SIMPLE BOX CONSTRUCTION

The recessed shelf detail is easy to make—just assemble open-faced boxes to fit within the stud cavity using ½-in. plywood or MDF. Mark the stud locations and cut openings into the drywall. Install boxes flush to the drywall and apply trim.

Pro Tip Whether you're painting or staining, finish the shelf boxes before installing them.

2 ADD ADJUSTABLE SHELVES

Increase storage and functionality with adjustable shelves. This can be done before installation or later as your needs grow. Use a shelf pin jig to drill the shelf pin holes accurately on both sides of the box. Cut the shelves ¼ in. narrower than the internal dimensions, and finish the shelves to match the shelf boxes.

PET LOUNGE

What better way to show some love for your pets than to make a space just for them! A dog just wants a bed of its own, and cats just want to reinforce their superiority by sitting higher than anyone else in the room. This plan suits both!

1 CARVE OUT A DOGHOUSE

You can simply cut a door into the wall, or frame out an entire under-the-stairs hideaway for your buddy. Add a dog pillow for creature comfort, plus bowls for food and water, then your pup will have a room to call its very own.

2 ADD A CAT PERCH

This cat perch is easy. Make a 14½-in. square box to fit between the studs, cut away the drywall and screw it in. Trim it to match the style of your room. Your feline will love running up the carpeted, L-shaped steps to its perch. Position steps over the studs for maximum strength.

HOME OFFICE SPACE

With more people working from home, the need has increased for a space to serve as "the office." Unfortunately, this is often the kitchen table, the couch, a spare bedroom—or, worse yet, our actual bedrooms. Let's be done with that! Convert unused space under a staircase into a small but functional home office complete with a work surface, filing cabinets, shelves and a task light.

1 INSTALL A WORK SURFACE

Design the space around an existing desk or design a desk to fit the existing space. A work surface is easy to make with particleboard and plastic laminate. Anchor it to the studs and it will be strong enough to stand on!

2 ADD CABINETS AND SHELVES

Add filing cabinets and shelves to fully outfit your new work-at-home digs. Store-bought filing cabinets with two drawers are typically 30 in. tall. Make sure they will fit under your work surface.

3 CONSIDER ADDING ELECTRICAL

Computers, printers and task lights all need power. An extension cord will do the trick, but it can be unsightly. Consider adding electrical outlets along the inside wall—you might be able to draw from an existing receptacle in an adjoining room.

DAYBED READING NOOK

This nook with a daybed is a perfect hideaway for alone time with a glass of wine and your favorite book. It can also double as a guest bed for kids' sleepovers. It's like adding an entirely new room without nearly as much work.

1 BUILD SHELVES

You know that teetering stack of books on your nightstand? You can move a few down here if you add shelves to the side wall. Build shelves into the stud wall and finish them with drywall for a clean look. A small nook on the back wall is perfect for a cup of coffee or tea.

2 USE STORAGE FOR MORE THAN BOOKS

In addition to the space for books along the front of the bed, the area underneath the mattress can be used for blankets and pillows.

WHAT IT TAKES

TIME	COST	SKILL LEVEL
2 days	$150 per window	Beginner

TOOLS
Table saw, pocket hole jig, drill/driver, miter saw, random orbital sander, drywall saw

FAUX DAYLIGHT

BRIGHTEN A DARK ROOM WITH AN LED "WINDOW"

BY BRAD HOLDEN

Want to bring daylight into a finished basement, but don't want the labor and cost of adding an egress window? If you don't need an egress window to meet code, here's a way to gain light along with the illusion of a beautiful new window. You won't get an outdoor view, but a basement window rarely gives much of a view anyway.

Thin LED panels with adjustable color temperature can be set in easy-to-build window frames. Getting power to the panels takes a little electrical work, but the lights are operated by remote control or a battery-powered switch that fits in a junction box, so you don't have to hard-wire a switch.

1

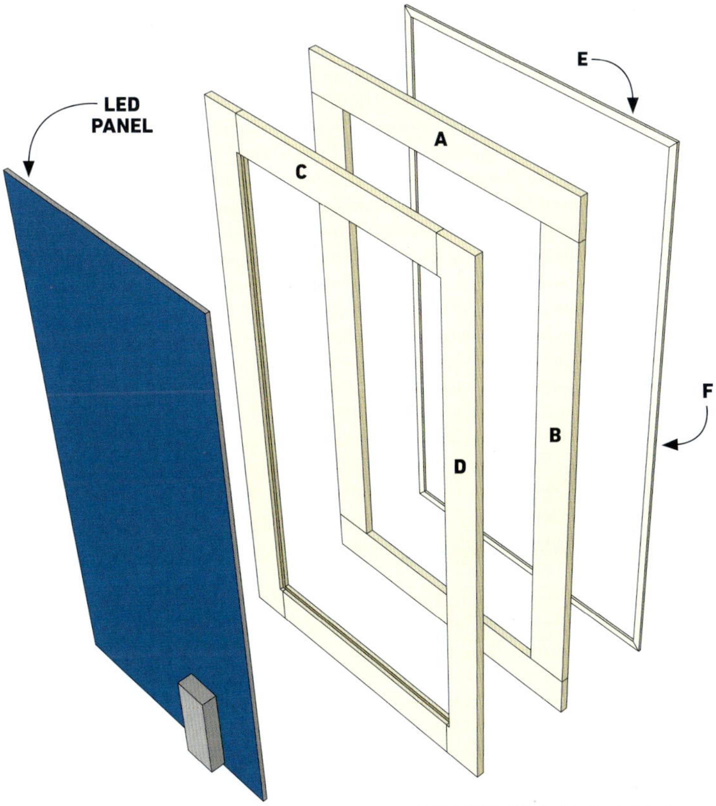

FIGURE A
LED WINDOW

OVERALL DIMENSIONS: 31" W x 55" H x 1¾" D

1 *BUILD THE FRONT FRAME*

The frame consists of a front and a back, each cut from ¾-in. MDF. Determine the frame size needed for your light panel, and then cut the front and back frame pieces. We chose to make a 4-in.-wide frame for our LED panel. You will have to decide what looks best in your room.

The front and back frames are identical in size, but the lengths of the parts are different so that the joints of the two frames overlap (see Figure A). Assemble the front frame using wood glue and pocket screws.

MATERIALS LIST

ITEM	QTY.
¾" x 48" x 96" sheet of MDF	1
¼" x ¾" screen molding	16'
Wood glue	
Sandpaper	
Paint and primer	
2' x 4' LED Even-Glow Tunable White Panel	
Light and remote control for LED panel from *superbrightleds.com*	
14-2 NM-B cable	

CUTTING LIST

KEY	QTY.	DIMENSIONS	PART
A	2	¾" x 4" x 31"	Front frame top and bottom
B	2	¾" x 4" x 47"	Front frame sides
C	2	¾" x 4" x 23"	Back frame top and bottom
D	2	¾" x 4" x 55"	Back frame sides
E	2	Cut to fit	Top and bottom trim
F	1	Cut to fit	Side trim

2 RABBET THE BACK FRAME

Cut rabbets on the back inner edges of the back frame. These rabbets should be deep enough to allow the LED panel to sit flush with the back side of the back frame. For our LED panel, the rabbets are about ⅜ in. x ⅜ in.

3 ATTACH THE BACK FRAME

Attach the back frame to the back of the front frame with glue and finish nails. If the top or bottom of your window frame will be visible, glue filler strips into the gaps created by the rabbets at the top and bottom.

4 ADD THE TRIM

Corner trim is typical for window trim. Because our window frame is painted, we needed trim only on the face of the frame, so we used pine screen molding. Attach the trim with brad nails and wood glue. Putty the holes and sand off the excess when the putty is dry.

5 PAINT THE FRAME

Sand the entire frame with 150-grit sandpaper, easing any sharp edges. After sanding, prime and paint the frame.

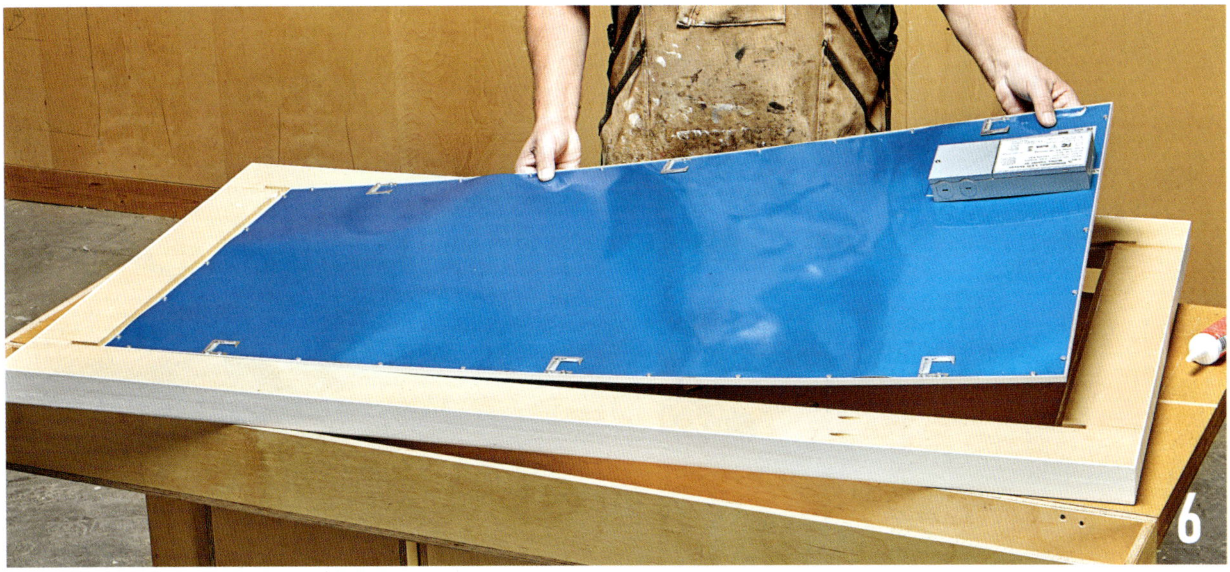

6 SET THE PANEL

Lay a light bead of silicone in the rabbet and set the LED panel into the rabbet. You can skip this step if your panel is snug in the rabbet and won't tip out while you're installing the window.

7 RUN THE CABLE

Once you have determined the location for your window, cut a hole in the drywall for the LED panel's wiring box. Turn off power to a nearby outlet, verifying that it's off with a noncontact voltage tester. Run NM-B cable from the outlet to the hole in the drywall. Leave enough extra cable to reach from the hole to the floor to make it easy to wire the panel. To learn how to bring over power from an outlet, visit *familyhandyman.com* and search for "add electrical outlet."

8 POWER THE PANEL

Hook up the conductors in the cable to their corresponding terminals on the LED panel. Secure the cable to the wiring box with a cable clamp.

9 HANG THE WINDOW

Using 3-in. trim screws, hang the window, driving the screws into the wall studs.

10 FILL THE HOLES

Fill the screw holes with wood putty or surfacing compound. When it's dry, sand it flush and prime. Give the entire window a final coat of paint.

11 HANG THE BLINDS

To complete the illusion, hang blinds inside the window frame. We found that having the blinds just slightly open really sells the look of daylight coming in.

MEET THE BUILDER

BRAD HOLDEN SAYS THAT THIS SIMPLE LIGHTING PROJECT IS ONE OF HIS ALL-TIME FAVORITES.

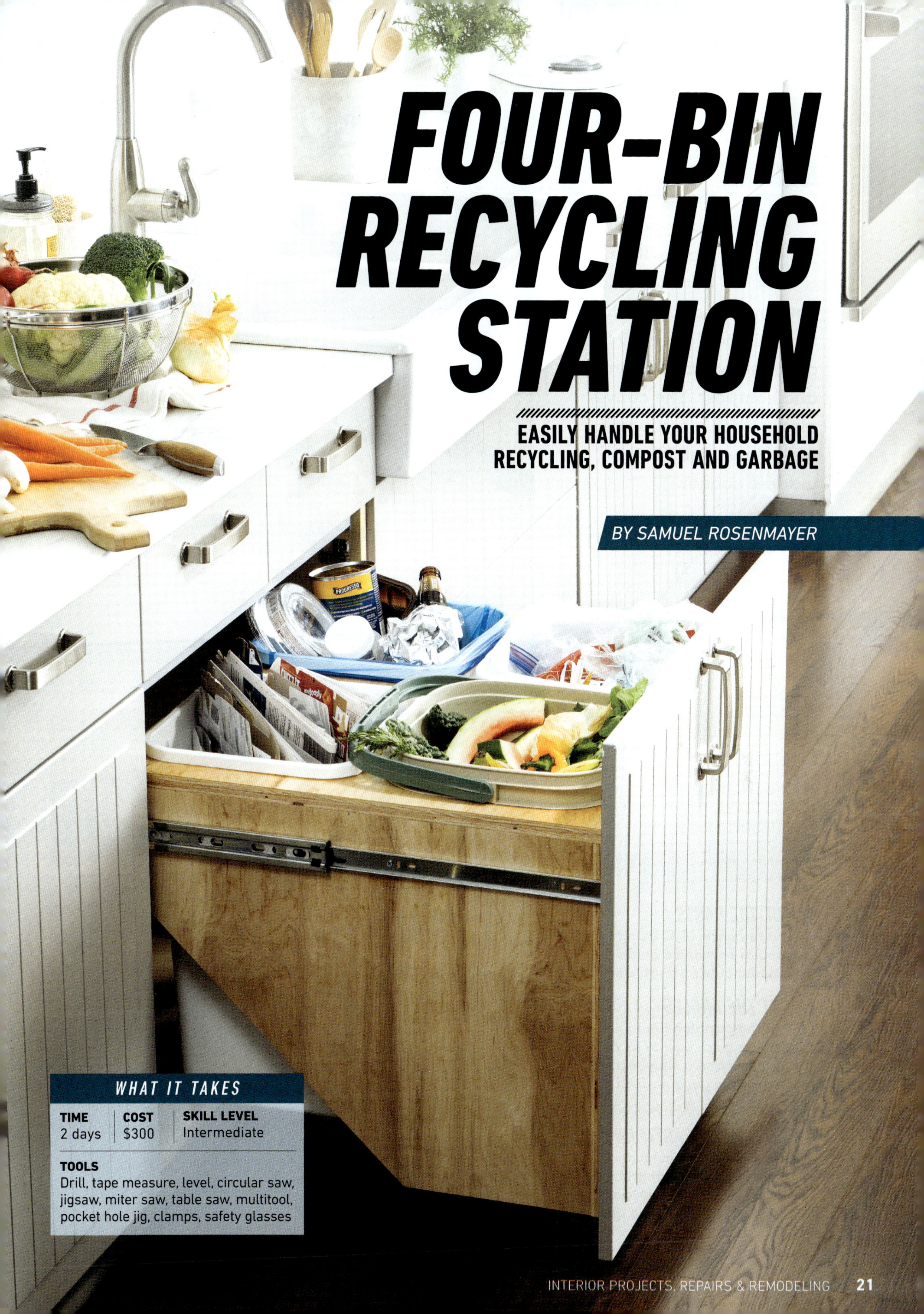

FOUR-BIN RECYCLING STATION

EASILY HANDLE YOUR HOUSEHOLD RECYCLING, COMPOST AND GARBAGE

BY SAMUEL ROSENMAYER

WHAT IT TAKES

TIME	COST	SKILL LEVEL
2 days	$300	Intermediate

TOOLS
Drill, tape measure, level, circular saw, jigsaw, miter saw, table saw, multitool, pocket hole jig, clamps, safety glasses

This project is just the thing to organize your kitchen waste. It isn't hard to build your own in-cabinet station that will hold not only your garbage but also recycling and compost. The convenience of this setup will make you wish you had made it sooner.

GETTING STARTED

To calculate your pullout size, remove the cabinet doors and measure the height, depth and width of the inside of the cabinet. For the pullout height, subtract at least 2 in. from the opening's height so that the bins will clear. Subtract 1 in. from the width to allow for the drawer slides. Your pullout's depth should be about ¼ in. less than the cabinet's depth.

Our cabinets don't have face frames. If your cabinets do, add a build-up strip behind the frames for mounting the drawer slides. Cut these strips to be flush with the inner edges of the face frames.

1 CUT THE PARTS

Cut the parts (A-E) using a circular saw and a guide. Finish the smaller cuts on a table saw.

2 CUT THE ANGLES

Cut the partition (B) angles using a track saw or any circular saw and a simple shop-made guide to get a perfectly straight cut.

3 ATTACH THE PARTITIONS

Mark the partition locations on the front (A) and predrill holes for the screws. Fasten the partitions (B) to the front using wood glue and No. 8 x 1½-in. wood screws.

4 ADD THE BACK

Attach the back (D) to the partitions the same way you attached the front, by predrilling holes, adding wood glue and using No. 8 x 1½-in. wood screws.

5 DRILL POCKET HOLES

Drill pocket holes in the inside dividers (C) to attach them to the angled sides and center partition.

6 FASTEN THE DIVIDERS

Fasten the dividers (C) in place between the partitions (B) using glue and 1¼-in. pocket screws.

7 MARK THE BIN PLACEMENT

On the underside of the top (E), lay out the bin locations and then trace the top lip of each bin. Measure the inside of the bins to find the cutout size; this will ensure there is enough overhang to support the bins. The amount you reduce depends on your bin overhang; for example, you can reduce the outline by ½ in. for support.

COMPOST BIN

We included the All Seasons Indoor Composter bin because of the convenience it provides—a good incentive for those new to composting. The 5-gal. bin is the right size for our recycling station, and it comes with an airtight lid.

8 CUT THE BIN OPENINGS

Drill a starting hole large enough to insert a jigsaw blade. Cut the outlines using a jigsaw, and then sand the openings smooth.

FIGURE A
FOUR-BIN RECYCLING STATION

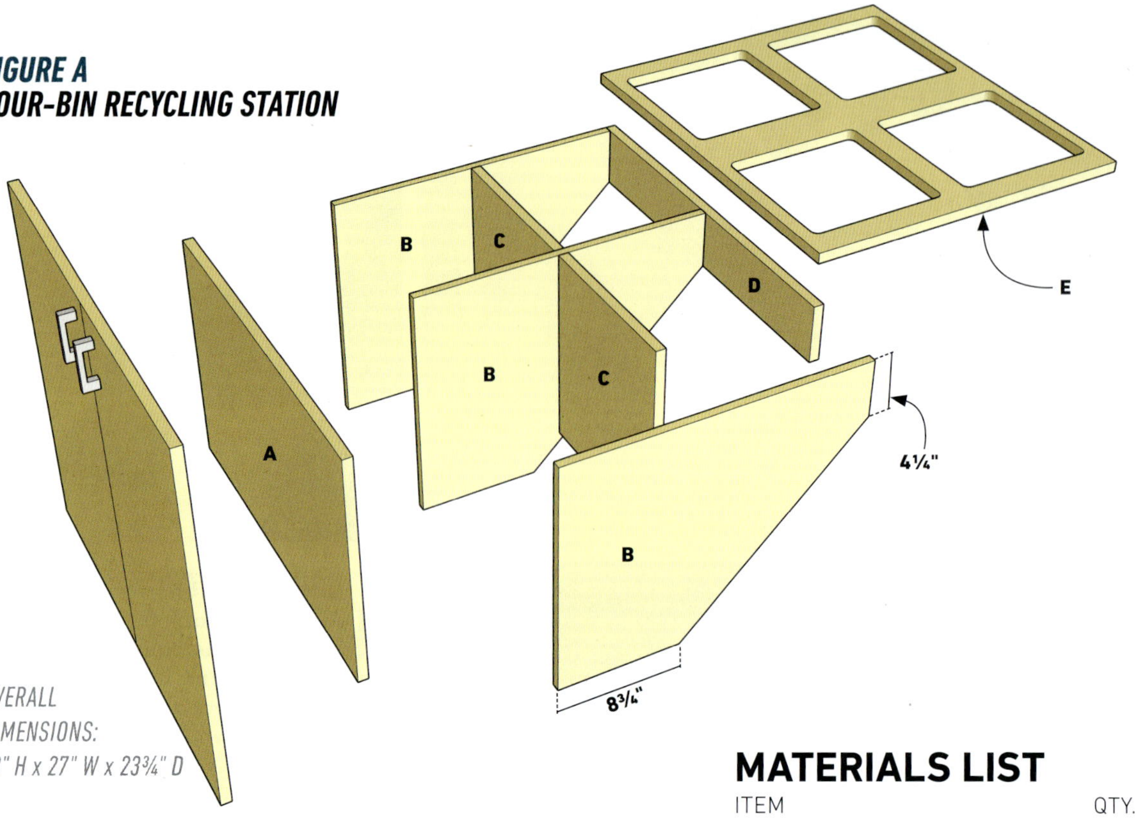

OVERALL DIMENSIONS: 18" H x 27" W x 23¾" D

CUTTING LIST

KEY	QTY.	DIMENSIONS	PART
A	1	¾" x 17⅜" x 27"	Front
B	3	¾" x 22¼" x 17⅜"	Partition*
C	2	¾" x 14⅝" x 12⁷⁄₁₆"	Inside divider
D	1	¾" x 27" x 4¼"	Back
E	1	¾" x 27" x 23¾"	Top

*See diagram for the angled cut

MATERIALS LIST

ITEM	QTY.
¾" x 4' x 8' maple plywood	1
22" soft-close side-mount drawer slides	Set of 2
Waste containers	3
Indoor compost bin	1
1¼" pocket screws	
No. 8 x 1½" wood screws	
Wood glue	
180-grit sandpaper	
Polyurethane	1 qt.

9 *CUT THE NOTCHES*

If your bins have stiffening ribs like the ones here, make marks on the top to show the locations of the ribs and cut a notch for each.

10 *ATTACH THE TOP*

To attach the top, drill pocket holes along the top edge of the front, back and partitions. Lay the top upside down, then glue the top edges of the pullout and set it in place on the top. Fasten the top with 1¼-in. pocket screws.

11 *PREDRILL HOLES*

Mark and predrill eight holes through the front—two of the holes evenly spaced at the top and bottom—to attach the cabinet doors.

MEET THE BUILDER

SAM ROSENMAYER, PROJECT EDITOR/BUILDER, IS HAPPY TO WRAP UP HIS FIRST PROJECT FOR *FAMILY HANDYMAN*.

12 ATTACH THE DRAWER SLIDES

Attach drawer slides to the assembled pullout, $2\frac{3}{4}$ in. down from the top and flush with the face of the pullout. It's best to use a spacer or jig to be sure the slides are mounted perfectly square.

13 APPLY A TOPCOAT

Apply three coats of polyurethane and allow each coat to dry for 12 to 24 hours. Sand lightly with 220- to 320-grit sandpaper between coats. Or, paint the pullout if you prefer.

14 ATTACH DRAWER SLIDES TO THE CABINET

Attach the drawer slides $15\frac{3}{4}$ in. up from the cabinet bottom. This measurement will depend on your particular cabinet. Predrill the screw holes and make sure the drawer slides are flush with the cabinet face. Again, use a spacer or jig to ensure the slides are square to the cabinet.

15 INSERT THE PULLOUT

Engage the slide members on the pullout into the slide members in the cabinet, then push the pullout completely in until you hear the slides click into place.

16 ATTACH THE DOORS

Drive screws into the predrilled holes from the inside of the pullout, just far enough so their points poke through the outside. With the pullout all the way in the cabinet, hold each door in place and push it into the screw points. With the pullout extended, locate each door on its screw indentations and drive two screws. Close the pullout and adjust the door alignment. Do this by loosening one of the screws, adjusting the door and driving in a different screw.

BASEMENT FLOORING

CHOOSE THE BEST MATERIALS AND PRACTICES FOR A MOISTURE-PRONE AREA

BY STEVE MAXWELL

When you're choosing basement flooring, style and comfort matter, but according to Chris Schmitz from ProSource Wholesale, your top consideration should be how well the flooring can handle moisture.

To start, you need to determine if your basement has any moisture issues. Obvious sources would be leaking pipes, water heaters, laundry tubs and floor drains. But, less obviously, moisture can also come in through the foundation or slab.

If you notice moisture entering through the foundation, you'll likely need to address the drainage around your home's exterior. Moisture coming in through the slab is less obvious; you'll need to run a test. Your flooring installer can do this for you, or you can perform the test on p. 43. If there's a moisture problem, the concrete must be sealed before you install any type of flooring.

The flooring you choose for a basement must be rated for below-grade installation. If you're not sure, check the product information and the manufacturer's website.

MEET THE EXPERT

CHRIS SCHMITZ IS THE MEMBER SERVICE MANAGER AT PROSOURCE WHOLESALE.

LUXURY VINYL PLANK AND LUXURY VINYL TILE

Luxury vinyl plank (LVP) and luxury vinyl tile (LVT) have several advantages for use in lower levels. "For basements, I recommend loose-lay flooring that doesn't click together. The flooring pieces simply butt together. If this flooring does get wet from above or below, you can lift out individual tiles or planks to let the area dry and then set them back into place. Also, because the pieces are just butted together, they're not waterproof, meaning moisture won't become trapped below the flooring," says Schmitz.

LVP and LVT are extremely durable. Both are made from the same materials, differing only in the shapes of the pieces: Planks are rectangular and tiles are square.

These types of vinyl flooring are flexible enough that they don't need a super flat surface as laminates do, which means they can easily lay over some undulations in a concrete floor. Unlike click-together vinyl floors, there's no expansion gap left at the walls. Instead, the tiles or planks depend on a close "compression fit" to stay in place. Also, each piece has a backing that prevents it from sliding.

CARPET

Many people install carpet in basements because it makes the concrete floor warmer and more comfortable. That's a fine goal, but never make the mistake of installing carpet and underlayment directly on basement concrete. One reason is summertime mustiness. When humid summer air enters the carpet pile and comes close to the concrete underneath, that air can cool to the dew point, releasing fine droplets of water within the carpet or underlayment. That's why finished basements smell musty.

Always install basement carpet and underlayment on concrete that has been sealed or on top of a vapor-impervious subfloor. This will raise the temperature of the floor in winter, make your carpet more pleasant to walk on and, most important, prevent humid air from reaching the concrete and triggering mold growth. A common mistake is to install a vapor barrier on top of the carpet pad. This will trap moisture and cause mold growth on the pad or even the concrete.

Carpet tile is an excellent flooring choice for a basement. These tiles wick moisture and release it into the air. Like many luxury vinyl tiles, they're "loose lay," so they don't click together. Many are adhesive backed, but it's a special adhesive that prevents only side-to-side sliding. They can be lifted up individually for drying if they do get wet. Schmitz doesn't recommend wool or natural fabric carpets for basements, as those tend to retain moisture.

LAMINATE

In 1994, a European company called Pergo introduced laminate flooring to North America, and it has been a popular choice ever since. Today's best laminates can feature real wood veneer on the surface and resist moisture.

The durability of laminate flooring is exceptionally good if you choose one with an abrasion class (AC) rating of 3 or higher on a scale of 1 to 5. The AC rating measures the resistance of laminate flooring to abrasion. You'll also need to verify that the flooring you choose is rated for below grade installation.

Laminates require a flat floor, which can be a problem for basement installations. Most manufacturers specify no more than ¼ in. of deviation from flat over a 10-ft. radius. Many concrete basement floors are not this flat, but it's possible to use floor-leveling compound to correct major issues. As is the case with most professional installers, Schmitz says, "We don't use 'waffle-backed' subfloor tiles. A sealed slab and the recommended underlayment for your laminate is sufficient."

CERAMIC AND PORCELAIN TILE

These tough, attractive, hard-wearing options are perfect for basements. "It's commonly believed that you should install basement floor tile on an uncoupling membrane to prevent tile from cracking as the concrete expands and contracts. This may be a good idea if your home is relatively new, as the concrete may still settle or move a bit, but if your home is 10 years old or more, that shouldn't be an issue. Properly installed, tile can be applied directly to the concrete without risk of cracking," says Schmitz.

One downside of tile is that it's cold to walk on. If you choose tile for a basement in a cold climate, Schmitz recommends installing electric heat cables. This will turn the tile into a radiant thermal mass, making your basement much cozier.

RUBBER FLOORING

This durable, moisture-proof and informal flooring makes good sense for basements, especially utility, play or exercise areas. It is unaffected by moisture, either liquid or vapor. Rubber flooring usually comes as interlocking tiles, and it can be easily removed or reconfigured after installation if your needs change. This type of flooring is very comfortable underfoot too.

BRING BACK THE SHINE

MAKE YOUR HARDWOOD FLOORS BEAUTIFUL AGAIN

If you have hardwood floors that are showing their age, you don't need to hire a pro to refinish them. As long as you are comfortable handling machines and can work carefully and patiently, you can tackle the job yourself. Be forewarned, however: It's a very dusty undertaking!

The floor we are working on as an example is called a pegged hardwood floor. Each board, depending on its width, has one or two pegs on both ends. In the traditional installation, these pegs were driven and glued into the joists below.

You'll see in this step-by-step journey that this job is just as much about careful decision making as it is about doing the actual job.

BY BRAD HOLDEN

WHAT IT TAKES

TIME	COST	SKILL LEVEL
3-4 days	$500	Intermediate

TOOLS (SOME YOU MAY RENT)
Floor drum sander, pry bar, floor edging sander, random orbit sander, carbide scraper, floor maintainer, hammer, nail set, box fan, vacuum

MATERIALS & SUPPLIES
40-, 60- and 100-grit sanding belts; 100-grit sanding discs for random orbit sander; tack cloth; plastic sheeting; painter's tape; 40-, 60- and 100-grit sanding discs for edgers; sanding screens; wood filler; sanding block; 220-grit screens for sanding block; floor polyurethane; polyurethane applicator pads; respirator; hearing protection; kneepads

1 PREP THE ROOM

Remove all furniture, then pull the quarter round from the baseboard so you'll be able to sand right up to the baseboard. Thoroughly vacuum and damp mop the floor. Next, seal off the room with plastic sheeting and painter's tape. We used a purpose-made plastic sheeting that includes a zippered door for easy access.

Sealing off the room is paramount for a couple of reasons. First, you want to keep dust from migrating throughout the house. Second, once you're applying finish, you want to keep any everyday dust that's floating around your house from settling into the wet finish. While you're sanding, take all the dust mitigation measures you can; wear a respirator and set a box fan in a window to exhaust as much dust outside as possible.

2 DECIDE: SCREEN OR SAND

Once your floor is clean, make a game-time decision: If your floor is in good shape, you can often get by just "screening" it with the floor maintainer (shown on left) and applying new finish. But if your floor has some deep scratches that you'd like to get rid of, you'll need to move right to the drum sander.

3 START DRUM SANDING

With a 40-grit belt on the drum sander, start in the middle of the room, as close to the wall as you can get, sanding in the direction of the flooring. The reason for starting in the middle is that as you stand behind the machine, you won't be able to get all the way to the wall that's at your back.

The drum sander has a lever that lowers the drum onto the floor. Start rolling the machine, then carefully lower the drum. As you're nearing the end of the room, raise the drum before you stop rolling. Think of an airplane landing and taking off. This avoids creating burns and dips. Work all the way across the floor, then turn around and sand the other half of the floor.

4 DO ANOTHER ROUND

Once you have removed the old finish and any major scratches using the 40-grit belt, repeat the sanding process, moving up to a 60-grit belt, then 100 grit. Without the old finish on the floor, it's much more difficult to see where you've sanded, so use landmarks on the walls or floor to keep track of where you are. Also, overlap your last pass by about one-third.

5 TACKLE THOSE EDGES

The first flooring boards against the wall often have been nailed through their face, leaving the nails visible or underneath a dab of putty. Before you start sanding the edges, sink any nails well below the surface using a hammer and nail set. If you don't, those nails will tear up your sanding discs fast, not to mention throwing sparks in a dry, dusty environment. Before you start edge sanding, put on kneepads and non-marring shoes (or just take your shoes off).

The edging sander has two swiveling casters near one side so that it rolls easily. To use the edging sander, press the "on" button while tilting the sander back on the casters. Carefully lower the spinning disc onto the floor, working right up to the baseboard. Always keep the sander moving while it's in contact with the floor. Work all the way around the room, working through the grit, just as you did with the drum sander.

6 SCRAPE THE CORNERS

None of the machines will get all the way into the corners. To get at those areas, use a carbide paint scraper. It's not as fast as 40-grit sandpaper, but it gets the job done.

7 FILL THE GAPS

Once the sanding is complete, it's time to fill any unsightly gaps. It can be difficult to find a filler that truly matches the floor and doesn't stand out. If your floor is in pretty nice condition, like this one, you can just spread wood putty in the larger gaps. If you choose to use a filler, apply it as directed and let it dry. Once it's dry, sand off any excess filler using a random orbit sander with a 100-grit sanding disc.

8 BRUSH THE ENDS

The pad you'll use for applying the finish gets right up to the wall on the edges of the stroke, but not at the ends. Start with a brush to apply the finish right up to the baseboard where the ends of the floor boards meet the wall. Work in sections of 3 to 4 feet at a time to keep the finish from drying before you get to it with the pad. Before you start applying finish, cover any vents with plastic if your HVAC is forced air.

9 APPLY THE FIRST COAT

As you do when you sand, you should apply finish in the direction of the flooring. Plan your finishing so you end up at a door. In other words, don't "paint yourself into a corner." Using a finishing pad on a pole, work carefully, making sure you're getting good coverage, but not too heavy. Multiple light coats are best.

Work across the room in reachable sections. Move as quickly as you can, so you're maintaining a "wet edge" in the finish as you work. As with sanding, overlap the last pass of each stroke of finish by about one-third. The raw floor will really soak up this first coat, so don't be alarmed when it's dry and looks blotchy.

10 SCUFF-SAND THE FIRST COAT

You can apply successive coats within six to eight hours after the previous coat without sanding, but after 10 hours, sanding is recommended. Even if applying back-to-back coats works with your schedule, it's recommended to wait and sand between coats. This gives you the opportunity to smooth out rough spots as you wait. After a light sanding using 220 grit, thoroughly vacuum the floor and then wipe it down with tack cloth. Using this method also ensures that you're picking up any dust that may have settled on the floor in the drying process.

11 APPLY THE NEXT COATS

With the floor scuff-sanded and cleaned, apply a second coat of finish just as you did the first. Allow the second coat to dry. Repeat the sanding and cleaning process, then apply a third coat. Three coats is sufficient for most floors, but you can apply more if you wish. After the last coat is applied, allow it to cure for at least 48 hours before moving the furniture back in.

MEET THE REFINISHER

WHILE NOT A FLOOR REFINISHING EXPERT, **BRAD HOLDEN** HAS REFINISHED THREE FLOORS IN HIS OWN HOME WITH GOOD RESULTS.

WHAT TO DO IF YOUR BASEMENT FLOODS

THE RIGHT STEPS CAN SAVE YOU *AND* YOUR HOME

BY ETHAN O'DONNELL

In addition to being a headache, a flooded basement requires immediate attention in order to prevent further damage. And as long as you take a few precautions, you can tackle this job. So take a deep breath and follow these steps for managing water removal and quickly restoring your basement to its preflood condition.

ENSURE THE BASEMENT IS SAFE

You have a mess on your hands, and of course you are anxious to start cleaning up. However, before you plunge into the flooded basement with waders on and a bucket in hand, you must determine if the location is safe to enter.

Avoid stepping into the basement if more than 2 in. of water is present throughout the entire space. Electricity and gas may pose safety issues. It is possible that the standing water has been electrified by wiring and appliances. Issues can also arise with gas-powered appliances such as furnaces or water heaters. The pilot lights may have gone out and gas may be flowing freely into the basement.

If you can access your electrical panel without getting wet, immediately turn off the power to the problem area. If not, call an electrician. Whenever you smell natural gas, immediately step outside and contact your gas provider to shut it off before proceeding.

IDENTIFY THE CAUSE AND REMOVE THE WATER

After you have determined that it is safe to begin working, focus on identifying the water source, stopping it if possible and removing the accumulated water.

Water should be shut off to broken pipes, or sump pumps should be repaired if they are faulty or floor drains are clogged. Then, using a wet vac, pump or squeegee, remove all the standing water. If the basement holds so much standing water that you must shut off the power to the whole house, you can rent a gas-powered pump at a rental store or home center to quickly remove the water.

DOCUMENT THE SCENE

Before you throw away any of your destroyed belongings, take a minute to document the damage. Taking photos of the flooded area, both inside and out, will greatly assist an adjuster if you decide to file an insurance claim. Document everything: damage to the dwelling, soaked boxes, electronics, furniture and furnishings, as well as the underlying cause of the flood.

CLEAN, CLEAN, CLEAN

If mold is present or likely, clean all vinyl or laminate flooring, solid wood, glass and concrete with a stiff-bristle brush, hot water and a household detergent. A solution of ⅓ cup bleach to 1 gal. water should be used when mold grows from overland flooding or sewage. Items such as carpet, drywall, insulation and paper that exhibit mold growth should be disposed of as soon as possible. During cleaning, avoid oversaturating the area. Be careful not to mix bleach with other chemicals, to use bleach in a well ventilated area, and to protect your eyes and skin from harsh cleaning products.

After cleaning, run a dehumidifier in the area for a couple of days. Keep an eye out for any signs of mold or mildew growth. Your eyes and nose are your most valuable assets during this time. Be on the lookout for common black or green mold spots, as well as pink or yellow staining on drywall, vinyl wall coverings and faux wall paneling.

A musty or earthy smell is often an indication of hidden moisture damage. If mold returns, fix the moisture problem and repeat the cleaning procedure. It is necessary to wait until the affected areas are completely dry before beginning to rebuild. The process may take several days, weeks or even months.

REMOVE WET ITEMS

Discard waterlogged and damaged items, particularly items that support mold growth, such as paper products, unwashable linens and fabrics, and furniture.

In order to reduce dampness in a basement, remove wet furniture as quickly as possible because cushions act as sponges and absorb liquids. If you intend to salvage other wet items, you should stage them in the garage or on the porch in order to allow the residual moisture in the basement to decrease.

During the interim, all plastic, glass, ceramic and metal items should be removed. Once they have dried and have been thoroughly cleaned, it's safe to put them back.

Caution: Inside any dwelling, no level of mold growth is considered safe. If you are unable to eliminate the odor or you discover a mold issue larger than 10 sq. ft., get in touch with an expert for mold remediation as soon as possible.

DRY OUT BUILDING MATERIALS

Once the area has been cleared of furniture and clutter, it is time to aggressively dry out your building materials. Rent floor blowers to dry carpet (assuming the floodwater wasn't contaminated), and purchase or borrow from family and friends as many fans and dehumidifiers as possible. Make sure all walls and flooring in the affected areas are dried out. Don't forget to empty the dehumidifiers and reposition carpet blowers and fans to reduce the humidity in your basement.

ADAPT YOUR APPROACH WHEN MOVING BACK IN

You should keep the flooding incident in mind when you begin to move your belongings back into your basement.

Improvements such as installing drainage tile and sump pumps, landscaping your yard or adding a subfloor with a membrane to the concrete basement floor can all help keep your basement dry. For more information, see "Fix a Leaky Basement," p. 42.

Consider simple solutions too. Store important documents high, use plastic totes instead of cardboard boxes on low shelves, and buy aluminum or plastic furniture rather than mold-prone particleboard. By doing this, you will save time, effort and money if your basement floods again.

FIX A LEAKY BASEMENT

PREVENT A WET LOWER LEVEL—PERMANENTLY

BY JEFF GORTON

If your basement leaks when it rains or is damp and smells musty in the summer, don't throw in the towel. There are all kinds of ways to dry a wet basement, ranging from simple weekend fixes to more difficult repairs that you may want to hire a contractor to do.

Here we will show you how to diagnose your wet basement problem and give you solutions to try yourself. Details on how to complete some of the more difficult jobs, such as installing an interior drainage system, won't be given, but you can see how systems work and what's involved in their installation.

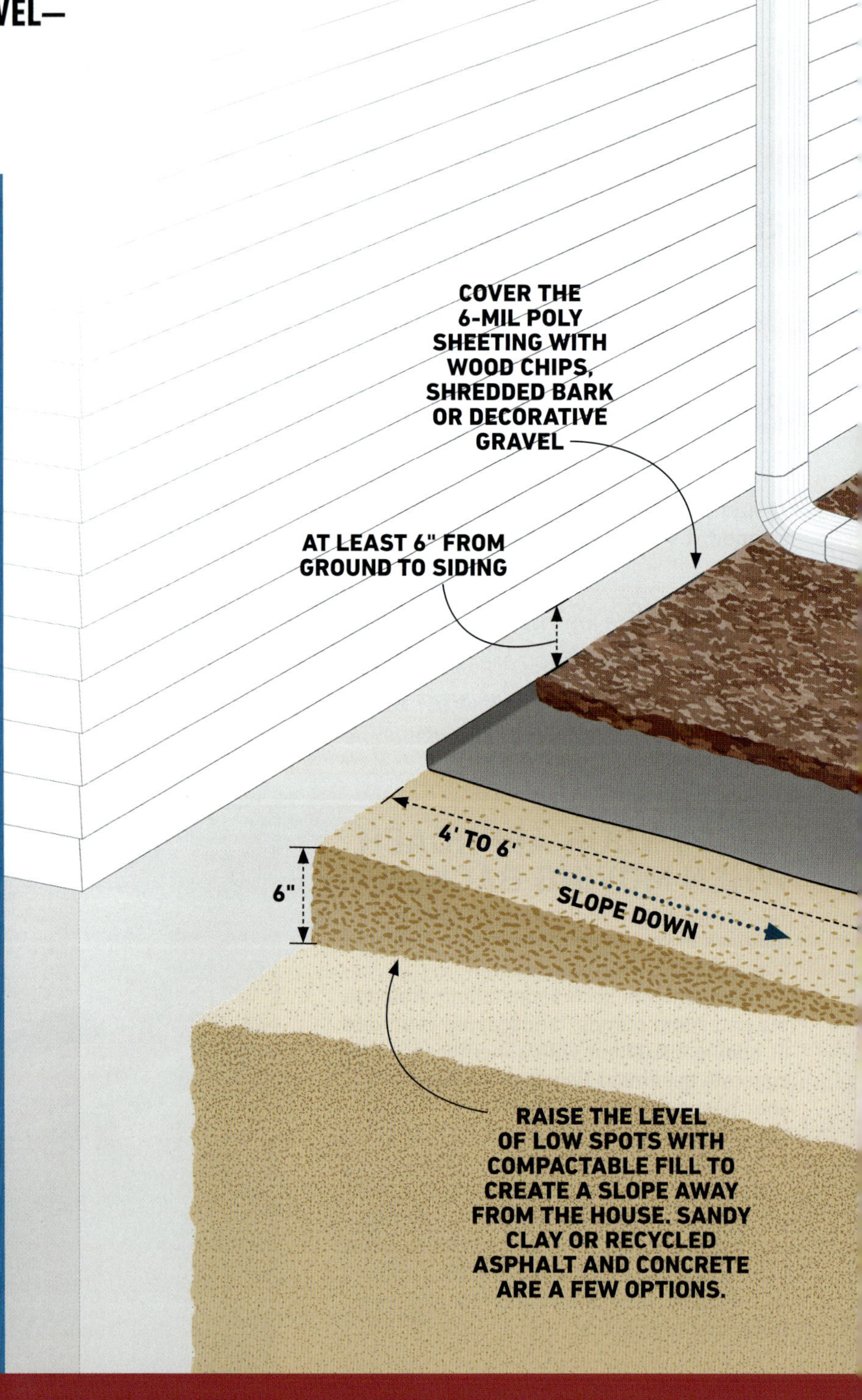

INSPECT YOUR FOUNDATION AND TAKE NOTES

It's important to do a thorough check of the ground around your foundation. For this you'll need a 4-ft. level, a tape measure and a notepad. First draw a simple sketch of your house and yard. Then use the level to check the slope of the ground around your foundation. Look for areas of sunken soil, garden beds with edging that protrudes to form a dam, and ground that slopes toward the house. Make notes on your sketch with arrows to show which way the ground slopes. This step will help you develop a plan for redirecting the water away from the foundation.

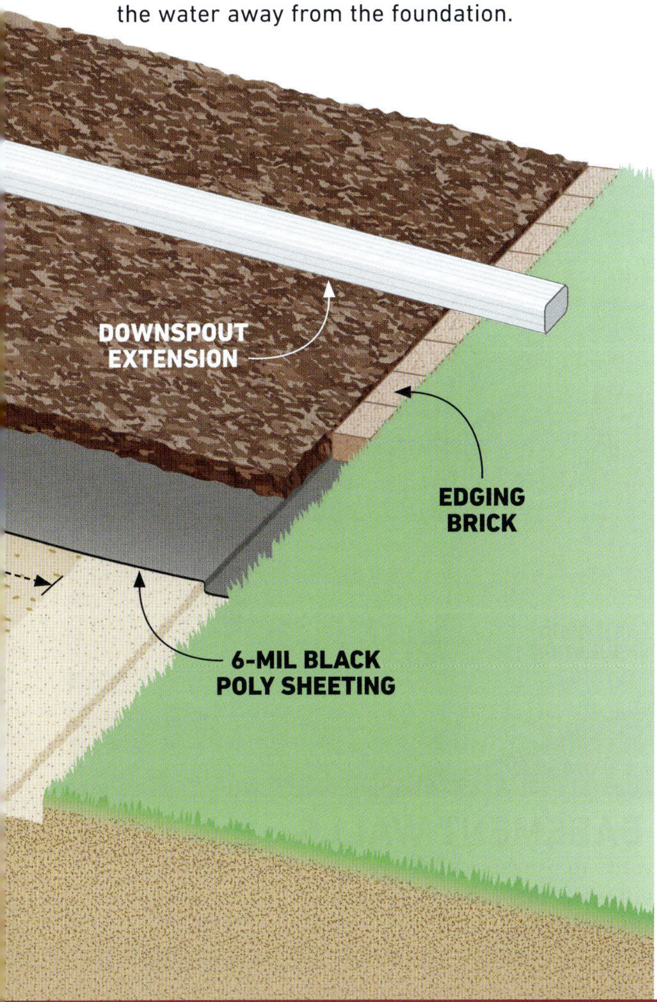

DETERMINE WHERE THE WATER IS COMING FROM

Water or moisture gets into basements through two sources. One is indoor humidity that condenses on cold surfaces, such as the sweat on a cold glass of lemonade on a hot and humid day. The other main source is water—or water vapor—coming in from the outside. Rainwater, melting snow or groundwater can saturate the soil around your foundation and leak in. Water can leak through cracks in the foundation or walls, or it can penetrate porous concrete or masonry walls in the form of water vapor.

To help you diagnose the problem, tape aluminum foil to your basement wall and inspect it a few days later. Moisture on the outside surface of the foil indicates high indoor humidity. Moisture behind the foil means moisture is leaking through the walls.

GET RID OF EXCESS HUMIDITY

Eliminate sources of humid air. Seal leaky dryer vents with foil tape to prevent unwanted humid air from entering your basement. Don't just use duct tape; it'll eventually fall off.

Add a vent fan to your basement bathroom and make sure your family members turn it on during showers. Keep your basement windows closed during humid weather. And if you're still getting condensation on cool surfaces, run a dehumidifier to lower the indoor humidity.

PLUG HOLES AND CRACKS IN THE FOUNDATION

Not all foundation cracks are created equal, so it's important to identify cracks that can contribute to leaks. Plugging them probably won't solve basement leaks, but it'll help. Hydraulic cement works great for this because it can set up even under water, and it expands as it sets to seal the hole and lock the plug in place.

Use a cold chisel or an angle grinder fitted with a masonry-cutting disc or diamond blade to enlarge the hole or crack into an inverted V, with the point of the V on the surface of the wall. Follow the package instructions for mixing and using the hydraulic cement.

INSTALL A SUMP PUMP

A flooded basement can cause expensive water damage and even be a health hazard. A sump pump transfers water from your basement to a place it can drain safely. Sump pumps must be installed at the lowest level of the floor. They don't have to be in a pit, but digging a pit in the basement floor is usually the best option. The pit is typically lined with a prefabricated plastic basin with a cover. Depending on the height of the water table, a submersible pump is installed in the pit or a pedestal pump is installed on the basement floor.

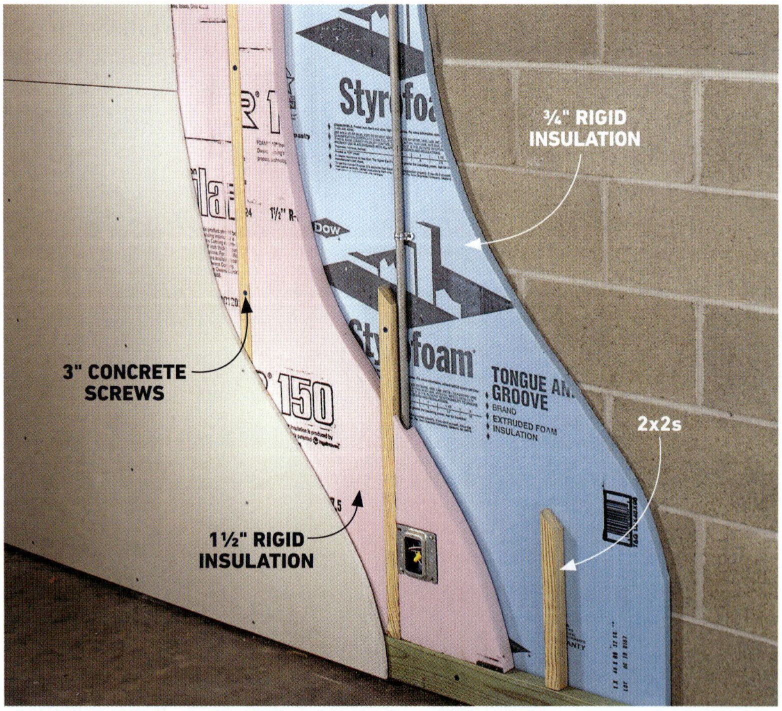

INSULATE BASEMENT WALLS

Insulate exterior walls to prevent condensation. In cold climates, insulating basement walls also saves energy and reduces your heating bill. But don't cover the walls with insulation if water is leaking in from outside; you'll just create a potential mold problem.

WATERPROOF BASEMENT WALLS

Paint-on waterproofing materials fill pores in concrete or masonry walls and prevent water from leaking in. To be effective, these coatings must be applied to bare concrete or masonry walls. Start by removing loose material with a wire brush. Then clean off any white powdery "efflorescence" with masonry cleaner.

Follow the safety and application instructions carefully. A common mistake when using masonry waterproofing products is to spread them too thin. The goal is to fill every pinhole to create a continuous waterproofing membrane. Brush the coating in all directions to completely fill every pinhole. Add a second coat after the first dries.

INSULATE PIPES

Condensation can build on cold pipes, leading to dripping and more basement water problems. Cover cold water pipes with foam pipe insulation to stop condensation. The foam insulation is inexpensive and easy to cut with scissors. It also helps prevent pipes from freezing in the winter, which can cause serious flooding problems.

INSTALL A DRAINAGE SYSTEM

The best permanent fix for chronic basement leaks is to install drainage tubing below the basement floor and to connect it to a sump basket and pump. You can install a system like this yourself, but breaking out the concrete floor, burying the tubing and patching the floor is a lot of backbreaking work.

ADD GUTTERS AND DOWNSPOUT EXTENDERS

If your basement leaks after it rains and you don't have gutters, consider adding them. Gutters catch the rainwater and channel it to downspouts, which direct it away from the house. Whether you're installing new gutters or already have them, be sure the downspouts have 4- to 6-ft. horizontal extensions to move the water away from the house.

GREAT GOOFS®

LAUGHS AND LESSONS FROM OUR READERS

USE YOUR HEAD, NOT YOUR HAMMER

My husband is a novice handyman with a great heart. So when I asked for a new sink in our upstairs bathroom, he got to work. After two weeks of struggle and leaking pipes, it was done. Whew!

But when I turned on the hot water, I heard water "hammering." He said he must have loosened a pipe, which was beating against a stud. He spent the next hour knocking holes in our nice drywall trying to trace the hammering. But he just couldn't find the problem. I then asked him if the hot water valve below the sink was fully open—problem solved. The contractor did a beautiful job of repairing our drywall.

MARI NELSON

MAN-EATING BEANBAG

When I remodeled my third-floor home office, I splurged on a new memory-foam beanbag chair, which came packaged in a highly compressed cube. No one was around to help, so I proceeded to carry it by myself up two flights of stairs and a narrow spiral staircase. The box wasn't big, but it was heavy—maybe 75 lbs.—and hard to get a good grip on. After the first flight of stairs, I ditched the box so I could hold on to the shrink-wrapped bundle.

Bad idea. After a couple of steps, I snagged the plastic on a piece of rough railing, and I knew I was in trouble when the foam started to expand. By the time I hit the spiral staircase, the beanbag had expanded so much that it sagged into a large, squishy dome around my head and shoulders, and I couldn't see where I was going! By the time I found the door to my office, I was completely stuck inside the chair. It took me 15 minutes to push it through the door and extricate myself.

JOEY BRAMLAGE

2 PLUMBING & APPLIANCES

PLUMBING IN OLDER HOMES

KEEP IT RUNNING WITH THESE EXPERT POINTERS

BY NINA BRICKO

Driving through southeastern Wisconsin, you'll hit the heart of Milwaukee and its neighboring suburbs. These areas are speckled with charming older homes, such as the bungalow of the 1920s, the Tudor of the 1930s, and the minimal, traditional style of the 1940s and '50s.

It's easy to see why a plumber like Jessie Cannizzaro, who specializes in older homes, would have a vibrant and flourishing business here. Though the Milwaukee-based expert hadn't intended to pursue a career in the trades, plumbing was in her blood and her hands craved to be worked. As is the case with so many, it just took a bit of time for her to find her own path.

INTRODUCTION TO THE WORLD OF PLUMBING

When she talks about how she got started, Cannizzaro's smile widens. "My dad."

Her father was a plumber. While growing up, she went with her dad to job sites. She was in charge of handing him tools and holding the flashlight. Though, according to him (Cannizzaro chuckles to herself), she never quite held it where he wanted it.

Cannizzaro's eyes light up as she describes a pipe job they did for a hotel in Menomonee Falls, Wisconsin. Every time she drives by it, she's reminded of the first time he trusted her with a propane torch.

"Of course, I always joke when I tell people the story, that OSHA [the Occupational Safety and Health Administration] would have had a fit if they would have seen it," she says. "That is not what a 7-year-old should be doing." But it gave her the taste for plumbing.

INITIAL CAREER PATH

As with many kids, Cannizzaro's aspirations were different than her father's. She was the first in her family to go to college. But while she was there, her father suffered a stroke. This made it difficult for him to do things by himself, so she helped.

Cannizzaro shuttled between assisting her dad on the job and going to class. Back at his side, she realized she "enjoyed working with [her] hands a lot more than doing paperwork."

She decided to finish her business degree and earn a plumbing license. This "parallel path" would take her on quite a journey, which eventually led to starting her own business, Milestone Plumbing.

Part of her success can be attributed to her deep appreciation for older plumbing. This is what she grew up with. But as with her dad, she also loves helping her clients become proactive so they can avoid larger disasters down the road.

JESSIE'S TOP TIPS
FOR MAINTAINING OLDER PLUMBING

1. PAY ATTENTION TO PLUMBING NOISES

THE PROBLEM: If you hear a glugging noise, "the drain system is starving for air to regulate the pressures and is not able to get the air, so it's pulling air," says Cannizzaro. This could be a blockage elsewhere in the system, such as a beehive in the vent pipe. But if water isn't going down the floor drain, it's sewer related.

THE SOLUTION: According to Cannizzaro, "the only time that this problem gets better on its own is if it's not an issue with your home." If it's something going on with the city sewer, once the issue is corrected, your home should be fine. However, don't wait to investigate. To determine if it's a city problem, Cannizzaro suggests asking your neighbors if they are having issues with their floor drain. "You [can also] call the city and ask them to check the city sewer." If it's not city related, call a plumber. They will troubleshoot the issue.

2. AVOID CHEMICAL CLEANERS AND DIY FIXES

THE PROBLEM: Chemical cleaners eat away at metal pipes that are common in older homes. They're also a temporary fix; often whatever is causing the blockage might continue to occur. If you try to dislodge the blockage with a drain cable, it could puncture a hole in the deteriorating pipes and cause an even bigger problem.

THE SOLUTION: Avoid causing blockages. If you have a garbage disposal, your older home is likely not equipped to handle it. Put things like stringy vegetables, coffee grounds, grease, and eggshells in the trash or compost bin. To help break down materials that are going down the drain, add a drain enzyme like Bio-Clean once a month. If there is already a blockage, you will most likely need to run a drain machine through the pipes. If you don't know what to use, call your local plumber for advice.

3. ASSUME LEAD PIPES ARE IN YOUR OLDER NEIGHBORHOOD

THE PROBLEM: Lead pipes are tricky in older neighborhoods. Lead doesn't necessarily have to be in your home to cause issues. "If there's work being done [in the city water system], let's say a block away, there could be lead shavings that are getting introduced" to your water. This becomes important especially when someone in the home is pregnant, or when babies and younger children are living in your household.

THE SOLUTION: Install a reverse osmosis system that will filter out lead and other unwanted containments. If you don't want a complete system, you can buy lead filters for kitchen faucets and refrigerator filters like Brita that can remove up to 99% of lead. This will ensure that your water is at least safe to drink.

EXTRA TIP:

WHEN PURCHASING AN OLDER HOME, HAVE A PLUMBER CHECK IT OUT

In today's real estate market, many home buyers are leaving out home inspections in their offers to help them be more competitive in their bids. However, without an inspection, you won't know the state of the home's plumbing. The pipes could be corroded or razor thin, or have small leaks. So, once you purchase a home, hire a plumber to get an idea of what is going on with your pipes, to discover the life expectancy of the system, or to make a maintenance plan to help prevent larger and more costly issues.

4. CHECK FOR DETERIORATING PIPES

THE PROBLEM: Water lines run along the ceiling of the basement, and a pinhole leak can be hard to spot on the top side of a pipe. Cannizzaro says she doesn't worry about the floor when looking for the leaks. "I'm with my flashlight and I'm looking right up at the ceiling to see what's going on." Water evaporates, so there might not be an actively wet spot; instead, she's looking for mineral deposits above the pipes. These are signs of a deteriorating pipe that needs immediate attention.

THE SOLUTION: If you see white or red mineral deposits above a waterline, it's time to get a plumber. Depending on the type of pipe or damage, a plumber might repair the leak or cut it out and replace that section.

5. INSTALL A BACKUP OR BATTERY-POWERED SUMP PUMP

THE PROBLEM: If you live in an area with a lot of groundwater and you lose power in a storm, it can take time to restart the sump pump.

THE SOLUTION: Get a backup sump pump or a battery-powered one that isn't affected by power outages.

6. BE AWARE OF ROOTS IN SEWER LINES

THE PROBLEM: In many older neighborhoods, roots from big, beautiful trees penetrate these older clay sewer systems that have concrete joints. The roots eventually crack the joints and enter the pipe, trapping materials such as "flushable" wipes, which then creates a dam. These bellies of water can build up and possibly collapse the sewage pipes.

THE SOLUTION: If you live in an area with lush trees lining the street, have your plumber check out your sewage system to establish care. For some homes, a plumber should come out once a year to do some root maintenance, and in other areas it might be every 10 years. Other than that, the best thing to do is to avoid flushing things down the system that could cause blockages.

EXTRA TIP:
JUST BECAUSE YOU HAVE AN OLDER HOME DOES NOT MEAN YOU CAN'T UTILIZE TECHNOLOGY

Moen recently came out with the Moen Flo Smart Water Monitor, which tracks water flow, pressure and temperature in your home. The monitor senses both larger water events and small leaks that could cause mold over time.

If the monitor senses that something is off, it can send an alert to your smartphone and shut off your water automatically.

Overall, being proactive is the best thing you can do for your older home to prevent any unwanted and costly repairs down the line. Replacing a pipe now is easier than dealing with a major leak or backed-up sewage later. It can be the difference between loving your older home and feeling overwhelmed by it.

MEET THE EXPERT

JESSIE CANNIZZARO IS A PRO PLUMBER AND OWNER OF MILESTONE PLUMBING IN WAUWATOSA, WISCONSIN.

UNCLOG A KITCHEN SINK DRAIN

CLEAR 95% OF YOUR STOPPED-UP DRAIN PROBLEMS WITH TWO SIMPLE TOOLS

BY PAUL GORTON

Save yourself the plumbing service call and unclog your drain yourself. We'll show you how to unclog a kitchen sink using a plunger and a drain snake.

PLUNGER

START WITH THE RIGHT TOOLS

When you shop for a plunger, keep in mind that those with larger rubber bells deliver more thrust, but most sizes will work for kitchen drains. Be sure the plunger has a stout handle so you can apply plenty of force as you learn how to unclog a sink.

A drain snake (also called a hand auger) is a long, serpentine tool that snakes into the drain to penetrate and pull out the clog. Drain snakes vary greatly in price, depending on their size, length and turning mechanism. For all-around use, the best drain snake is a $\frac{3}{8}$-in. model that's about 20 ft. long. It's easy to turn down into the drain. Shorter $\frac{1}{4}$-in. types will work for most clogs too. Unclogging stubborn drains probably won't be a regular activity in your home; consider renting a high-quality drain snake instead of buying a cheap one.

Keep these other items handy: a bucket or plastic bin that fits under your drain, rubber gloves and a bright flashlight.

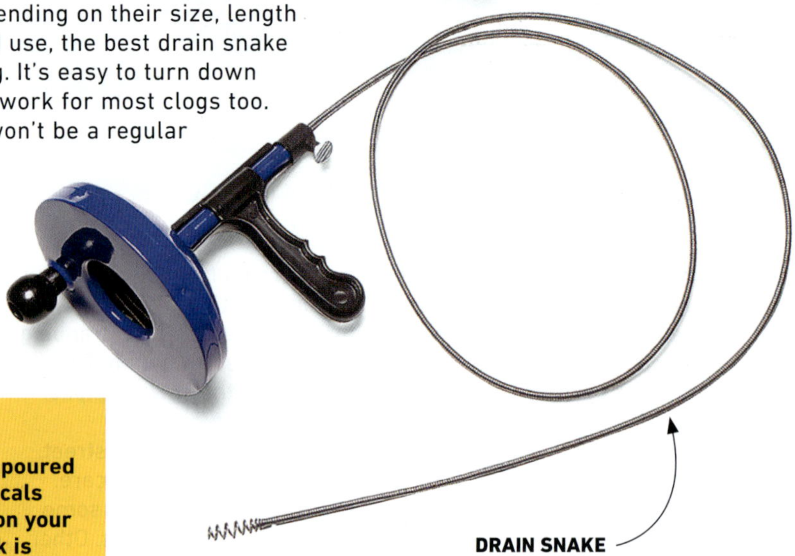

DRAIN SNAKE OR AUGER

CAUTION

Don't plunge or snake a drain if you've poured drain cleaners into the sink. The chemicals can cause serious burns if they splash on your skin. Use drain cleaners only if the sink is draining slowly and not completely clogged.

1 CHECK THE GARBAGE DISPOSER FIRST

If the side of the sink that has the disposer doesn't drain, plunge it first to remove the clog or force it down the drain.

One of the most common causes of a clogged drain is a clogged garbage disposer. If you flip the switch to turn on your garbage disposer and all you hear is a low humming sound, your disposer is probably jammed. Switch it off and unplug the unit. You can usually free it by turning the blades manually by inserting an Allen wrench in the hole on the bottom of the disposer.

If the disposer doesn't make any sound when you turn it back on, an internal breaker on the motor has probably tripped. Give the disposer a minute to cool off. Then press the reset button located on the bottom of the unit and turn it on again.

2 CLAMP OFF THE DISHWASHER

If you have a dishwasher, tighten a clamp over the flexible part of the drain line before plunging the drain. This prevents dirty water from flowing back into the dishwasher cabinet.

3 GET BUSY WITH THE PLUNGER

If the problem isn't in the disposer, plunge the drain. Plunging can be quick and easy, or it can be a wet mess. Keep some towels handy to soak up spills.

Fill the sink with 3 to 4 in. of water to ensure that the plunger seals around the drain. Hold a wet rag tightly over the other drain opening in a double sink or use the basket strainer to seal it (3A).

Plunge up and down vigorously for about 20 seconds. Roll the head of the plunger into the water so you force water, not air, into the drain. On your last upstroke, pop the plunger off the mouth of the drain for extra pressure (3B). If the water doesn't swirl straight down the drain, continue plunging for several minutes.

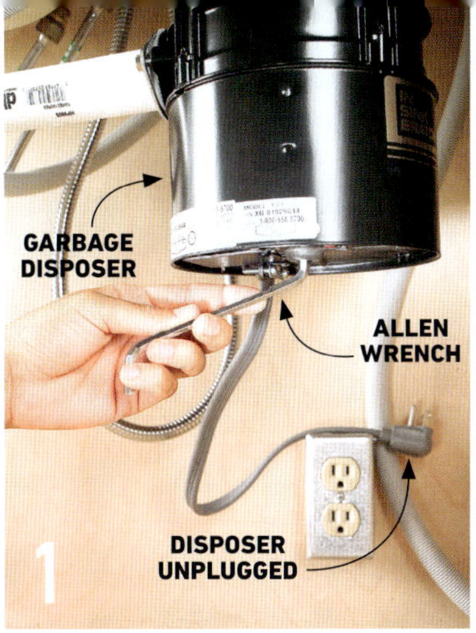

4 DISASSEMBLE THE P-TRAP

If intensive plunging doesn't remove the clog, disassemble and clean out the P-trap. Clogs that occur in the P-trap and trap arm of the drain most often occur when grease or coffee grounds build up.

Begin by sponging the water from the sink to reduce the flow under the sink when you pull off the trap. Keep your pan or bucket underneath; dirty water will flow out. Loosen the slip nuts, unscrewing the slip nut between the P-trap and the trap arm assembly first, then the nut at the bottom of the continuous waste tee. Wiggle the P-trap free.

We show plastic drain lines, but many older kitchen sinks have metal traps and pipes. Metal slip nuts are usually more difficult to loosen than plastic, but both will probably require the use of slip-joint pliers to break them free. Loosen the slip nuts gently to avoid cracking or bending the trap assembly.

5 CLEAN OUT THE TRAP

Clean out any debris from the P-trap. Inspect both the P-trap and the trap arm for cracks or weak walls. If it's worn, replace it to avoid problems. Reinstall the P-trap and test the line with warm water. Don't overtighten the slip nuts. Hand-tight plus a quarter-turn with pliers should be enough.

6 REMOVE THE TRAP ARM

If the P-trap isn't clogged, move on; remove the trap arm and clean it. To remove the trap arm, loosen the slip nut and slide the trap arm from the drain line stub-out. You will likely need pliers to remove the nut.

Next, run a screwdriver around the inside of the pipe stub-out and pull out any debris that may have collected in the opening. If you still haven't found the clog, reach for the snake!

7 INSERT THE DRAIN SNAKE

Loosen the setscrew at the tip of the snake and pull out 6 to 10 in. of cable. Then tighten the setscrew and spin the drain snake into the drain stub-out (7A). Initially, you may feel an obstruction, but it's likely that the tip of the snake is just turning a corner. Loosen the setscrew, pull out another 6 to 10 in. of cable and continue to feed the snake into the line. Tighten the setscrew and turn the crank clockwise to feed it into the drainpipe.

Continue to turn the snake when you encounter resistance. The snake tip is designed to corkscrew through clogs and around corners (7B).

8 RETRACT THE DRAIN SNAKE

When you feel the cable hit an obstruction, continue cranking and pushing the cable through the clog until you feel the tip bite through. This should be obvious because the tension in the cable will drop.

When you are through the clog, turn the crank counterclockwise and pull out the cable. Clean the cable as you pull; it'll probably be covered with incredibly dirty gunk. You may get a large plug of material at the end of the snake, so keep that bucket handy.

Repeat the process until you no longer feel a blockage, then reassemble the trap and run plenty of warm water to flush the line.

CLEAN THE DRAIN

After the drain is open, pour ½ cup of baking soda and ½ cup of white vinegar into the drain. Cover both openings and let it sit for a few minutes. Then run another gallon or so of warm water behind it to flush out the mixture. The combination of baking soda and vinegar will break down any leftover fat deposits and will leave your drain smelling fresh. Reinstall the P-trap and run water to test the drain.

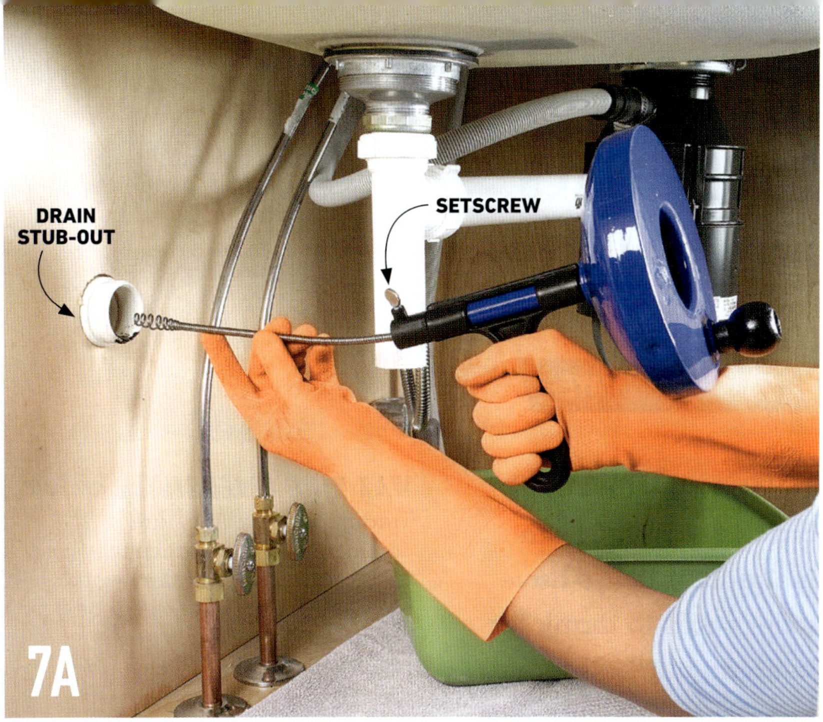

7A

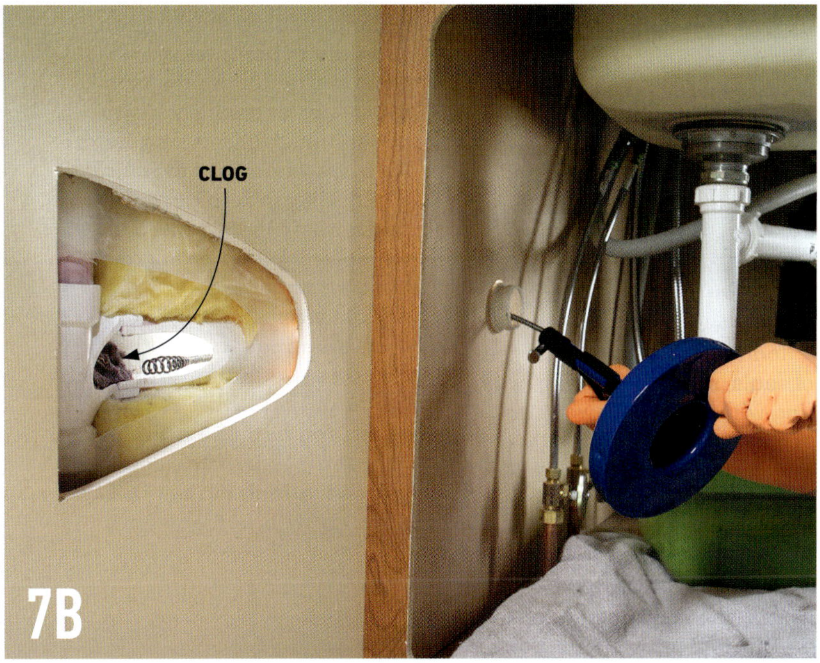

7B

8

TOILET SEALS: COMPARING TYPES

BY SAM ROSENMAYER

Toilet seals are small, but they are far from insignificant. We have toilet seals to thank for keeping our bathroom floors free of dirty toilet water when we flush.

A toilet seal works like a gasket around the base of the toilet by attaching to the toilet flange and the opening of the waste line. You'll need to buy a toilet seal when you're installing a new toilet or resetting the original toilet after remodeling, or if your current seal is compromised.

Today there are various types of seals, such as wax ring, wax ring with sleeve, felt wax ring, sponge gasket, wax-free gasket and wax-free foam gasket. Most of these seals come in different thicknesses. In order to have a good watertight seal, you may also have to add flange extenders to raise the height of a recessed flange if it is not ¼ in. above the floor.

Here are the most popular toilet seal options on the market:

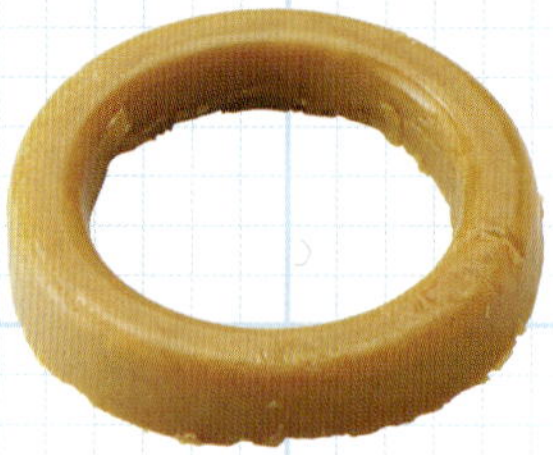

WAX RING (EVERBILT)

Traditional wax rings are commonly used because they are inexpensive and they work. They're made of vegetable- or petroleum-based wax, sometimes with a polyurethane additive. The wax material resists bacteria and mold growth while providing a tight seal.

Unlike rubber, wax doesn't deteriorate. But it can be a bit messy, especially if you haven't installed a ring before. Also, it's important to install a wax ring that is at room temperature. If the wax becomes too cold, it could crack and become unusable.

Most wax rings fit 3- and 4-in. openings, and if the distance between the flange and the floor is a little less than ¼ in., you can use a thicker wax seal. Wax rings cost less than $5, which makes them popular with homeowners.

WAX-FREE SPONGE GASKET (FLUIDMASTER)

If you're trying to avoid using a wax seal, another great option is Fluidmaster's 7530 Universal Better Than Wax Toilet Seal. This seal is made of sponge rubber, which makes it more durable and unaffected by temperature change.

Included with the seal is a rubber gasket, spacer and hardware for easy installation. The purpose of the spacer is to provide an airtight seal if the flange sits below floor level. This is a great option if you know your floor is uneven. You can set the toilet and reposition it more than once without damaging the seal since it is rubber, not wax. Like the foam gasket, this is a universal seal that will fit a 3- or 4-in. drainpipe. This seal costs about $10.

The right seal for you depends on your situation and budget. Before you buy a seal, make sure you take proper measurements of the drainpipe and of the distance between the flange and the floor.

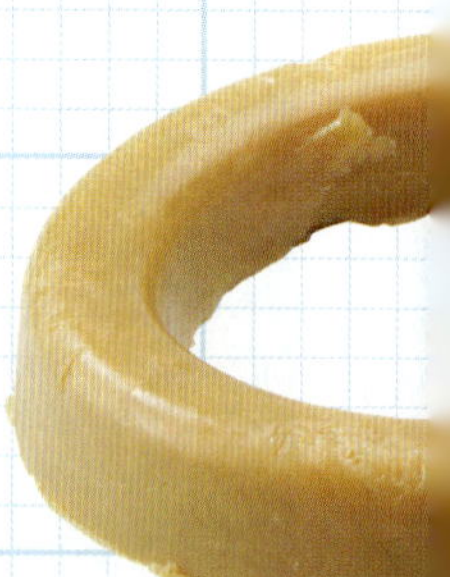

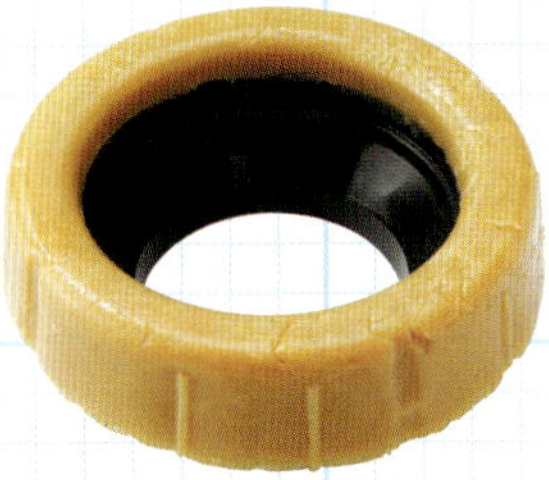

WAX RING WITH SLEEVE (OATEY)

This seal has the same properties and thickness options as traditional wax rings. The difference is the ring has a sleeve attached that fits into the waste line and provides more stability.

Again, if the distance between the flange and the floor is a bit less than ¼ in., you can use a thicker wax seal. This is a good option if your floor is a little uneven. Wax rings with a sleeve cost less than $10.

WAX-FREE SEAL (FERNCO)

A strong alternative to traditional wax seals is the wax-free toilet seal made of flexible PVC. An obvious advantage is you won't have to deal with the potential mess of wax. The PVC provides a strong seal, and once installed, it allows minor movement without compromising the seal.

This seal is ideal for situations when the floor is raised above the toilet flange no more than ¾ in. because no additional extensions are required. There are sizes to fit a 3- or 4-in. drainpipe. They cost less than $10.

WAX-FREE FOAM GASKET (KORKY)

Like the wax-free seal, the wax-free foam gasket is a less messy alternative to wax. Whether your flange sits below, at or above floor level, this seal is designed to fit and create a tight seal. Its two-piece foam is flexible enough to fit on the flange and creates a watertight seal.

Another advantage is that this universal seal will fit either a 3- or 4-in. drainpipe. You will need to attach the seal to the flange with the hardware provided. A drawback of this seal is the higher cost, about $13 to $17.

REVERSE THE SPIN OF A CEILING FAN

Help your home stay warm this winter just by flipping a switch

A ceiling fan can help keep your home cool in the summer, and warm in the winter. Did you know you should change the direction your ceiling fan spins from season to season?

While most people are familiar with the cooling effect that circulating air can have during warm weather, they may not realize that circulating air can help keep a home warm when the temperatures drop. This makes ceiling fans great to use all year. Spinning the fan the right direction at the right time can help keep everyone in your home comfortable and save money on your utility bills.

SUMMER AND WINTER SETTINGS

Your ceiling fan should spin counterclockwise (forward) during the summer. A ceiling fan that spins counterclockwise forces air downward, providing cooling relief when it's hot. As temperatures get higher, you'll naturally choose to run the fan faster to increase the cooling airflow.

Conversely, the ceiling fan needs to spin clockwise (reverse) during the winter. Because warm air rises, the air near the ceiling can be three to four degrees warmer than air near the floor. A ceiling fan that spins clockwise will draw cooler air up and force warmer air near the ceiling down and out toward walls. It's best to run the fan on a low speed so that it doesn't create too much of a cooling breeze.

MOMENTARY CHANGES TOO

Keep the fan direction in mind when you're looking to cool down or warm up a room. For instance, run the fan counterclockwise if an oven heats up your kitchen beyond what's comfortable or if body heat from a gathering of people makes a room toasty. Conversely, run a fan clockwise to amplify the heat from a fireplace or any other heat source in a room.

HOW TO SWITCH THE DIRECTION

Most ceiling fans have a switch on the motor that lets you change the direction by sliding the switch one way or the other. You will most likely need a ladder to reach it. Be sure your fan is turned off and completely still before getting on the ladder. Some ceiling fans have remote controls that let you easily change not only the speed of the fan but the spin direction as well—without getting on a ladder.

AMANDA PRISCHAK CONTRIBUTING WRITER

DOUBLE THE LIFE OF A WATER HEATER

A water heater needs to be flushed at least once a year to remove sediment on the bottom of the tank. That's especially true if you have hard water. This task is easy to blow off, but skipping it is costly. The buildup reduces the heater's efficiency and causes premature failure.

One sign of excessive sediment buildup is a popping or rumbling sound caused by steam bubbles percolating up through the muck.

If you've never flushed your water heater or haven't done it in years, sediment will likely clog the drain valve when you open it and keep you from fully closing the valve after the heater is drained. Then you'll have a leak too. We'll show you how to drain the sediment and skip a service call. You'll need to get a few plumbing parts from a home center, a garden hose, a wet vacuum, pliers and a pipe wrench.

BUY THE PARTS

The key is to build a new full-port drain valve so you can remove the debris. You'll need a ¾-in. full-port brass ball valve with threaded ends, a 3-in. x ¾-in. galvanized nipple, and a ¾-in. MIP x G.H. garden hose adapter (such as the BrassCraft/Plumbshop No. HU22-12-12TP).

Then build a shop vacuum adapter. If your vacuum has a 2½-in. hose, buy a converter to reduce it to 1¼ in. (the Shop Vac No. 9068500 is one option). Make a vacuum hose-to-plumbing adapter (Photo 1) with a 1¼-in. x 1½-in. female PVC trap adapter, a ¾-in. MIP x ½-in. barb fitting, a second ¾-in. x 3-in. nipple and a 24-in. piece of ½-in. I.D. vinyl tubing.

DRAIN THE TANK

Shut off the gas or electricity to the water heater and open a hot water faucet. Let it run full blast for about 10 minutes to reduce the water temperature in the tank. Then shut off the cold water valve at the top of the tank, attach a garden hose to the existing drain valve and route it to a floor drain. (Catch the sediment with a colander so it doesn't clog the drain.) Open a hot water faucet on an upper floor and the water heater drain valve. Let the tank drain until sediment clogs the valve and reduces the flow. Then close the upstairs hot water faucet and water heater drain valve.

Next, remove the blow-off tube and temperature pressure release (TPR) valve, and apply suction to the tank so you won't get soaked when you yank the old valve (Photo 2). Then swap the valves (Photo 3). Remove the vacuum hose from the TPR port and finish draining the tank.

Most of the sediment will flush out. To remove the rest, open the cold water valve at the top of the tank in short bursts to blast it toward the drain. If necessary, vacuum out the last of it (Photo 4).

When you're done, close the ball valve and remove the lever handle to prevent accidental opening. Then reinstall the TPR valve and blow-off tube. Refill the water heater and turn on the gas or electricity.

RICK MUSCOPLAT CONTRIBUTING WRITER

YUCK!

This is what the sediment looks like.

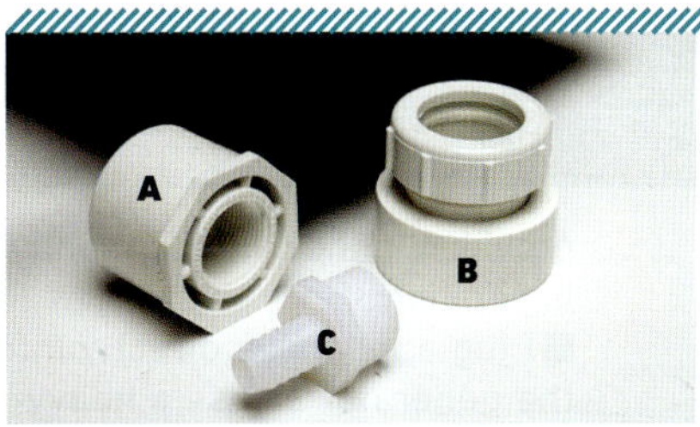

1 Glue a 1½-in. PVC x ¾-in. FIP adapter (A) onto a female PVC trap adapter (B). This allows you to attach your vacuum to ¾-in. pipe (see below). The barbed fitting (C) connects to tubing (Photo 4).

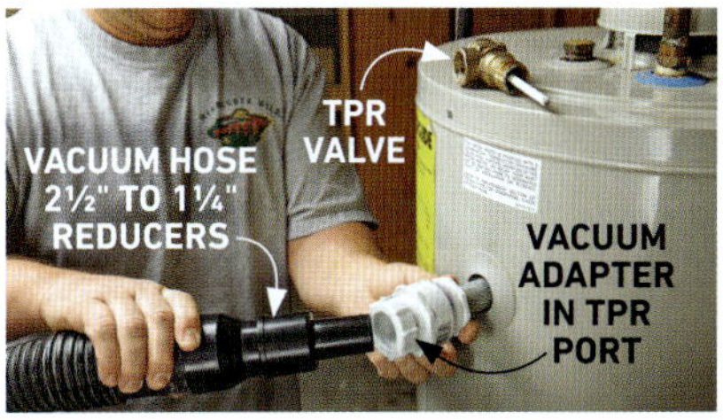

2 Remove the temperature pressure release (TPR) valve. Screw in the vacuum adapter. Attach the shop vacuum hose and turn on the vacuum.

3 Unscrew the old drain valve and install the full-port valve (closed position). Attach one end of the garden hose to the valve; run the other end into a colander and on to the floor drain.

4 Remove the full-port valve and suck out the remaining sediment with your shop vacuum adapter and vinyl tubing. See the final steps above.

USE YOUR GENERATOR SAFELY

One portable generator can produce as much carbon monoxide as hundreds of cars. With people increasingly relying on portable generators for backup power, the Consumer Product Safety Commission issued an alert: Gasoline-powered portable generators create a risk of carbon monoxide (CO) poisoning, which can kill in minutes.

Using data from 2017 to 2019, the CPSC report says "about 85 consumers die in the U.S. each year from CO poisoning caused by gasoline-powered portable generators." It goes on to say that about 81% of the deaths occurred in residential settings.

Among the households reporting fatalities, the three top reasons for generator use were weather-related power outages, power shutoffs and providing power to temporary locations such as cabins and campgrounds.

Because CO is odorless and colorless, it's possible to inhale a fatal dose and lose consciousness before exhibiting symptoms of poisoning, which include dizziness, nausea and weakness.

PROPER VENTILATION IS CRUCIAL

Never use a generator indoors—not even in a garage, outbuilding or tent. Always keep it at least 20 ft. from the house and far from doors and windows.

It can be tempting to run a generator on a porch or in an unused part of the house, especially if it's raining or snowing. Don't. Generac, a leading generator manufacturer, says that it's impossible to provide adequate ventilation in an enclosed space, even if you open all the windows and run a fan.

If you must run a generator during heavy rain, put it under the overhang of a shed or garage roof as far as possible from windows. You could also put it under a table or build a makeshift roof with four posts. Never cover a generator with a tarp.

SOME MODELS FEATURE AUTOMATIC CO SHUTOFF

The CPSC report includes these guidelines:

- Buy a generator with an automatic CO shutoff. Models conforming to the latest safety standards can prevent 87 to 100% of deaths from CO poisoning.
- Maintain the generator regularly to minimize emissions. Clean the air filter before each use, top off the oil, and frequently clean or replace the spark plug.
- Install battery-operated CO detectors or hardwired detectors with battery backup on each level of your home and also in all sleeping areas.

USE THESE SAFETY TIPS

Be sure that you read and understand all the safety precautions provided in the owner's manual. In addition:

- Plug appliances directly into the generator or use a heavy-duty outdoor extension cord rated for the total current draw of all appliances plugged into it.
- To prevent burns, don't touch any part of the motor while the generator is running.
- Don't smoke or use lighters near a running generator.
- Avoid gas spills. Don't overfill the tank, and don't add gas while the unit is running. Turn off the unit and let it cool first.
- Don't feed a generator directly into your electrical panel by yourself. Leave that to a licensed electrician.

CHRIS DEZIEL CONTRIBUTING WRITER

GREAT GOOFS®

LAUGHS AND LESSONS FROM OUR READERS

THE NEW FANDANGO

While I was installing our expensive new ceiling fan, I noticed a red caution tag, but I was eager to proceed so I figured I'd read it later.

I followed the directions and included the extra bracing. When I was done, I proudly called in my wife. As I flipped the switch, the fan immediately unscrewed itself from the threaded support pipe, came whirling down and crashed to the floor. The fan was destroyed, there were ugly scratches in our new hardwood floor and you can guess what my wife had to say!

When I got around to reading the red tag, here's what it said: "After the pipe is screwed in, use the locking screw provided to lock the pipe onto the main support."

STEPHEN FINEGAN

WHAT A TURKEY

The week before Thanksgiving, my office gave each employee a free turkey as thanks for our hard work during the year. I rushed home with my frozen bird, and my wife told me to put it in the basement freezer since the kitchen freezer was full. I took the turkey downstairs and opened the door to find the freezer compartment almost completely iced over. There was no time to defrost it, so I thought I would chip away just enough ice to fit the turkey inside.

I grabbed a small hammer and a screwdriver to begin tapping on the ice—one, two ... but on my third tap, there was a loud hiss. I had ruptured a refrigerant line that was just below the ice. The estimate to repair the line and replace the coolant was about the same as the cost of a new freezer: $350. I bought a new freezer and put my very expensive "free" turkey inside it.

PAUL HILPERT

3 WOODWORKING & WORKSHOP PROJECTS & TIPS

TAMBOUR CABINET

BUILD A SIMPLE, ELEGANT CABINET WITH EASY SLIDING DOORS

BY BRAD HOLDEN

Inspired by a roll-top desk, found in many grandparents' homes, we designed a stylish cabinet that features two sliding tambour doors. The way the slats of wood—or tambours—curl out of sight seems almost magical.

We milled the tambours using a special set of router bits. To assemble the tambours, we used, and will show you, the traditional method of backing them with canvas—it's what makes the magic happen!

MEET THE BUILDER

BRAD HOLDEN IS A FIRST-TIME TAMBOUR DOOR MAKER. YOU CAN DO IT TOO!

1 MAKE THE TOP AND SHELF

Edge-glue boards together to make the top and the shelf. Leave them slightly longer than the final dimensions. If needed, use cauls covered with packing tape to keep the glued-up panels as flat as possible. When the glue is dry, cut them to the final dimensions and sand them flat.

2 BEVEL THE EDGES

Make a simple tall sliding fence. The fence's carriage should fit over your saw's fence, sliding freely but not loose. After cutting the top and shelf to the final dimensions, tilt your saw blade 10 degrees and clamp a panel into the jig. Set the fence and slide the panel through. Rotate the panel 90 degrees after each pass and run it through, repeating until all the edges are beveled. Do the same with the other panel.

3 MAKE THE TRACK TEMPLATES

Cut out a melamine template blank that's 12 x 14 in. Give the corners a 3-in. radius, then sand to the lines to smooth the curves. You'll use this to rout the track. Next, cut a triangular template with a 22-degree angle; this is for cutting the access slot.

4 ROUT THE TAMBOUR TRACK

Center the track template on the top side of the shelf and tack it with 1-in. brad nails. Rout the track 7⁄16-in. deep using a 3⁄8-in. router bit with a guide bushing. Add the access-slot template and rout the "on ramp." Remove the templates and repeat the process on the underside of the top, making sure the top track is oriented to mirror the shelf track.

WHAT IT TAKES

TIME	COST	SKILL LEVEL
2 days	$500	Intermediate

TOOLS
Router, router table, tambour router bit set *(rockler.com)*, 3⁄8-in. router bit, dado set, clamps, drill press, miter saw, two miter gauges, table saw, tall fence for table saw, tapering jig, doweling jig

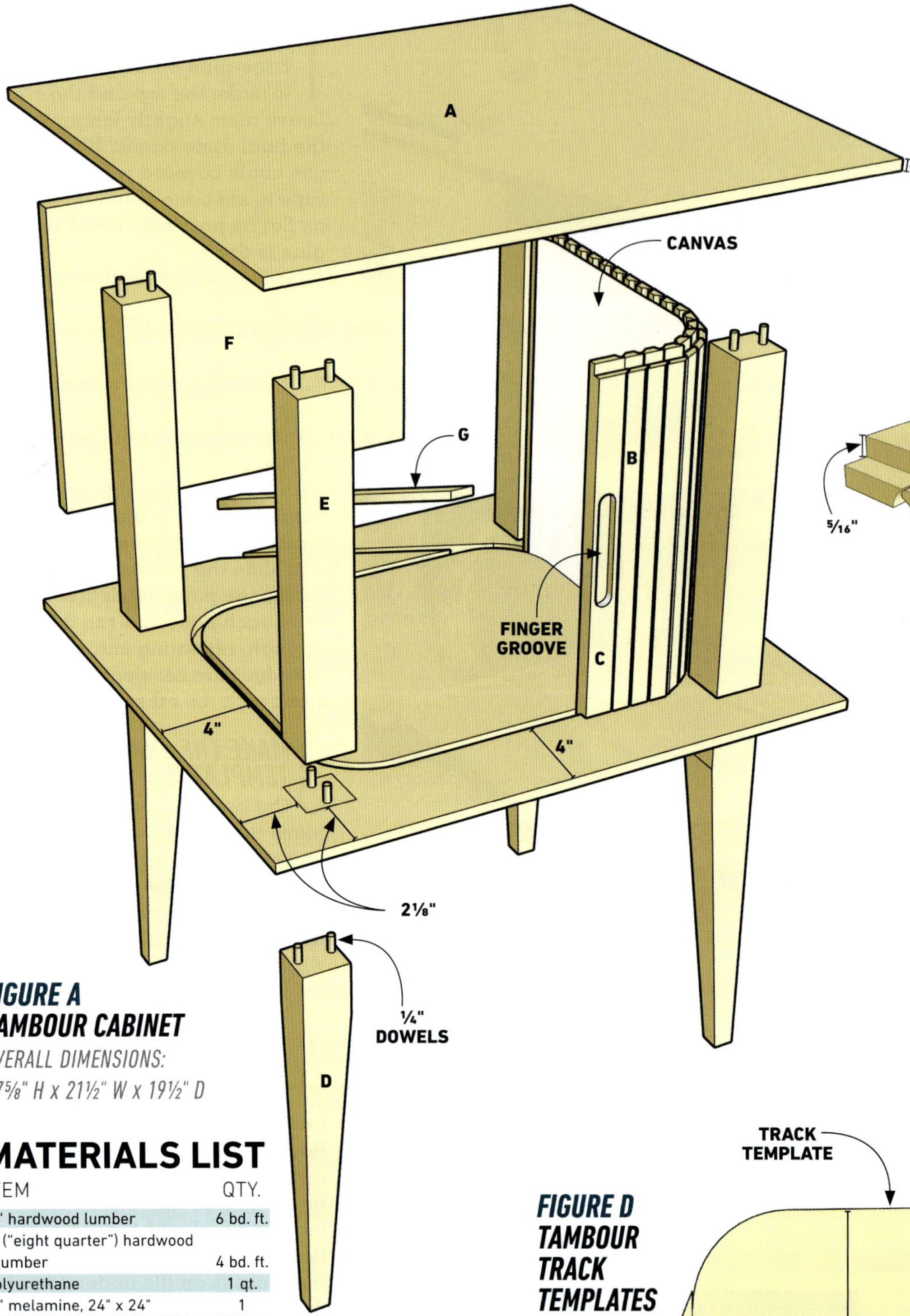

FIGURE B
RABBET CLOSE-UP

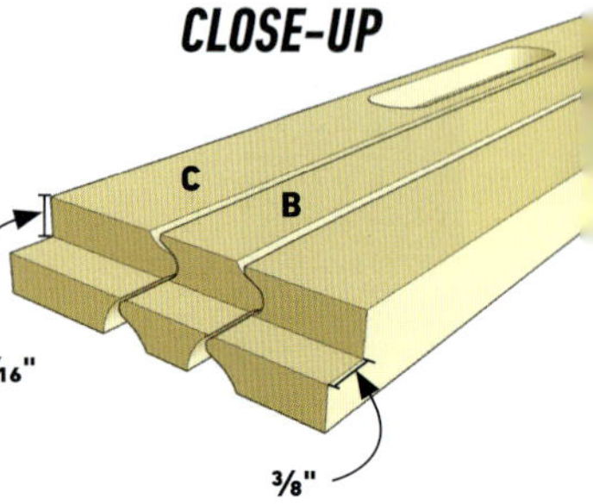

FIGURE C
LOWER LEG

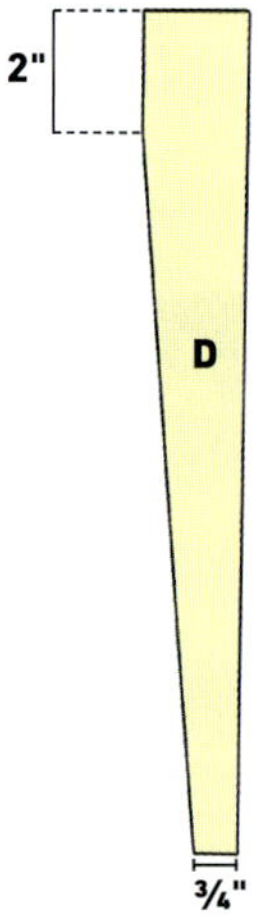

FIGURE A
TAMBOUR CABINET

OVERALL DIMENSIONS:
27 5/8" H x 21 1/2" W x 19 1/2" D

MATERIALS LIST

ITEM	QTY.
3/4" hardwood lumber	6 bd. ft.
8/4 ("eight quarter") hardwood lumber	4 bd. ft.
Polyurethane	1 qt.
1/2" melamine, 24" x 24"	1
1/4" dowels	24
Wood glue	
Canvas	
Pocket hole jig	
Pocket hole screws	

CUTTING LIST

KEY	QTY.	DIMENSIONS	PART
A	2	3/4" x 19 1/2" x 21 1/2"	Top/Shelf
B	38	5/8" x 1" x 12 3/4"	Tambours
C	2	5/8" x 1 1/4" x 12 3/4"	End tambours
D	4	1 3/4" x 1 3/4" x 14"	Lower leg
E	4	1 3/4" x 1 3/4" x 12"	Upper leg
F	1	3/4" x 14 3/4" x 12"	Back
G	2	3/8" x 3/8" x 10"	Access stops

FIGURE D
TAMBOUR TRACK TEMPLATES

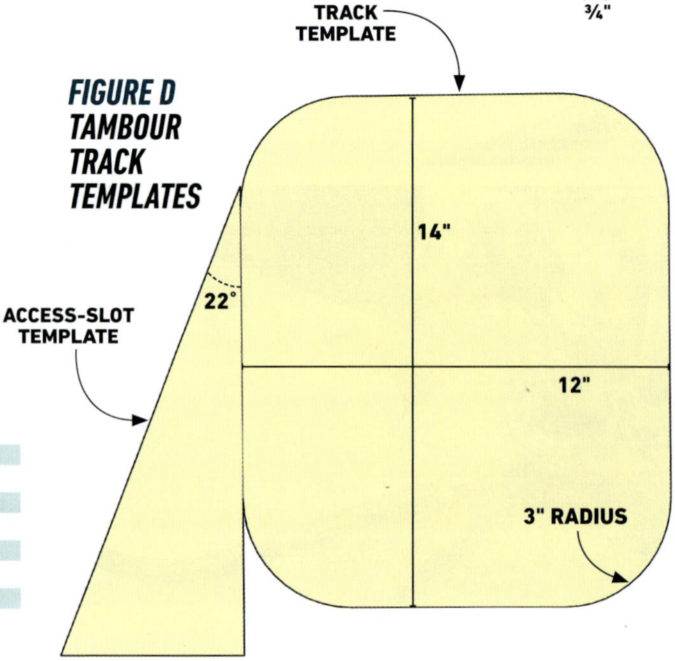

5 ROUT THE FIRST SIDE OF EACH TAMBOUR

After cutting all the tambour blanks, set up the first router bit to cut the convex side of each tambour. For safety and consistency, install featherboards and/or stock guides on the table and fence. Run all the blanks through to shape the first sides.

BIT 1

6 THEN ROUT THE SECOND SIDE

Set up the second bit to cut the concave side of each tambour. Again, using featherboards, run blanks through to cut the second sides. Route only one side of the last tambours on each panel, which includes the wider-end tambours with the finger pulls. Because the panels are mirror images, the outer tambours will be routed with opposite bits, leaving the other edges flat.

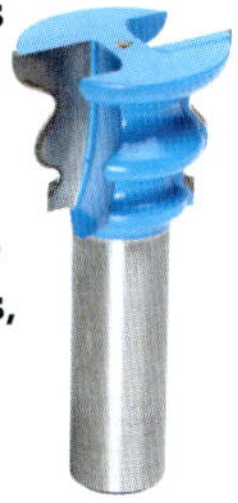

BIT 2

7 RABBET THE TAMBOUR ENDS

Attach a long fence across two miter gauges. Install a 1/2-in. dado blade in your saw and make a cut through the fence, dialing in the 5/16-in. depth. To the fence, add a stop positioned to cut the 3/8-in. dimension of the rabbets. The stop allows you to quickly and accurately cut rabbets on the ends of each tambour. See Figure B for the rabbet dimensions.

8 ROUT THE PULLS

To cut a 4-in. finger groove centered on each of the end tambours, set up a fluting bit in your router table and attach stops on the fence that limit the tambour's travel. Starting at one stop, carefully lower that part onto the bit, then slide it to the other stop.

9 FINISH THE TAMBOURS

Apply the finish of your choice to the tambours. Leave the backs unfinished so the wood glue can adhere the tambours to the canvas. Allow the tambours to dry while you work on the cabinet.

10 TAPER THE LEGS

The lower legs are tapered on two sides. Using a shop-made tapering jig, cut the first taper on each leg (see Figure C). Set the jig for the second taper and cut that taper on all the legs. Next, cut the square upper legs.

11 DOWEL THE LEGS

Drill two dowel holes in both ends of each upper leg using a doweling jig. Drill dowel holes in the tops of the lower legs in the opposite direction from the upper legs so they don't interfere during assembly.

12 DRILL THE TOP AND SHELF DOWEL HOLES

Using dowel centers in the leg dowel holes (12A), carefully position each leg in its marked location. Press down firmly so the dowel centers mark the hole locations in the shelf and top. Drill each hole using a depth stop on your drill bit (12B). Don't use a tape flag on the bit in this case—tape won't stop a drill bit!

13 ATTACH THE LOWER LEGS

With the shelf upside down, insert glued dowels into the holes. Put glue on the ends of the legs and in the leg dowel holes, and press the legs into place. Drill a clearance hole for a screw through the shelf, centered on each leg, and a pilot hole into each leg. Drive one 3-in. wood screw into each leg for stability.

14 ADD THE UPPER LEGS

Install the upper legs in place on the top of the shelf as you did the lower legs, using glue and dowels.

15 ADD THE TOP

Glue the dowels into the tops of the upper legs. Position the top on the dowels and press the top into place using a clamp at each corner. When the glue is dry, sand and finish the whole cabinet.

16

17

16 FRAME THE TAMBOURS

Build a frame on a piece of melamine to hold your tambours snug and perfectly square. Place the tambours face down in the frame. Apply painter's tape around the edges, masking off about ¾ in. all the way around.

17 APPLY THE CANVAS

Cut a piece of canvas slightly larger than the tambour area. Spread a coat of wood glue on the canvas and the backs of the tambours. A foam roller works well for this. You don't want the glue to run down the edges of the tambours, so don't apply a heavy coat. Weigh down the canvas evenly while the glue dries.

18 TRIM THE CANVAS

When the glue is dry, trim off the excess canvas at the tape line with a straightedge and a utility knife. Repeat these steps to make the second door.

19 WAX THE TRACK

Apply paraffin canning wax to the ends of the tambours to ensure they slide freely in the track.

18

19

20

21

20 INSTALL THE DOORS

Slip the tambour assemblies into their tracks via the access slot at the back of the cabinet.

21 ADD THE ACCESS STOPS

Insert the access stops in the tracks and fasten them with ⅝-in. wood screws. Don't glue the stops in place.

22 INSTALL THE BACK

Fasten the back into place between the two back legs using only pocket screws and no glue. If the sliding doors ever need repair or rewaxing, you'll be able to easily remove the access stops and the back to remove the doors.

22

BY JAY CORK

WHAT IT TAKES

TIME	COST	SKILL LEVEL
2 hours	$140	Beginner

TOOLS
Straight and curved carving knives

CARVE A SPOON

GET THE SCOOP—THIS IS SO FUN *AND* EASY!

Simple or fancy, a hand-carved spoon adds a unique flair to your utensil collection. Spoon carving is something anyone can learn, and it can become a rewarding hobby. With a few simple tools and a few simple cuts, you can be on your way to carving an everyday utensil, a thoughtful gift or your next family heirloom.

THE KNIVES YOU NEED

ONE STRAIGHT KNIFE

For most carving projects, you can use a straight knife such as this Flexcut roughing knife (about $30 at Woodcraft). How a knife feels in your hand is more important than a brand. If you're able, try before you buy.

ONE OR TWO CURVED KNIVES

For carving spoons, you need curved hook knives (about $45 each online). The right-handed knife is pulled toward your body with your right hand or pushed with your left. The left-handed knife works the opposite way. You may want both to work with changes in grain direction.

KEEP YOUR KNIFE SHARP

Carvers use a secret weapon to keep their knives sharper longer—a strop. Make a habit of routinely drawing your blade on the strop as you carve and you won't have to go to the stone nearly as often. Try using a little oil on a leather strop.

MEET THE EXPERT

CHARLIE EILER HAS BEEN CARVING WOOD SINCE HE WAS 6 YEARS OLD AND TAUGHT HIS FIRST CARVING CLASS AT THE RIPE OLD AGE OF 14. HE'S NOW A LOT OLDER THAN THAT.

PRO TIP
If your pattern doesn't fit the wood blank, trace the top and bottom of the profile, then draw the stem to fit.

1 DRAW THE PATTERN

With a pencil, trace the pattern on a ¾-in.-thick wood blank.

2 ROUGH-CUT THE BLANK

A band saw makes this step a breeze, but you can do the rough cut with a scroll saw or even by hand with a coping saw. Cut as close to the line as you can.

3 CARVE THE INSIDE OF THE BOWL

Carve the concave bowl of the spoon first. With a curved hook knife, start in the middle and work your way to ¼ in. from the edge.

PATTERNS

The fun thing about patterns is that you can use one for the spoon bowl and another for the stem. Mix and match to create unique designs. Feel free to use this one or to come up with your own, and share your results with us at submissions@familyhandyman.com.

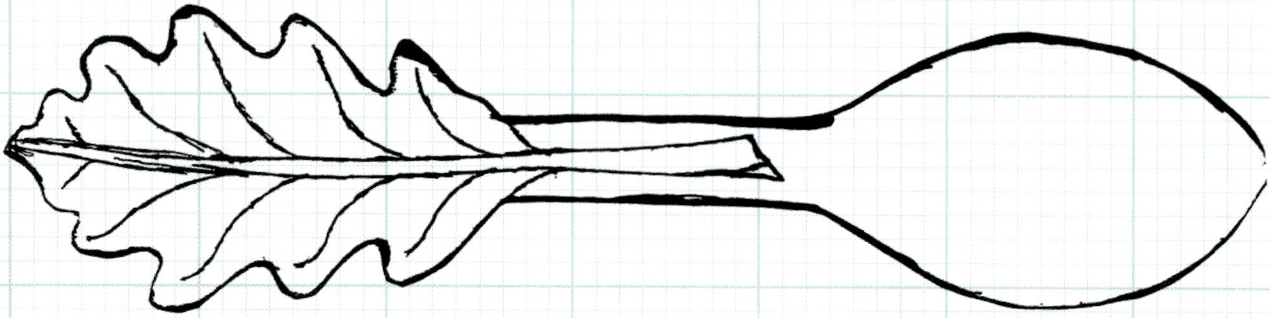

4 MATCH THE OUTSIDE TO THE INSIDE

Once the inside bowl has been carved to the desired depth, start shaping the outside of the bowl with the straight knife. Leave the bottom about ¼ in. thick.

5 THIN THE LIP

Taking small cuts, trim the inside edge of the spoon bowl to create a thin lip.

6 EASE THE HANDLE'S CORNERS AND EDGES

Ease the edges on the back of the leaf with the straight knife. Use your opposing thumb to push the knife in short cuts, creating a slightly rounded profile.

7 GROOVE THE CENTER

Cut a groove down the center of the back with the knife tip. Draw it down one side, and then come in from the opposite side to trim the "V" to the desired depth.

8 CARVE THE TOP OF THE LEAF

Pressing at an angle, chip the scooped detail of the leaf petals. Cut one side, then cut the other until you've achieved the desired shape.

9 FINISH THE BOTTOM OF THE LEAF

After the top is complete, carve the back using the same technique as for the top.

10 FINISH THE STEM

Use a pencil to shade in the areas to be cut off. Trim the bottom of the stem with a straight first cut. For the next cuts, trim the sides of the stem down to the spoon handle. Bevel the stem's edges to your liking.

11 SAND IT SMOOTH

Before finishing, sand the inside bowl of your spoon with 220-grit sandpaper. Typically, you don't need to sand any other part of the spoon. Remember, carvings don't have to be perfect; little flaws add character!

FINISHES

Our expert uses only one finish on spoons. Tung Oil Finish from Minwax is easy to use, dries fast and can be reapplied as needed.

PRO TIP

Wash your spoons by hand using only warm water and dish soap—never put them in the dishwasher!

HAND-CUT DOVETAILS

LEARN THIS CENTURIES-OLD JOINERY METHOD

BY BRAD HOLDEN

At *Family Handyman*, we have cut lots of dovetails, both by hand and using dovetail jigs and a router. When doing a run of drawers, we'll use the jig and router 10 times out of 10. But for a small project, we'll cut them by hand. Why? First, in the time it takes to get the jig and router set up and dialed in, you could be well into the process of cutting them by hand. Second, hand-cutting dovetails is fun and rewarding. We'll show you just one method. It's important to work as accurately as you can, but don't be concerned with perfection. Enjoy the truly handcrafted look!

LEAVE YOUR LAYOUT MARKS! THEY'RE THE HALLMARK OF A HAND-CUT DOVETAIL.

FIGURE A
DOVETAIL ANATOMY

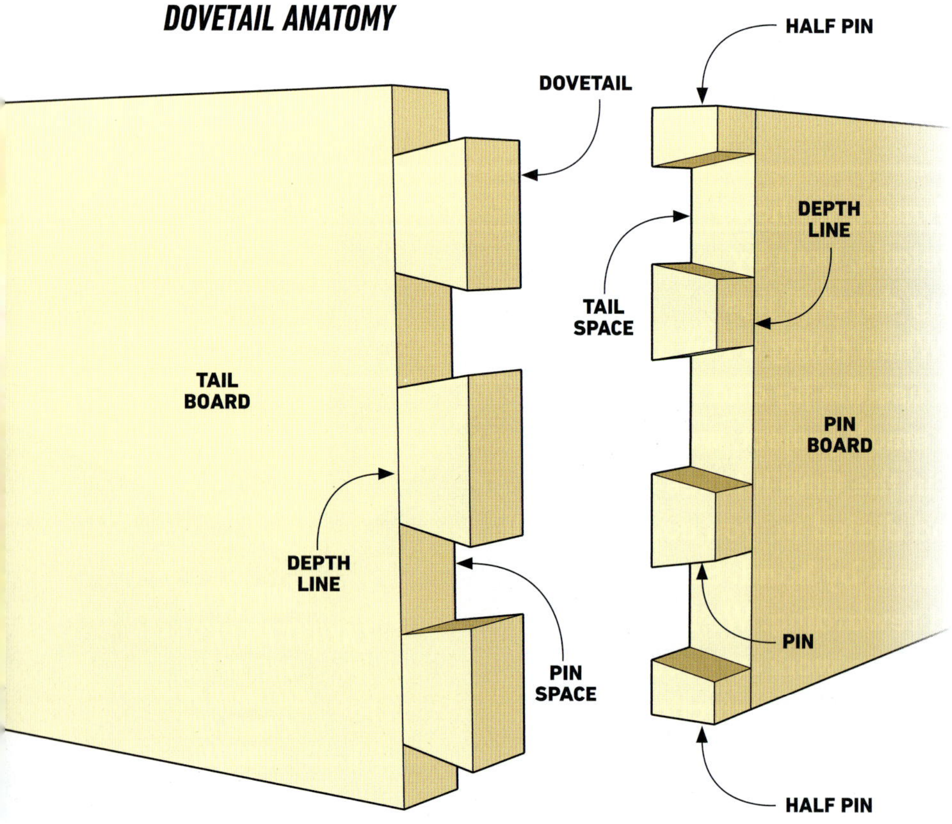

TOOLS & MATERIALS

In addition to hardwood lumber and wood glue, you'll need a dovetail saw, chisels, sharpening stones, a sharpening guide, a sliding T-bevel, a square, a marking gauge, a marking knife, and a woodworking vise or clamps.

HOW IT WORKS

A dovetail joint is made by cutting interlocking parts on two pieces of wood. The tail board has the dovetails. The pin board has pins that slide in between the dovetails. Each outer edge of the pin board has a half pin, meaning only one face of the pin is angled.

It's a strong joinery method because the parts mechanically resist being pulled apart and have a lot of gluing surface.

1 MARK THE DOVETAIL DEPTH

After milling your parts to their final dimensions, use a marking gauge to lay out the depth of the dovetails on each piece. For "through" dovetails like these, that depth is equal to the board's thickness.

2 LAY OUT THE TAILS

With the sliding T-bevel on the end of your board, set the dovetail angle—given in a "rise and run" format instead of degrees. Softwoods are traditionally 1:6, and hardwoods 1:8. Lay out the tails with a marking knife. Unlike a line marked by even a sharp pencil, a line marked by a knife is exact. You can choose your dovetail size, but there should be a half pin on both edges of the pin boards.

3 TRANSFER THE LINES

Using a square and a marking knife, transfer the tail marks across the ends of the tail boards. From there, bring the angled tail layout lines down the other face of the tail board.

4 CUT TO THE LINE

Staying just outside your layout marks, saw down each line to just shy of the depth line. If you like, mark the waste areas to be cut out so you don't cut on the wrong side of the lines. (No, of course we've never made that mistake.) Cut off the half-pin space waste on the outer edges now as well.

5 CHISEL TO LAYOUT LINE

This is where your sharp chisels come into play. Starting inside the depth line, just wiggle the chisel up to the line. Next, set the chisel on the layout line, press down lightly and then wiggle the chisel up to the depth line again. This method sets the dovetail depth accurately. If you chop in hard right on the line, the chisel will push its way past your depth mark.

6 CHOP OUT THE FIRST SIDE

Once you've chiseled down about ⅛ in., you can chop more aggressively. Leave the outer ends of the pin waste intact and proceed until you're about halfway through the board's thickness. The outer ends will give the pin waste support when you're chopping from the other side, helping to prevent tear-out.

7 THEN DO THE SECOND

Flip the pin boards over and start the second side as you did the first, just wiggling up to the line. Then chop each pin space all the way through. Go lightly as you reach the end.

8 PARE THE TAILS

Clamp your tail boards in a vise and use a chisel to pare the tails to their layout lines. Be sure to look at the layout lines on both sides of the board so you keep the tails perfectly square.

9 TRANSFER TAILS TO THE PIN BOARD

Set your tails on the ends of the pin boards and transfer their layout with a marking knife. Next, use a square to mark the pins down to the depth lines on both sides of the pin boards.

10 CUT TO THE LINES

Cut the pins as you did the tails, staying just outside the layout lines and stopping just short of the depth line.

11 CHOP OUT THE FIRST SIDE

Chop out the first side of the tail waste exactly as you did the pin waste, wiggling the chisel to get an accurate start.

12 THEN DO THE SECOND

Flip the tail boards and chop out the rest of the tail waste. It's trickier than pin waste; you're chopping an angled cut.

13 PARE TO THE LAYOUT LINES

Pare the pins to their layout lines. Again, be careful to pay attention to both sides of the board to keep everything square.

14 TEST THE FIT

Press the joint together to check the fit. Chances are you'll need to adjust it. Mark the areas that need material removed and carefully pare off a bit at a time, checking the fit often so you don't overdo it. A good fit requires only a light tapping with a mallet.

15 ASSEMBLE THE JOINT

Once you're satisfied with the fit, apply glue to all the mating surfaces and press the joint together. With the glue applied, you may have to be a bit more forceful with your mallet.

16 SAND AND FINISH

Once the glue is dry, sand and apply finish.

MEET THE BUILDER

BRAD HOLDEN IS A FORMER CABINETMAKER AND A SELF-PROFESSED HAND-POWERED TOOL SNOB.

WHAT IF THERE ARE GAPS?

Rest assured, there will almost always be a couple of gaps that bug you, especially if you are new to this or out of practice. Don't worry. You can fill them and make them disappear.

CUT WEDGES

CUT SMALL WEDGES from an extra board. Make several vertical cuts, then saw the wedges free by cutting in from the side. Make wedges with grain going vertically as well as horizontally so you can easily match the grain at the gaps.

GLUE IN THE WEDGES

SPREAD A LITTLE glue on a wedge and slip it into the gap. When the glue is dry, cut off any extra material and sand the repaired area.

HARDWARE ORGANIZER

STORE ITEMS IN FLEXIBLE, PORTABLE BINS

BY GARY WENTZ

This bin system is the perfect project to get you organized. It's modeled on the systems used in cabinet shops, plumbers' vans and mechanics' garages.

The materials cost for the bins shown is about $90 to $125, depending on the plywood you choose. We built these bins from leftovers and didn't spend a dime.

FRENCH CLEATS MAKE IT NEAT

This simple hanging system—made from 1x4s cut at a 45-degree bevel—lets you grab a bin and take it to the job, or rearrange bins instantly as your needs change.

WHAT IT TAKES

TIME	COST	SKILL LEVEL
4 days	$125 or less	Beginner

TOOLS
Table saw, miter saw, brad nailer

Begin by measuring the items you want to store. We found a basic bin just right for most stuff: nuts and bolts, as well as plumbing and electrical parts. For larger items, we made a few bins wider but didn't change the bin sides (A) since doing so requires more fuss.

With sizes chosen, rip plywood into strips on your table saw. If you're following our plan, you'll need strips 1¾, 3½ and 6 in. wide. Then cut the strips to length, making parts for one bin only. Test-assemble the bin to check the fit of the parts. If all parts are the right size, mass-produce them by chopping the strips to length (Photo 1).

1 CUT THE PARTS

Rip strips of plywood to width on a table saw, then cut them to length with a miter saw. Clamp a scrap of plywood to the saw's fence to act as a stop block. That lets you cut identical lengths from several strips with one chop.

2 CUT THE DIVIDER SLOTS

Set your table saw blade to a height of 3/16 in. Screw a long fence to your miter gauge and run the fence across the blade to cut a

FIGURE A BASIC BIN

INSIDE DIMENSIONS: 4" W x 6" H x 3" D

MATERIALS LIST

ITEM	QTY.
4' x 8' x ½" plywood	1
2' x 4' x ⅛" hardboard	1
1x4 x 8' pine	3
1" brads	
2½" screws	
Wood glue	
Watco Danish Oil (Natural)	

CUTTING LIST

KEY	QTY.	DIMENSIONS	PART
A	2	3½" x 6½"	Sides
B	1	4" x 6"*	Bottom
C	1	3½" x 4"	Back
D	1	1¾" x 5"	Front
E	1	3" x 4⁵⁄₁₆"	Divider
F	1	¾" x 1½" x 5"	Cleat

Dividers are hardboard. Cleats are pine. All other parts are plywood.
**"Half-inch" plywood is slightly less than ½ in. thick, so the bin bottom (B) needs to be slightly longer than 6 in. Start at 6⅛ in., then trim as needed.*

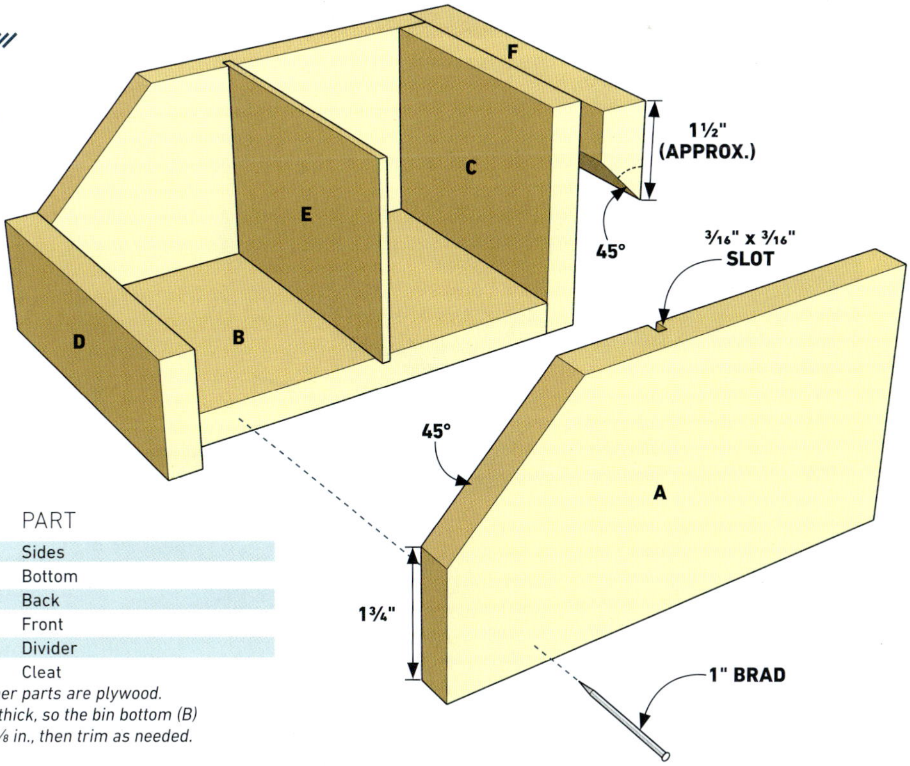

notch on the fence. Position a stop block 3¼ in. from the center of the notch. Place a side (A) against the block, run it across the blade, rotate it 180 degrees and cut it again (Photo 2). Check the fit of a divider in the slot and reposition the block if needed to adjust the width of the slot. It may take several tries to get it right.

When you're done cutting slots, it's time to clip off one corner of each bin side. Set your miter saw 45 degrees to the right. Clamp on a stop block and "gang-cut" sides just as you did when cutting parts to length (similar to Photo 1). Note: Slotted sides require left/right pairs. For every side that you cut with the slot facing up, cut another with the slot down.

3 CUT THE CLEATS

Tilt the blade to 45 degrees and set the fence so that the bin cleat is 1½ in. wide. Getting the fence positioned may take some trial and error, so cut a test scrap first. The 45-degree bevel cuts will leave sharp edges, so crank the table saw blade back to zero degrees and shave ⅛ in. off each cleat before cutting them to length.

4 ASSEMBLE THE BINS

Join the parts with glue and brads. The glue will provide plenty of strength, so drive only as many brads as needed to hold the parts together while the glue sets. Using an 18-gauge brad nailer, first tack the back (C) to the bottom (B); then add the sides (A), the front (D) and finally the cleat (F). After assembly, we wiped on two coats of Watco Danish Oil.

5 MOUNT THE WALL CLEATS

Mark the stud locations with tape and screw on the lowest cleat, making sure it's level. Then cut spacers at least 1¾ in. tall and use them to position the remaining wall cleats (Photo 5). Larger cleats will create more space between rows of bins, making it easier to reach in and grab stuff. Bins filled with hardware put a heavy load on the cleats, so drive a screw into every wall stud.

WORKSHOP LESSONS

THINGS YOU LEARN ALONG THE WAY

BY JAY CORK

Whether you share a shop with cars and a lawn mower or you have your own dedicated woodworking space, make the most of your time there. While working in tight spaces as well as spacious shops, you'll learn enough tips, tricks and techniques to write a book. Here are just a few of our favorites.

PORTABLE DUST CONTROL

You can buy box fans with attached filters, like the one shown, or you can simply attach a filter to the back of an old box fan. Either way, having one of these portable dust-control devices on hand lets you keep it close to the dust. You can also use the device as a downdraft table when sanding!

MEET THE EXPERT

JAY CORK ENJOYS SHARING HIS BEST PRO TIPS WITH YOU, WHETHER YOU LIKE IT OR NOT.

REMEMBER TO BRUSH YOUR TEETH

Clean teeth stay sharp longer. To ensure you're getting the best cuts from your saws, clean the pitch and resin from your blades. Set the blade in a special container that holds circular saw blades. Then spray the blade with a blade and bit cleaner and scrub it with a brass wire brush.

STORE CHEMICALS AND SOLVENTS PROPERLY

Most DIYers have a hard time getting rid of anything. But when it comes to solvents, finishes and cans of paint, it's best to recycle them once they're too old to use. For the solvents that are still usable, follow these simple rules:

- Keep them in their original containers with a legible label.
- Store out of reach of children and pets.
- Keep them out of extreme temps—freezing will spoil them; heat will make them more dangerous.
- Consider a lockable, fire-safe storage cabinet.
- Know what to do in case of an emergency. Call hazardous waste management or poison control immediately.

MAKE CHIP-FREE CUTS

If you're cutting plywood with a jigsaw or a circular saw, chip-out is just part of the game. Here's our preferred way to reduce it. First, start with a sharp blade. Next, apply a strip of painter's tape where you are cutting. Mark your cutting lines right on top of the tape, then make the cuts.

KEEP YOUR ROUTER BITS SHARP

Sending router bits out to be sharpened is risky. Profile bits might get slightly altered, and flush-cut bits may no longer match the bearing diameter after a traditional sharpening. Instead, use a diamond card. Carefully run the flat, back face of the carbide bit along the diamond card to sharpen the carbide edges. Keep the card handy and give your bits a quick tuneup before each use.

MAKE DUST COLLECTION FITTINGS FIT

Vacuum hoses, tool-specific dust fittings and hose adapters can be frustrating to piece together. But there are a few tricks to make most fittings work. If the inside diameter of a fitting is too large, wrap duct tape around the smaller fitting until they fit snugly. When a dust fitting is just slightly too small—which seems to happen all the time—soften the fittings with a heat gun to save the day.

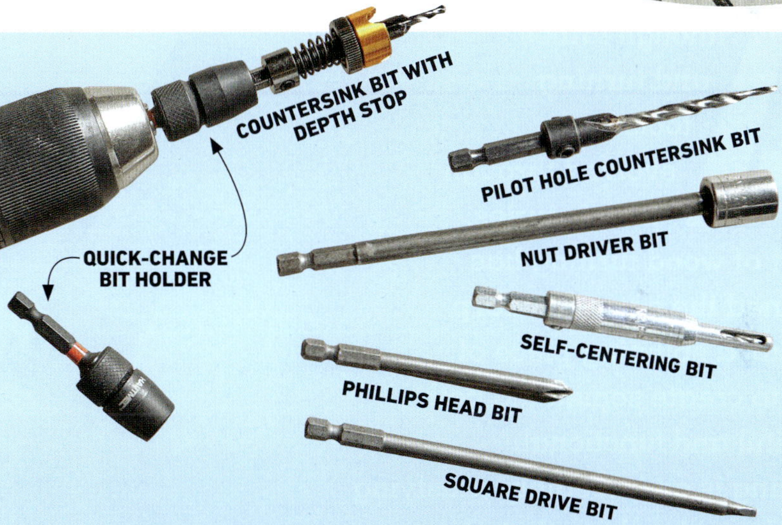

CHANGE BITS FAST

If you are constantly switching between a countersink bit and a driver bit, this one change to a cordless drill setup will save time and frustration.

The secret is a quick-change bit holder. Similar to an impact driver's chuck, this bit eliminates the need to loosen a drill's chuck. You can release the bit from the bit holder and swap it for your next task.

DON'T BURN DOWN YOUR SHOP—OR HOUSE!

It's often considered a myth that oily rags spontaneously ignite. But they do and they will. We've witnessed it firsthand. When you're finished with a rag soaked in solvents like stain or oil-based finishes, drape it over your waste bucket or on a pair of sawhorses. Tossing it into a bin with sawdust and wood scraps could turn into a barrel fire.

TURN A ROLLING PIN

GIVE YOUR SKILLS A WHOLE NEW SPIN

BY JOE CRUZ

Although lathes and turning tools have evolved through the centuries, the art of wood turning has remained the same: A sharp tool cuts a spinning piece of wood to create something both beautiful and functional.

Turning is an incredibly satisfying form of woodworking that gives you the ability to create anything from spindles and handles to ornate bowls and hollow vessels. But in order to create ornate patterns, you have to first learn the basics. Here we'll show you how to turn a simple rolling pin using carbide lathe tools.

MEET THE EXPERT

BITTEN BY THE WOODTURNING BUG AT AGE 9, **JOE CRUZ** HAS BEEN CREATING USEFUL ART ON THE LATHE EVER SINCE.

WHAT IT TAKES

TIME
2 hours

COST
$400 for the turning tools

TOOLS
Wood lathe, turning tools, calipers

MATERIALS
2½" x 2½" x 24" maple turning blanks

SHOPPING FOR MATERIALS

Often in your scrap bin you can find wood to turn, but the tools and machinery are best sourced at specialty woodworking outlets such as Rockler and Woodcraft.

CHOOSE THE RIGHT TOOLS

Years ago, the only option was "traditional" high-speed steel tools such as spindle gouges, bowl gouges, skews and scrapers. Today the novice turner has a better choice: carbide tools. Easy Wood Tools and Hunter Tool Systems' carbide tools have flattened the learning curve so you can get to turning faster without the need to purchase (and the need to learn to use) expensive sharpening equipment.

PICK THE PERFECT WOODS

Domestic hardwoods such as cherry, maple and walnut are easy to turn and readily available. Exotic hardwoods such as purpleheart, padauk and cocobolo produce beautiful turnings, but these woods will dull your tools faster and the dust may irritate your lungs and eyes.

PARTS OF A LATHE

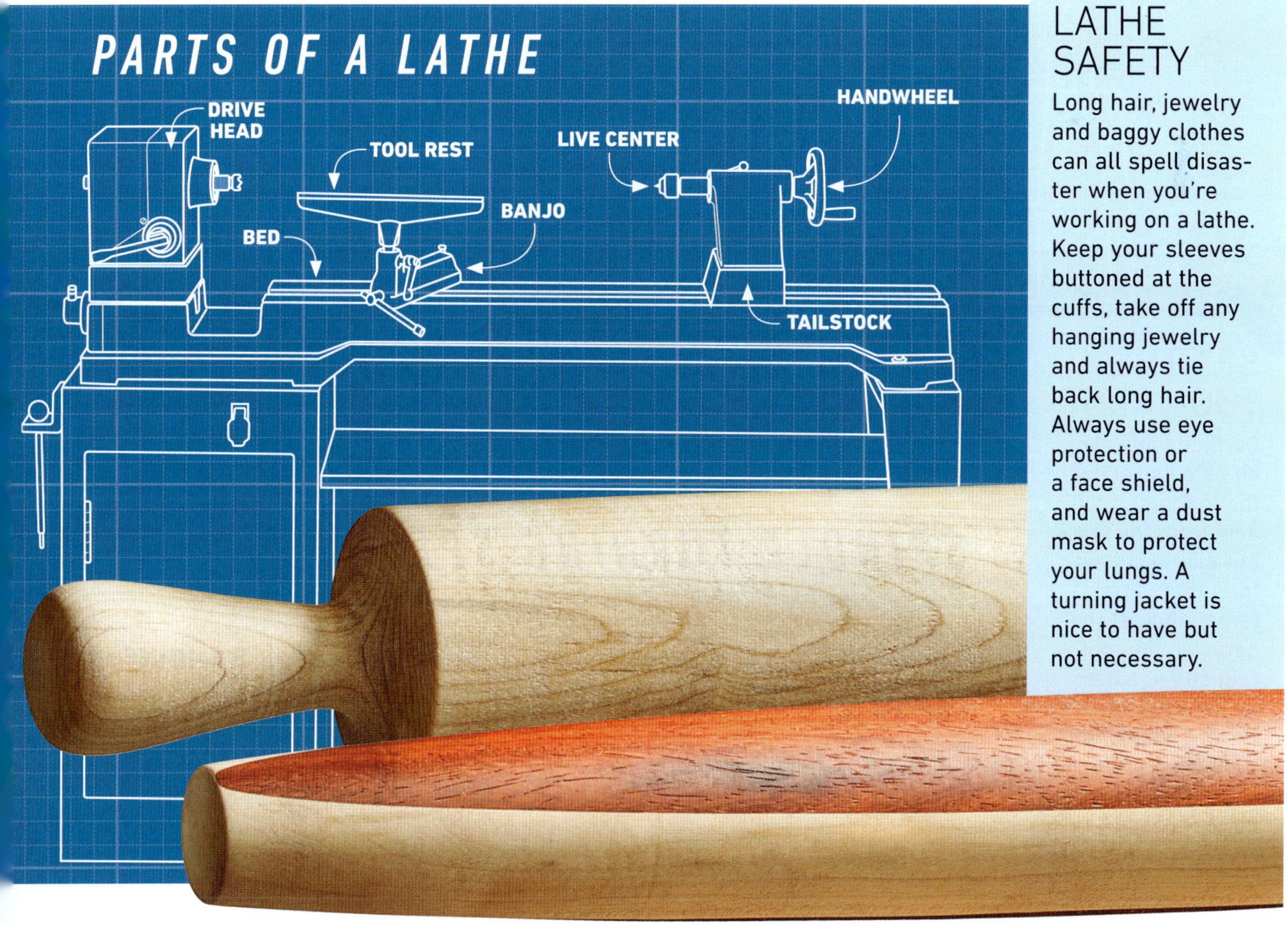

LATHE SAFETY

Long hair, jewelry and baggy clothes can all spell disaster when you're working on a lathe. Keep your sleeves buttoned at the cuffs, take off any hanging jewelry and always tie back long hair. Always use eye protection or a face shield, and wear a dust mask to protect your lungs. A turning jacket is nice to have but not necessary.

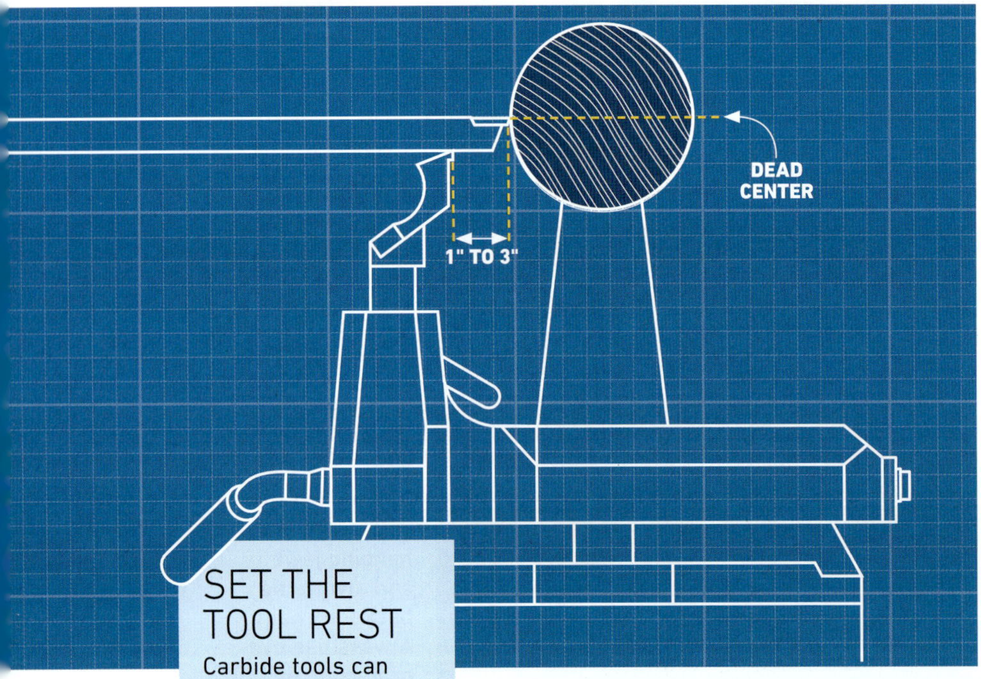

SET THE TOOL REST

Carbide tools can be safely used with the tool rest a full 3 in. from the stock, but a little closer than that is preferred. Adjust the banjo so the tool rest sits about an inch away from the turning blank. Set the height of the tool rest so the carbide cutter is dead center on the turning blank.

1 MARK THE CENTER

On one end of your turning blank, draw two lines corner to corner. Set your drive center on the intersection of these two lines and strike it with a hammer. Repeat this process on the other end. This creates impressions that will help you center the blank on the lathe.

2 MOUNT THE TURNING BLANK

With the drive center mounted on the turning blank, slide the tapered end of the drive center into the drive head. Holding the blank with one hand, slide the tailstock up to it, aligning the live center to the impression. Lock down the tailstock to the bed and tighten the handwheel until the drive center and the live center are fully seated.

SPINDLE TURNING SPEEDS

Use this chart to help you set the spindle speed of your lathe:

	ROUGHING	SHAPING	SANDING
UP TO 2"	800	1,300	3,000
2"-4"	650	1,100	2,500
4"-6"	500	900	1,700
6"	350	700	1,000

3 ROUGH OUT THE TURNING BLANK

With the lathe set to 650 rpm, slowly draw the roughing tool from one end to the other. Take shallow cuts to begin with, gradually increasing the depth of the cut to about ⅛ in. As you reduce the square stock down to a cylinder, remember to occasionally readjust the banjo so the tool rest stays close to the work.

4 FINISH THE PROFILE

For finishing the profile on a shape like this, continue to use the roughing tool; the cutter head is slightly curved so it works very well. For tighter curves, use the finishing tool. Increase the spindle speed to 1,100 to 1,300 rpm. Press lightly and move the tool across the work with a slow, steady speed until you've achieved the desired profile.

5 CUT FOR PARTING

Easy Wood Tools does make a parting tool, but you can use the detail tool to cut a groove in the spindle. Cut inward until there is about ¼ in. left to go. This will give you plenty of room for a slender saw blade when it is time to completely part off in Photo 8.

PRO TIP
It's best to sand on top of the spindle with the lathe in reverse. The dust will fall down and away from you. If your lathe doesn't have reverse, hold the sandpaper from underneath—and hold your breath!

6 SAND IT SMOOTH

Set the spindle speed to about 2,500 rpm and quickly move the sandpaper back and forth across the rolling pin. Start with 120-grit sandpaper and work your way up to 320.

7 APPLY A FINISH

With your project still on the lathe, finishing is easy. Shellac and wax work very well. But for rolling pins, mineral oil is a great choice. It is food-safe and can be reapplied with ease.

8 PART OFF THE ROLLING PIN

When the finish is dry, it is time to part off the rolling pin. Roll the spindle by hand and complete the part with a handsaw or Japanese-style pull saw. Once it is parted, sand the ends and touch them up with finish.

ADDING HANDLES

Here's how to lay out handle profiles for a rolling pin. Follow these steps to make the handles symmetrical.

LAY OUT THE HANDLES

Define the length of the handles of your rolling pin with pencil marks on the cylinder. With the lathe on slow speed, rest your pencil on the tool rest and touch it to the wood. This will draw a line around the circumference of the blank.

SHAPE THE HANDLES

With the finishing tool, start at the outside and cut toward the deepest part of the profile. Once you've achieved the general shape, increase the spindle speed and finish the profile with very light cuts.

SHOW YOUR STUFF

BUILD THIS SIMPLE DISPLAY RACK

1 MAKE THE BACK PANEL

We made the back panel from walnut because it contrasted well with our rolling pins. Cut the panel to an appropriate size, round over the edges and sand it to 220 grit.

2 CUT THE PEGS

The pegs can be simple straight dowels, or you could take it one step further. Using a spindle sander, make half-round saddles for the rolling pins to sit in. Mount the saddles to the panel from the back with 1¼-in. screws.

3 APPLY A FINISH

Once the display rack is complete, apply your favorite finish. We used a wipe-on gel urethane from General Finishes.

KIDS' GROWTH CHART

CREATE A MASTERPIECE WITH THIS WOOD INLAY TECHNIQUE

BY MIKE BERNER

As with many projects on a parent's "want to do" list, this growth chart languished for a long time—about six years—before *Family Handyman* tackled it!

Our editors wanted something unique, so we designed this version on a live-edge slab of cherry, adding custom maple inlays to mark each foot measurement. You can use this same inlay technique to make a variety of personalized projects.

Once the growth chart is done, your kids won't be able to wait to show everyone how much they've grown!

MEET THE FAMILY

MIKE AND STEPHANIE ARE THE VERY BUSY PARENTS OF THESE ADORABLE BUNDLES OF ENERGY.

1 CLAMP A STRAIGHTEDGE DOWN THE CENTER

Establish a line near the center of the slab, from the bottom to the top, then clamp a straightedge along it. This will allow you to make perpendicular hash lines to identify inches and feet, and it'll give you a plumb reference when you hang the chart on a wall.

2 SCRIBE ALONG THE EDGE

Set the ruler on your combination square to 2 in. and use it as a guide to scribe down the edge of the slab. This line will give you a stopping point from the edge of the slab for the many hash marks you will be making. You could also use a compass or tape measure.

3 MARK THE INCHES

Hook your tape measure on the bottom of the slab and make a mark near the straightedge at each inch on the tape. These marks help keep the chart's hash marks perfectly spaced. They don't indicate where the marks will be but provide a reference for lining up the Speed square in the next step.

4 CUT THE HASH MARKS

Use a 60-degree V-groove bit in a compact router to make ⅛-in.-deep cuts for the inch and foot hash marks. We did this by aligning a Speed square against the straightedge at each inch mark, stopping the bit at the scribed line. For each foot hash mark, we pushed the router to the straightedge.

60° V-GROOVE

5 MAKE THE PATTERN

It may take some trial and error to choose a size and font for the numbers to be inlaid. Once chosen, print them, cut them out and use spray adhesive to adhere them to a ¼-in.-thick maple board. This will give you a perfect pattern to follow to cut out each number.

6

6 CUT OUT THE INLAYS

A scroll saw is our preferred tool for cutting out inlays; the small blade makes it easy to turn tight corners and follow curves. When you go slowly, it's easy to move and turn the maple board to follow the pattern. Try to cut out an entire number at once without stopping; a continuous cut will require less sanding afterward.

7 DRILL OUT THE HOLES

To cut out the enclosed parts of a pattern, start at the drill press with a Forstner bit the same size of the hole. To make a shape that isn't a perfect circle, remove the blade from the scroll saw, feed the blade into the hole and finish cutting the shape.

7

WHAT IT TAKES

TIME	COST	SKILL LEVEL
2 days	$100-$200	Intermediate

TOOLS
Straightedge, clamps, drill/driver, compact router, ⅛-in. downward spiral bit, chisel set, basic hand tools, marking knife (optional)

8 SAND THE EDGES

With the shapes cut, smooth out the rough saw marks and any jagged edges left by the scroll saw. You can do this by running each shape over a sheet of 150-grit sandpaper on a workbench. Use smaller strips or rolled-up sections for the hard-to-reach details.

9 TRACE YOUR INLAYS

Position the numbers on the slab and temporarily hold them in place with double-sided tape. Use a fine marking knife to trace the outlines. The knife scores the slab, precisely transferring the shapes into the wood.

Scoring the fibers of the wood like this will also help give you a clean cut when you remove the material with the router. If you don't have a marking knife, no worries—a sharp pencil will work just fine.

10 DRILL FOR BIT ACCESS

To make it possible to use a router to create the recesses for the inlays, drill a ⅜-in. hole that is ⅜ in. deep within each of the shapes. Plunging the router into solid wood wouldn't be safe (unless you're using a plunge base).

MAKE A CUSTOM ROUTER BASEPLATE

Even with a compact router, routing fine details is challenging. To remove the material for these inlays, fashion a custom acrylic baseplate that will let you see what you're cutting. The dowel handles allow you to safely grip the tool for more controlled, precise movements.

FASTEN ACRYLIC TO THE ROUTER BASE

START WITH a 6 x 10-in. piece of ¼-in. acrylic. Place the router's original baseplate in the center and transfer the screw locations onto the acrylic. Drill the mounting holes with a countersink bit and a center hole with a 1-in. Forstner bit. Then use the router's mounting screws to fasten the new baseplate to the router base.

ADD HANDLES

YOU CAN use just about anything for a handle—a cabinet knob, even just a small scrap—but we chose a short length of ¾-in. dowel. No matter what you choose, drill two more countersink holes, one on each side of the router, and fasten the handles through the bottom of the base.

11 ROUT OUT THE SLAB

You can rout out the material within the inlay outlines in two steps. First, set up the router with a ¼-in. downward spiral bit to a depth a hair less than the thickness of the inlays. Lower the bit into the hole that you drilled in Step 10 and carefully remove the bulk of the material, staying well inside the outline. Then switch to a ⅛-in. downward spiral bit to get even closer to the outline.

PRO TIP

Any straight bit would work, but the bit shown here pushes the wood fibers down, making clean edges that are free of splinters and chip-out.

DOWNWARD SPIRAL

11

12 SQUARE THE CORNERS

The ⅛-in. bit can get right up to the outline of the inlay, but it will always leave a rounded corner. Sharpen the corners and any other areas that need slight trimming with a sharp chisel. Line up the chisel with the outline, then chop downward to remove the material.

13 CHECK THE FIT

Once all the material is removed and the edges and corners of the recesses are cleaned up, it's time to check how the inlays fit before gluing them in permanently. To prevent the inlays from getting stuck, make two tape tabs for each, enabling you to check the fit and to pull the inlays out with the tabs.

14 SET EACH INLAY

Spread a layer of glue on the bottom of the recess. Be sure to spread the glue to the corners and up the sides of the recess, then carefully press in the inlay until it sits just about flush with the surface of the slab. Wipe away any excess glue, scrape the paper off the inlay and sand the inlay flush.

CREATE A BETTER DIY WOOD FILLER

Let's face it—gaps happen, especially with patterns that have tight corners and curves. Many woodworkers like to mix sawdust and wood glue for a homemade filler to match the wood species. But the wood glue won't accept stain or finish, and the repairs will stand out against the beautiful wood grain. Instead of wood glue, use shellac, which can be stained and will blend in with the rest of the wood after the finish is applied.

MAKE THE FILLER

START WITH a pile of sawdust from your orbital sander. Use a small stir stick to drip shellac onto the sawdust and mix it until it forms a wet paste. Work in small batches, and work quickly—shellac dries quite fast. Note: For a near perfect match, use sawdust from the project you're working on.

FILL THE GAPS AND THEN SAND

SPREAD THE filler into the gaps with a gloved finger or putty knife. If the filler starts to dry, just add a few drops of shellac and mix it in. When the gaps are filled, wait a few minutes for the filler to dry. Sand the filler smooth during your final sanding.

15 *APPLY YOUR FINISH*

We applied several coats of shellac. It works well over homemade filler, and because it dries so quickly, you can do several coats in a day. It's also a very easy finish to repair, which is key for a project in a kid's room. Once the finish is cured, the chart is ready to hang. You can use a permanent marker to mark heights, or choose your own marking system.

BY JAY CORK

MEET THE EXPERT

JAY CORK HAS TAUGHT CLASSES ON BENDING WOOD WITH STEAM. AND, TRULY, NO ONE IS MORE FULL OF HOT AIR.

SHAPE WOOD WITH STEAM

FIND A NEW WOODWORKING SKILL RIGHT AROUND THE BEND

Steam bending has long been employed to build boats, ships and wagons, even toboggans and snowshoes. A time-honored method of manipulating wood, steam bending will be a fun and rewarding addition to your woodworking skill set.

To begin your wood-bending journey, you'll need a few basic items: an inexpensive steam generator, an easy-to-make plywood box and MDF to make a form. Bending wood takes patience and practice; a simple round mirror frame is the perfect place to start.

HOW CAN WOOD BEND?

Some wood species—such as ash or oak, even cherry or walnut—can be bent by softening their lignin with heat. Think of lignin as the glue holding the wood fibers together. As both the lignin and fibers are heated, they become pliable for a short time and the wood can be bent around a form.

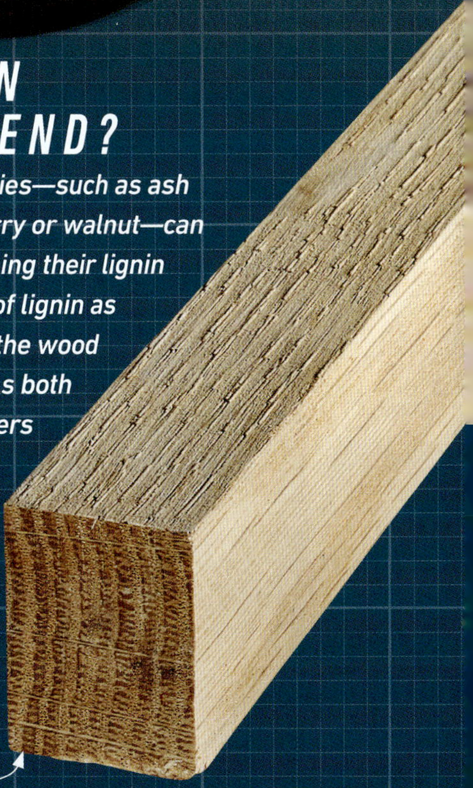

WHAT IT TAKES

TIME	COST	SKILL LEVEL
2 days	$300*	Intermediate

TOOLS
Steam generator, table saw, band saw, router, basic shop tools

*Not including the wood and mirror

AIR-DRIED IS BEST, BUT ...

It's a common misconception that only air-dried lumber bends well. This is only partly true. Kiln-dried lumber has a bad reputation because during the drying process, the lignin gets cooked and becomes stiff. Despite this, kiln-dried wood can indeed be bent if it's steamed for a longer period.

1 CUT THE BOX PARTS

Size the steam chamber to the parts being bent; any larger will be wasting heat energy. The box can be made from any wood—we used CDX (exterior) plywood.

2 DRILL HOLES FOR SUPPORT DOWELS

It's important to suspend the wood inside the steam chamber—to allow the heat to fully penetrate the wood. We used 3/8-in. dowels for this and drilled 13 holes, 4 in. apart. Screw the two sides together while drilling so the holes are perfectly aligned.

3 ASSEMBLE THE BOX

Assemble the box with 1½-in. screws. Make sure the holes for the support dowels are oriented near the bottom of both sides of the box.

4 INSERT THE SUPPORT DOWELS

Cut the dowels to the width of the steam chamber. With the chamber on its side, guide the dowels into the holes, securing them with CA glue.

SHOPPING FOR MATERIALS

You can find steam generators at woodworking outlets such as Rockler or Woodcraft, but big box stores sell them too, as wallpaper steamers. (They are the same thing.) We purchased a Wagner model at The Home Depot.

5 ADD THE LEGS

Adding legs provides space for the steam generator to sit underneath the steam chamber. Cut legs at a slight angle and attach them with 1¼-in. screws.

6 DRILL HOLES FOR THE THERMOMETERS

Installing thermometers isn't absolutely necessary, but having them allows you to monitor that the internal temperature is a constant 220 degrees. We used two thermometers designed for grills; the threaded neck made each easy to install in the plywood box. Drill ½-in. holes and thread the thermometers in.

7 DRILL THE HOSE PORT

After shortening the steam generator's hose, drill a ⅝-in. hole in the side of the chamber to accept the smaller, inner hose.

> **PRO TIP**
> The long hose that comes with the steam generator poses a problem—the steam condenses inside the hose, eventually clogging it. Cut the hose to about 18 in.

FIGURE A
THE STEAM CHAMBER

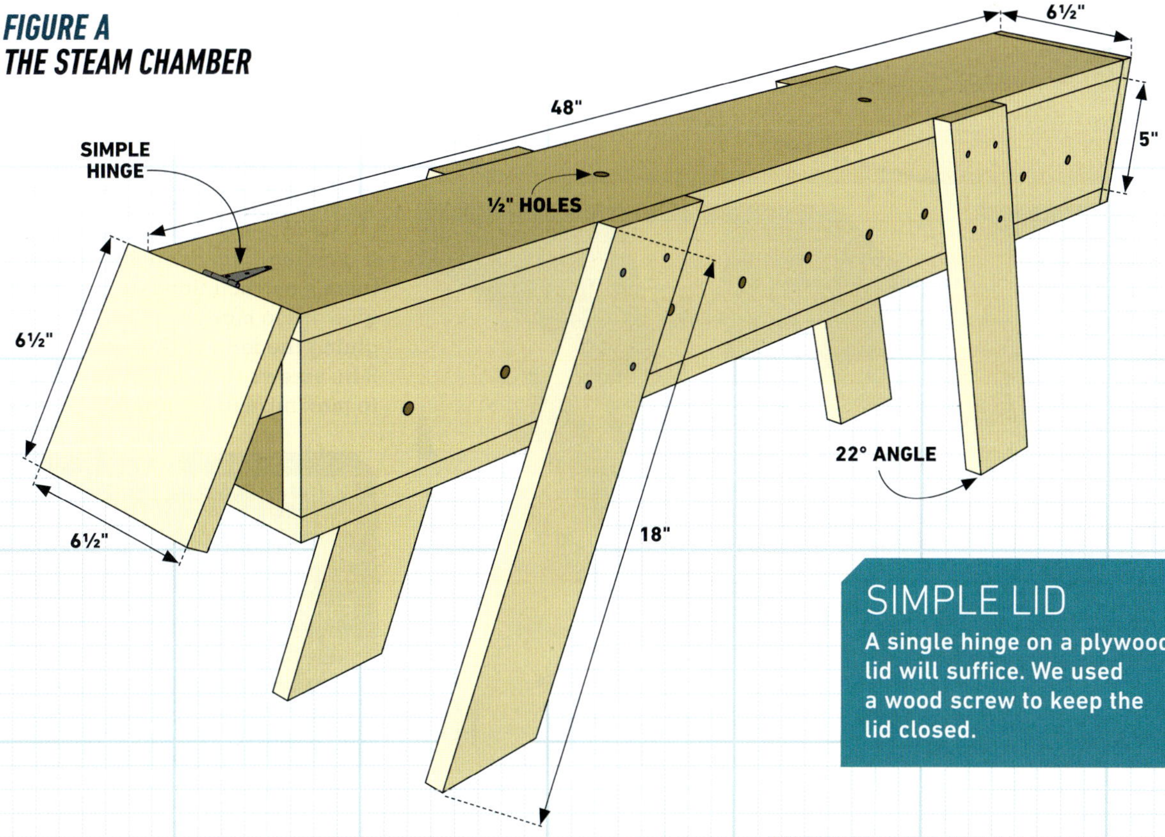

> **SIMPLE LID**
> A single hinge on a plywood lid will suffice. We used a wood screw to keep the lid closed.

8 ROUT THE SHAPE

The frame we're bending for the mirror will form a partial circle. With a circle-cutting jig, cut the round shape with a plunge router. Cut this in multiple passes with a ¼-in. solid carbide spiral bit, going about ¼ in. deeper on each pass.

9 GLUE THE FORM

Once the form has been routed, trace the outline on another piece of MDF. Cut out this part close to the line—we used a band saw, but a jigsaw works just fine. Glue and screw the two parts together and trim the excess flush with a router.

10 ATTACH THE FORM TO THE BASE

When you're attaching a bending form to an MDF base, there's no such thing as too much glue or too many screws. After gluing the form to the base, use 2-in. screws through the bottom to maximize its strength.

PRO TIP

Once the form is glued together, drill evenly spaced holes around the circumference with a 2-in. Forstner bit. This provides space for the clamps needed to help bend the wood. The edge of each hole should be 1½ in. away from the edge of the form.

11 ADD AN ANCHOR BLOCK

When bending wood, it is important to anchor it firmly. We prefer to use a lag bolt. Cut two lengths of hardwood to the same thickness as your workpiece plus the thickness of the backing strap. Drill a hole for the lag bolt in the longer piece and attach both to the form as shown using CA glue and 2-in. screws.

12 DRILL AN ANCHOR HOLE

With a 5⁄16-in. drill bit, drill a hole in one end of the bending stock to match the hole in the anchor block.

13 PREPARE THE BACKING STRAP

We used a Veritas bending strap jig (about $100 at *leevalley .com*) but made our own backing strap. We used a rotary tool to cut it to length and drilled a hole to match the anchor hole in the wood.

14 STEAM THE WOOD

The rule of thumb is to leave the wood in the steam chamber for one hour per inch of thickness, but this assumes you're using air-dried lumber with a moisture content of over 20%. Kiln-dried lumber should be steamed for twice that long. This 1¼-in.-thick kiln-dried walnut steamed for two hours.

15 WORK FAST!

Once the wood comes out of the steam chamber, quickly get it on the form and start the bending process. You have less than two minutes before the lignin cools and starts to reset.

16 CLAMP AS YOU GO

Here's where a helper comes in handy! As you pull the wood around the form, have someone follow you, tightening clamps against the form as you go.

LEAVE IT ALONE

The rule of thumb is to allow the wood to sit in the form for 12 hours before removing it. If you're making many parts and want to speed things up, you can make a frame to hold the now-bent piece of wood. After letting it cool for an hour or so in the form, transfer it to the frame. Then your form is freed up, ready for another part to be bent.

FIGURE B THE BENDING FORM

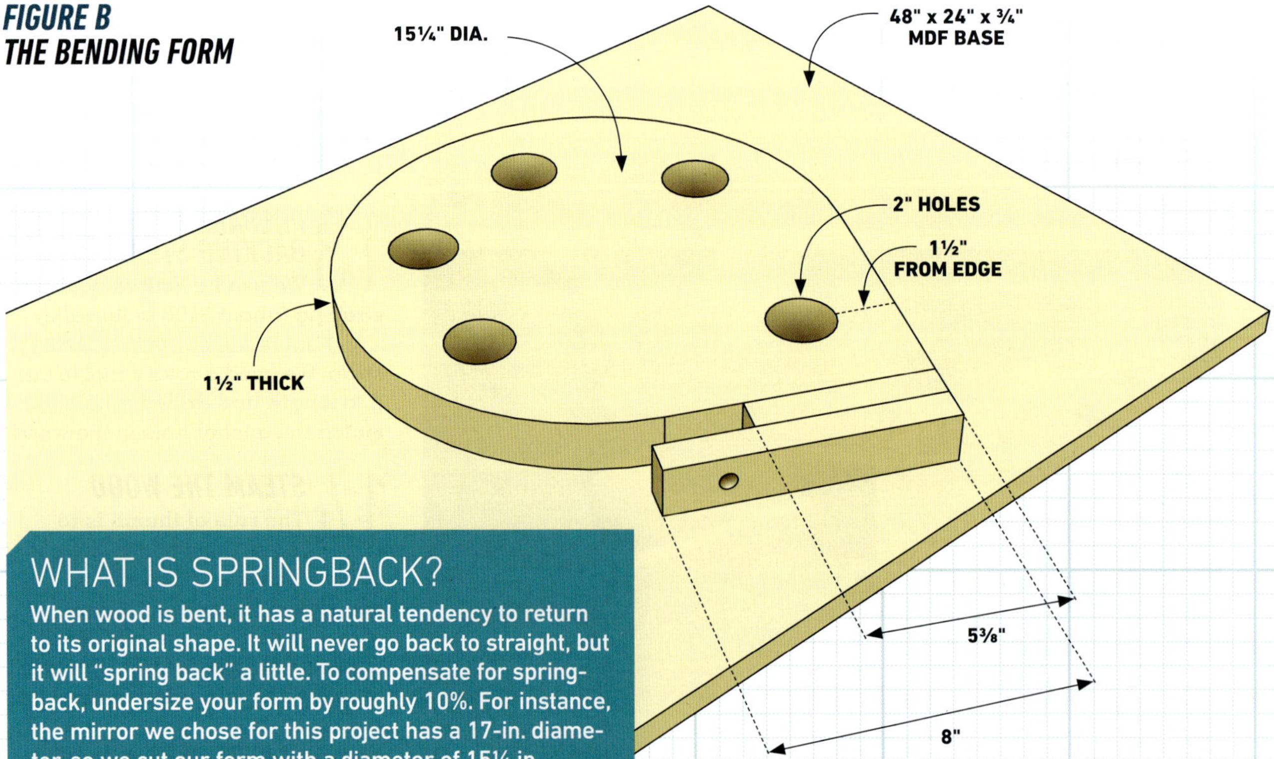

WHAT IS SPRINGBACK?

When wood is bent, it has a natural tendency to return to its original shape. It will never go back to straight, but it will "spring back" a little. To compensate for springback, undersize your form by roughly 10%. For instance, the mirror we chose for this project has a 17-in. diameter, so we cut our form with a diameter of 15¼ in.

17 CUT THE RABBET

On a router table, cut a ½-in. wide by ¼-in. deep rabbet around the back of the curved frame. This will provide plenty of room for the thickness of the mirror and the adhesive that will keep the mirror in place.

18 PROFILE THE FRAME

Here's where you let your creative side take over. Profile the frame in any way you find appealing. We rounded over the inside edge with a ¼-in. round-over bit and the outside edge with a "tabletop" bit—a slightly oblong round-over.

19 APPLY A FINISH

Apply the stain and finish of your choice. We used iron oxide stain, which will turn the wood almost black without obscuring the grain, and shellac, which dries very fast.

20 ATTACH A HANGER

Because we chose an acrylic mirror—not glass—we felt comfortable gluing the hanger to the back with construction adhesive. The hanger doesn't have to be perfectly centered—the frame is round, so there is no perfect up or down.

21 SET THE MIRROR

After the finish is dry, set the frame face down on a workbench. Place the mirror in the rabbet and glue it in place with construction adhesive.

REFINISH FURNITURE WITHOUT STRIPPING

GET BETTER RESULTS WITH LESS TIME, LESS EFFORT AND LESS MESS

ASSESS THE FINISH WITH MINERAL SPIRITS

Before you start any repairs or touch-up, wipe on mineral spirits to help you decide what your next steps should be. The mineral spirits temporarily saturate the finish to reveal how the piece of furniture will look with nothing more than a coat of wipe-on clear finish.

Don't worry; this won't harm the finish. If it looks good, all you have to do is clean the surface and apply an oil-based wipe-on finish. If the surface looks bad even when wetted with mineral spirits, you'll have to take other measures to restore the finish. We show some of these in the following steps.

Stripping furniture is a messy, time-consuming process. And sometimes the results aren't as great as you had hoped. Fortunately, you don't always have to resort to stripping the furniture to restore it to the original luster.

To show you an easier alternative, we enlisted Kevin Southwick, a furniture restoration specialist. We'll show you Southwick's tips for cleaning, repairing and restoring finishes without all the messy chemical strippers and tedious sanding. You'll save tons of time. And since you'll preserve the patina and character of the original finish, your furniture will retain the beauty of an antique. One word of caution, though: If you think your piece of furniture is a valuable antique, consult an expert before you do anything.

BY JEFF GORTON

CLEAN IT UP

A thorough cleaning is an important first step in any furniture renewal project. Removing decades of dirt and grime often restores much of the original luster. Southwick says it's hard to believe, but it's perfectly OK to wash furniture with soap and water.

Southwick recommends liquid Ivory dish soap mixed with water. Mix in the same proportion you would to wash dishes. Dip a sponge into the solution, wring it out and use it to gently scrub the surface. A paintbrush works well for cleaning carvings and moldings. When you're done scrubbing with the soapy water, rinse the surface with a wrung-out sponge and clear water. Then dry it with a clean towel.

FIX WHITE RINGS

White rings can be easy to get rid of, or they can be a real nightmare. First, slather the ring with petroleum jelly and let it sit overnight. The oil from the petroleum jelly will often penetrate the finish and remove the ring or at least make it less visible.

If that doesn't work, you can try a product such as Homax White Ring Remover (about $10 online) or Liberon Ring Remover (about $30 at woodworking stores or online). This often works but may change the sheen. If these fixes don't work, consult a pro to see if there may be other options.

SCRAPE PAINT WITHOUT DAMAGING THE FINISH

Paint spatters are common on old furniture, and most of the time you can remove them easily without damaging the finish. Here's a trick we learned from Southwick to turn an ordinary straightedge razor into a delicate paint scraper. Wrap a layer of masking tape around each end of the blade, then bend the blade slightly so it's curved.

The masking tape holds the blade slightly off the surface so you can knock off paint spatters without the blade even touching the wood. Hold the blade perpendicular to the surface. The tape also keeps you from accidentally gouging the wood with a sharp corner of the blade. The curved blade allows you to adjust the depth of the scraper. If you tilt the blade a little, the curved center section will come closer to the surface to allow for removing really thin layers of paint.

GET RID OF DENTS

You can often get rid of small dents by wetting them. The moisture swells the crushed wood fibers back to their original shape. (You can't fix cuts or gouges this way, though.)

Moisture must penetrate the wood for this to work. Because finishes prevent water from penetrating, Southwick suggests using a razor blade to make a bunch of tiny slits to allow the water to penetrate. Use the corner of the blade, keeping the blade parallel to the grain direction. Then fill the dent with water and let it dry. If the dent is less deep but still visible, you can repeat the process. As with most repairs we talk about here, the repaired surface may need a coat of wipe-on finish to look its best.

REPLACE MISSING WOOD WITH EPOXY

If you discover missing veneer, chipped wood or a damaged molding, you can fix it easily with epoxy putty. Southwick showed us the process he uses, and the resulting repair is so realistic that it's hard to spot. When it's hardened, the epoxy is light colored and about the density of wood. You can shape, sand and stain it like wood too, so it blends right in. QuikWood and KwikWood are two brands of this Tootsie Roll–shaped epoxy. You'll find it at home centers and specialty woodworking stores for about $14 a tube.

To use this type of epoxy, slice off a piece with a razor blade or utility knife and knead it in your gloved hand. When the two parts are completely blended to a consistent color and the epoxy putty starts to get sticky, it's ready to use. You'll have about five or 10 minutes to apply the epoxy to the repair before it starts to harden. That's why you should slice off only as much as you can use quickly.

1

2

3

4

5

1 FILL THE DAMAGE WITH EPOXY
After the epoxy putty is thoroughly mixed, press it into the area to be repaired.

2 SMOOTH THE PUTTY
Use your wetted finger to smooth the putty. Press the putty until it's level with the surrounding veneer.

3 ADD WOOD GRAIN
On open grain wood such as this oak, use a razor blade to add grain marks.

4 SAND THE EPOXY
Sand carefully to avoid removing the surrounding finish. Make a detail sander by gluing sandpaper to a thin strip of wood.

5 STAIN THE EPOXY TO MATCH
Stain the patch with gel stain to match the color and pattern of the grain. Match the stain color to both the light and dark areas of the wood. Create a range of colors by blending them. Then use an artist's brush to create the grain. If the sheen of the patch doesn't match the rest of the wood when the stain dries, recoat the entire surface with wipe-on finish to even it out.

RESTORE THE COLOR WITH GEL STAIN

It's amazing what a coat of gel stain can do to restore a tired-looking piece of furniture. The cool part is that you don't need to strip the old finish for this to work. Southwick demonstrated the tip on this round oak table. The finish was worn and faded. He loaded a soft cloth with dark gel stain and worked it into the surface. Then he wiped if off with a clean cloth. It was a surprising transformation. Of course, gel stain won't eliminate dark water stains or cover bad defects, but it will hide fine scratches and color in areas where the finish has worn away.

There are other products, but Southwick prefers gel stain because he finds it easier to control the color and leave a thicker coat if necessary. Also, since it doesn't soak in quite as readily as thinner stains, gel stain is somewhat reversible. Before it dries, you can remove it with mineral spirits if you don't like the results. Gel stains offer some protection. But for a more durable finish or to even out the sheen, let the stain dry overnight and then apply a coat of wipe-on finish.

RENEW THE LUSTER WITH WIPE-ON FINISH

The final step in your restoration project is to wipe on a coat of finish. After you clean your furniture piece and do any necessary repairs and stain touch-ups, wiping on a coat of finish will restore the sheen and protect the surface. Any wipe-on finish will work—Minwax Wipe-On Poly is a common brand (about $20 a pint). But Southwick prefers a wipe-on gel finish like General Finishes Gel Topcoat (about $35 a pint). It's thick, so it's easy to put on with a rag. One coat is usually all you need to rejuvenate an existing finish. To find a store near you that sells General Finishes Gel Topcoat, go to *generalfinishes.com.*

To apply wipe-on finish, first put some on a clean rag. Apply it in a swirling motion as you would car wax. Then wipe off excess finish, going in the direction of the grain. Let the finish dry overnight, and you'll be ready to proudly display your furniture restoration project.

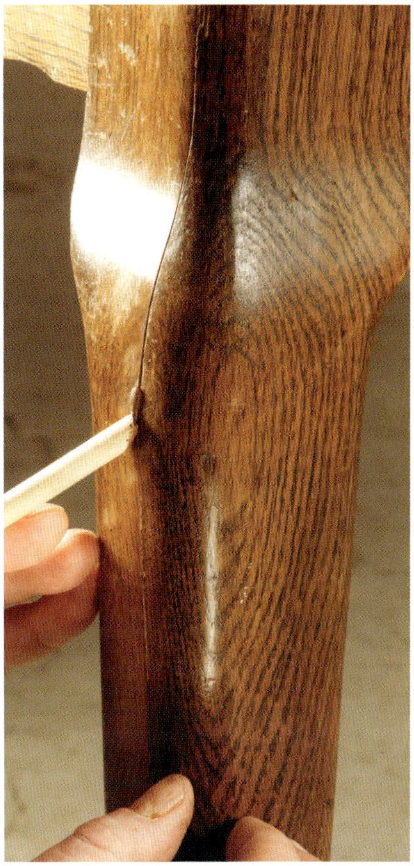

FILL SMALL CRACKS

If you find nail holes or tiny cracks after applying the final finish, fill them with colored wax fill sticks, wax repair sticks or fill pencils, found at home centers and paint stores.

The directions tell you to rub the stick over the defect. But Southwick recommends breaking off a chunk and warming it in your hands. Then shape it to fit the flaw and press it in with a smooth tool. He uses a ⅜-in. dowel with an angle on the end. For cracks, make a thin wafer, slide it into the crack and then work the wax in both directions to fill the crack. Buff with a soft cloth.

MEET THE EXPERT

KEVIN SOUTHWICK SPECIALIZES IN THE CONSERVATION AND RESTORATION OF ANTIQUES AND IN CUSTOM WOOD FINISHES.

4 PET OWNER PROJECTS & IDEAS

A NEW DEN FOR YOUR BEST FRIEND

BUILD YOUR DOG A REAL PIECE OF FURNITURE

BY MIKE BERNER

If you're looking for an alternative to the mostly plastic crates and metal kennels available at pet stores, check out this dog crate designed using red oak lumber and copper pipe. We dyed the frame black with India ink and added a slick sliding door. Charlie, the lucky dog, jumped right in and has been calling (barking) it home since the day it was done.

WHAT IT TAKES

TIME	COST
2 days	$500

SKILL LEVEL
Beginner/Intermediate

TOOLS
Circular saw or miter saw, drill/driver, drill press, 18-gauge nailer, clamps, basic carpentry tools

1 DETERMINE THE SIZE

To size the dog crate, measure the length and height of your dog, and as a rule of thumb, add 4 in. to each dimension. We will place a bed in the bottom of the crate, so we used this rule to determine the proper-size bed. With the dog bed in hand, we placed it on a sheet of ¾-in. plywood and marked its length and width. This plywood will be the bottom of the crate.

2 FASTEN THE PANELS

Cut the bottom, side and back panels from ¾-in. plywood. We used a sheet of red oak veneer plywood. Fasten the side to the bottom panel with glue and a pair of pocket hole screws; keep the pocket holes within 2 in. of each edge. Next fasten the back panel to the bottom with pocket screws and use trim screws to fasten the corner.

3 CUT THE FRAME PARTS

The front and opposite side are face frame panels. It's essential that all the parts are the exact same size, so stack the boards on the miter saw and clamp the ends to keep them together. Cut the ends flush, then cut the outer and inner stiles and rails to length.

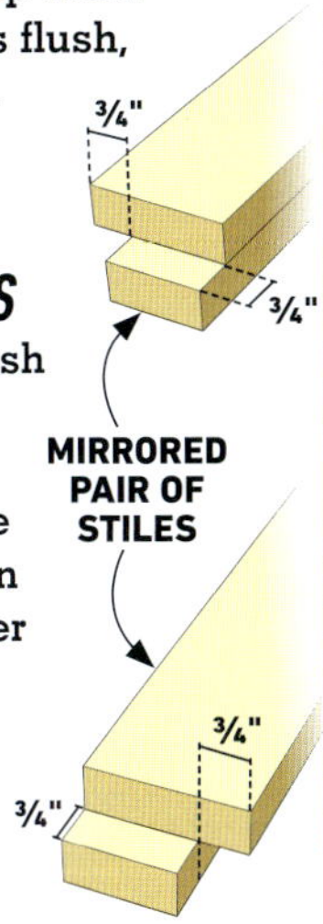

4 GLUE THE STILES

Glue the stiles flush on the edge and use a 2½-in.-wide spacer on the top side of the stiles to position the boards. The spacer ensures the rails will fit precisely when you assemble the face frame. Build a pair of stiles that mirror each other for each panel.

FIGURE A
DOG CRATE

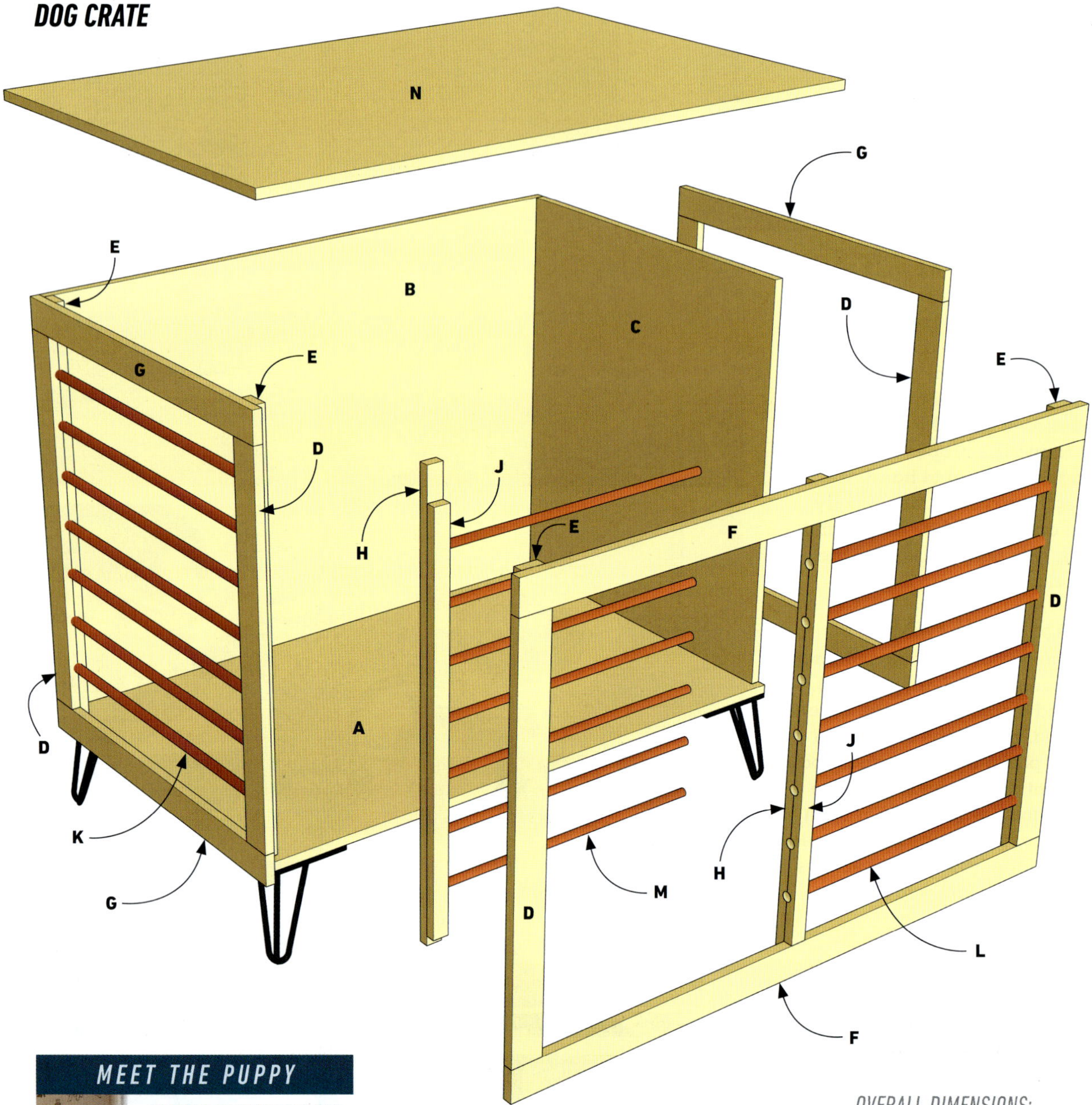

OVERALL DIMENSIONS:
51½" L x 33½" D x 39¼" H

MEET THE PUPPY

CHARLIE, MIKE'S 2-YEAR-OLD GERMAN SHEPHERD MUTT, IS 40 IN. LONG AND 29½ IN. TALL, AND THIS MODERN DOG CRATE WAS CUSTOM BUILT FOR HIM.

MATERIALS LIST

ITEM	QTY.
1x3 x 8' red oak boards	8
¾" x 4' x 8' red oak plywood	2
½" x 10' copper Type L pipe	2
¾" x 10' copper Type L pipe	3
Figure-eight desktop fasteners	8
1½" trim screws	
Peel-and-stick wallpaper	
1¼" pocket screws	
4" hairpin legs	
India ink	

CUTTING LIST

KEY	QTY.	DIMENSIONS	PART
A	1	¾" x 30" x 48"	Bottom
B	1	¾" x 34½" x 48"	Back
C	1	¾" x 23¼" x 33¾"	Side
D	6	¾" x 2½" x 30½"	Outer stiles
E	4	¾" x 1¾" x 33¾"	Inner stiles
F	2	¾" x 2½" x 48½"	Front rails
G	4	¾" x 2½" x 30¼"	Side rails
H	2	¾" x 1¼" x 33¾"	Inner door stiles
J	2	¾" x 1¼" x 30½"	Outer door stiles
K	7	¾" diameter x 26½"	Side panel copper pipe
L	7	¾" diameter x 21¾"	Front panel copper pipe
M	7	½" diameter x 21¾"	Door copper pipe
N	1	¾" x 33½" x 51½"	Top

5 MARK FOR THE COPPER PIPE RAILS

Position the stiles with the inside edges facing up, and hook your tape measure to the top of the outer stile. Make a mark every 4 in. from the top to the bottom on each stile. We used the spacer from the previous step to support the stiles while making the marks.

6 DRILL THE PIPE HOLES

Set up a drill press with a ¾-in. Forstner bit and a waste board clamped to the table. Then drill ½-in.-deep holes at each of the marks on the stiles. The copper pipes that will make up the rest of the side and front panels will fit into these holes.

7 POLISH THE PIPES

Before fitting the side panels together, polish the copper pipes with steel wool to get rid of marks and give the pipes a nice shine. Wipe them down with acetone, rinse them off with soapy water and let them dry.

8 ASSEMBLE THE FRAMES

Use a soft-face hammer to pound the pipes into the holes of the side panel frame, and then glue and nail the rails to the stiles to hold everything together. Make sure the rails are flush to the outside edge of the stiles, and then check that everything is square. The front face frame is built the same way but without the pipes.

9 ATTACH THE FACE FRAMES

Fit the side face frame panel, followed by the front, and make sure all the corners line up. Then fasten them with glue and nails.

10 DRILL THE CENTER STILE

We made two door stiles the same way we made the corner stiles—gluing the inner and outer door stiles together, with the only difference being their width. For the door stile that is fixed to the front face frame, we drilled the same ¾-in. holes as the other stiles but then drilled a ½-in. hole all the way through the stile. This allows the door to telescope into the crate when it's closed.

11 ADD THE FIXED STILE AND PIPES

Fit the ¾-in. copper pipes in the fixed center stile, then nest ½-in. pipes into the other side of this stile. Position the stile along the front panel and work the pipes into the adjacent holes in the corner stile. Check that it is square to the frame, and glue and nail the fixed center stile into place.

Note: Because our work surface is level, we used a level to check that the stile was plumb to make sure the assembly was square. Alternatively, use a framing square or check that the distances from the corner stile are equidistant top and bottom.

12 ADHERE THE DOOR PIPES

Drill ½-in. holes 4 in. apart into the center door stile, place it in a closed position and use five-minute epoxy to adhere the ½-in. pipes into the door stile.

13 FASTEN THE LEGS

Next, flip the crate frame over and add 4-in. hairpin legs to each corner.

14 DYE THE WOOD

We nailed trim boards (D and G) to match the face frame on the opposite side panel and then dyed the wood surfaces with India ink. We left the inside of the panels unfinished. India ink is less expensive than wood dye and gives a very dark finish, which looks especially stunning in open grain woods such as oak.

15 APPLY WALLPAPER

On the inside of the crate, we applied peel-and-stick wallpaper, starting from one side and working across the back and side, lining up the edges and cutting the roll to fit.

Be sure to clean the panels well; peel-and-stick wallpaper won't stick to sawdust-covered surfaces. We learned that the hard way.

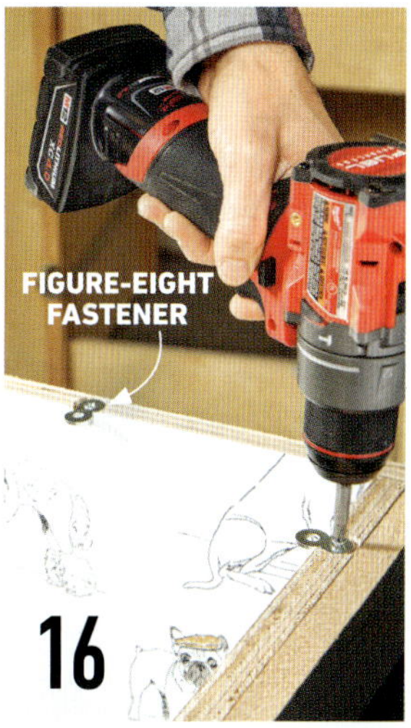

16 FASTEN THE TOP

Cut the top of the dog crate 1½ in. longer than the crate's length and ¾ in. wider than its depth. Drill two recesses on the top edge of each side using a ⅝-in. Forstner bit and attach the figure-eight desktop fasteners.

Position the top flush with the back and allow a ¾-in. overhang on the sides and front. Secure it through the figure-eight fasteners with ½-in. screws.

17 APPLY EDGE BANDING

Cover the plywood edge of the top with matching iron-on edge banding, trim the edges, sand the top and apply a finish. Once it dries, it's ready for a comfy dog bed and your furry best friend.

CAT TREE & TOWER

MAKE YOUR OWN STURDY SET IN A WEEKEND

BY ALLY CHILDRESS

Ever have the urge to take in a new kitten? Maybe your older cat will be game, and even give the kitten a little nuzzle, but it's possible your dogs will be apoplectic. If that's the case, you'll need a cat tree, pronto.

Cat trees and towers allow cats to survey their domain from above, plotting their next moves far from the chaos below. The standard fare from the pet store may work for a while, but the dream of building a sprawling habitat of ramps and hammocks isn't going to start with a boxed cat tree. Such a set needs to be built to scale.

If you want to build your cat an aerial hangout, check out the steps on these pages. Because we worked with an open floor plan and really high ceilings, we needed a cat tree that wouldn't be dwarfed in the space, so this one is quite large.

If you need a smaller tree, you can scale this down by building a smaller base and reducing the towers from three to two. You can also base the size on the lumber you have on hand—this is a great project for using leftover materials.

WHAT IT TAKES

TIME	COST	SKILL LEVEL
2 days	$200+	Intermediate

TOOLS
Circular saw, drill bits (various sizes), drill or impact driver, hammer, hot melt glue gun, jigsaw (optional), level, miter saw or miter box and handsaw, scissors, Speed square, tape measure, utility knife and an extra set of paws

MATERIALS LIST

ITEM	QTY.
2x2 for shelf/hammock supports	1
1x4 softwood boards	2
4x4s for towers	2
1x6 softwood boards	2
90-degree angle brackets	2
2x4s for base	3
Bath mats or carpet and/or fabric (for shelves and hammock)	
Drywall anchors	
Grommets	
Hooks and eyes to hang toys and hammock	
Hot melt glue sticks	
MDF or plywood for shelves	
Sandpaper	
Screws or nails (2" and 3")	
Sisal rope	
Tek screws	

1 BUILD THE BASE

Cut 2x4s into two pieces 4 ft. long and into six pieces 21 in. long. Use two 4-ft. pieces and two 21-in. pieces to form a rectangle. Place the 21-in. pieces inside the longer ones. The perimeter should be 2 by 4 ft. Add a 21-in. 2x4 crosspiece in the middle. Square the corners, and screw or nail the base together.

2 ATTACH THE MIDDLE POST

Cut 4x4s to the desired heights, depending on your cat's agility level. We did 2, 4 and 6 ft. Stand the tallest post up at the intersection of the back and the crosspiece. Screw the post into the base and the crosspiece. Next to the post, add another 21-in. 2x4, into which the floor will be screwed.

3 FINISH THE BASE AND ADD THE POSTS

Using the shortest post as a spacer inside the base at left, add a 21-in. 2x4 next to the post and screw it into the base. Repeat with the medium (4-ft.) post, standing it in the right corner of the base. Add a 6-in. floorboard at the front, in line with the front of the trim board. Align the left post behind the first floorboard and screw or nail it into the base and crosspiece. Add two courses of floorboards and repeat on the right side.

Cut a 4-in. board 4 ft. long and attach it to the front of the base to cover the screws.

4 MAKE SHELVES

Decide how big you want your shelves and cut them to rough size with a circular saw. Sketch the shelf shapes with a pencil and cut them out with a jigsaw. We wanted free-form shelves, but you can leave them rectangular if you prefer.

MEET THE BUILDER

ALLY CHILDRESS IS A LICENSED ELECTRICIAN AND FREELANCE WRITER.

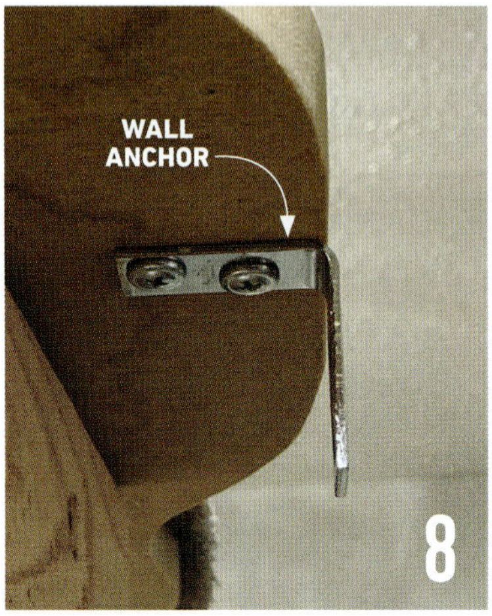

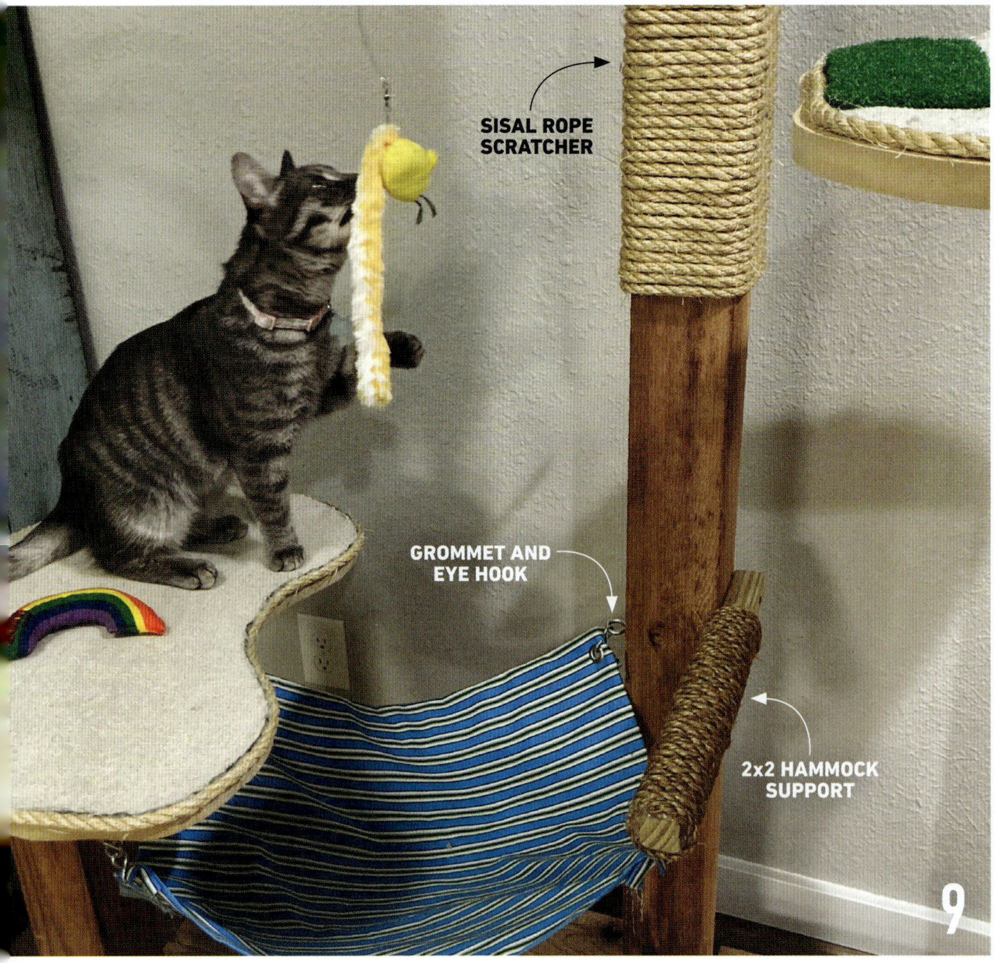

5 INSTALL SHELVES

Cut shelf supports from 2x2s and 2x4s. We used four 2x2s for the lower shelves and two 2x4s for the biggest, highest one. Cut these shorter than the shelves. Screw them into the sides of the posts level with the top. Add trim to cover the 2x4 if desired.

6 CARPET THE SHELVES

Cut your shelf covering to size, but don't attach it yet. If you are short on material, you can add a scratcher to a shelf (Photo 7). Place the shelves on top of the supports and screw the shelves into the posts and supports. Cover the shelves with carpet, gluing it in place. Glue sisal rope around the perimeters.

7 MAKE THE SCRATCHERS

Wrap and glue sisal rope around the posts at the desired heights. Start by tying a knot at the back and wrapping the rope around the loose end.

Optional: Drill a line of ½-in. holes side-by-side about 1 in. from the edge of the shelf. Cut out the wood segments between the holes with a jigsaw, and sand the edges. Wrap sisal rope through the holes and around the edge of the shelf, and glue or screw the rope into place.

8 ANCHOR THE CAT TREE

Attach a 90-degree angle bracket to the top and middle shelves. Use drywall anchors to secure the cat tree to the wall. Join the two tallest posts with a 2x2 brace to prevent wobble if desired.

9 ADD TOYS AND HAMMOCK

Hang cat toys from shelves with hooks. Attach a 1-ft. section of 2x2 perpendicular to the middle post for hammock support. Make a hammock with sailcloth, denim or other sturdy fabric. A hot-melt glue hem and grommets work fine. Screw eye hooks into the posts, the 2x2 and under the lower shelf at the same height. Wrap the support with sisal rope; hang the hammock.

3 SIMPLE PET PROJECTS

CREATE A BED, A FEEDER—AND A HOUSE!

If you are looking to build your woodworking skills, here are three practical items you can make for the dogs and cats in your life.

RAISED PET BED

Many of us like to keep our pets off the furniture, yet also up off the cold floor. Here's a simple platform bed you can build in an afternoon. You'll need a few basic carpentry tools, paint, finish nails, sandpaper and glue. The materials—a 12-ft. poplar (or other hardwood) 1x8 and a 4 x 4-ft. piece of ¾-in. plywood—cost about $50.

1 CUT THE PLYWOOD PARTS (NOT SHOWN)

Cut the bottom (A). From the remaining plywood, cut the long cleats (B) and short cleats (C).

2 CUT THE LEG BLANKS

Cut the front (D), back (E) and sides (F) to length.

3 LAY OUT THE SIDES

Make a mark on the bottom edge of the sides, 1 in. from each end. Draw a line 3¼ in. up from the bottom across the length of each board. Starting from the

FIGURE A RAISED PET BED

OVERALL DIMENSIONS: 41½" L x 31½" W x 7¼" H

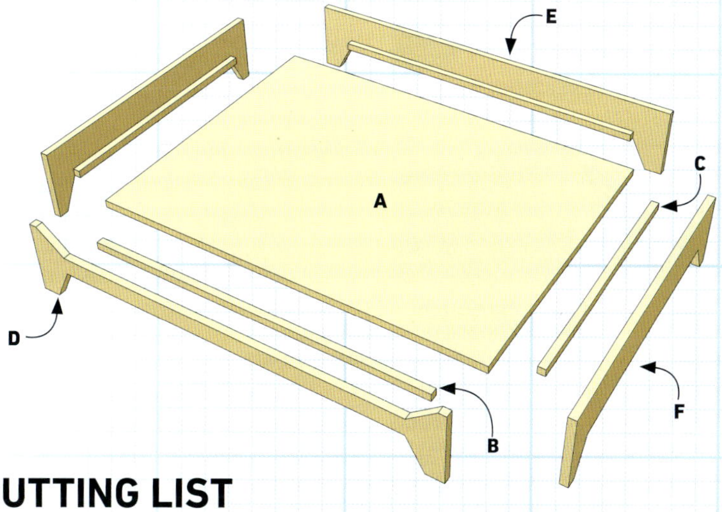

CUTTING LIST

KEY	QTY.	DIMENSIONS	PART
A	1	¾" x 30" x 40" plywood	Bottom
B	2	¾" x ¾" x 34½" plywood	Long cleats
C	2	¾" x ¾" x 24½" plywood	Short cleats
D	1	¾" x 7¼" x 41½" hardwood	Front
E	1	¾" x 7¼" x 41½" hardwood	Back
F	2	¾" x ¾" x 30" hardwood	Sides

FIGURE B SIDE

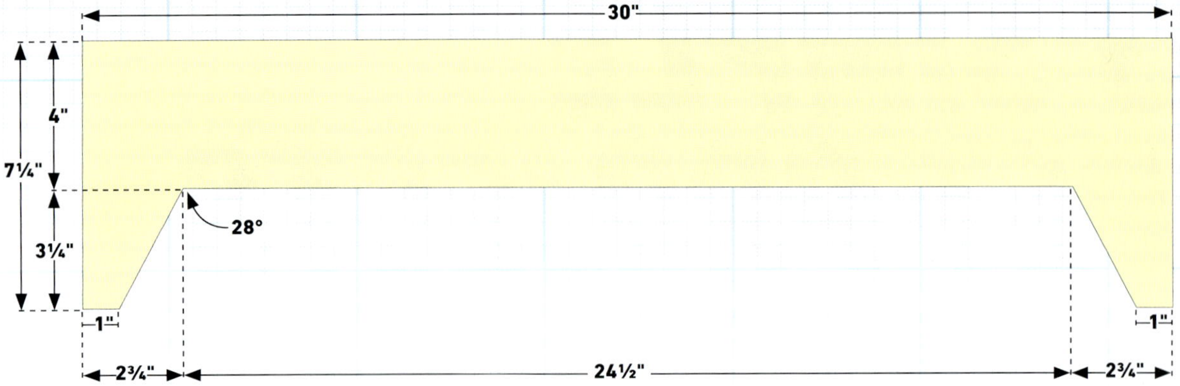

end marks along the bottom edge, connect the lines at a 28-degree angle using a template cut with your miter saw.

4 CUT THE SIDE SHAPES

Cut the angles with a circular saw or miter saw, making sure not to cut past the horizontal line. Cut the horizontal line by making a plunge cut with a circular saw and straightedge, or on the table saw. Be sure to stop the cut before you reach the angled cuts. Finish the cuts with a handsaw or jigsaw.

5 LAY OUT THE BACK

Make marks on the bottom edge of the back 1¾ in. from each end. Lay a side on top of the back as a template, lining up the inside of the leg with the marks you made. Trace the pattern onto the board.

6 CUT THE BACK

Cut the back as you did the sides, finishing the cuts with a handsaw or jigsaw.

7 LAY OUT THE FRONT

For the bottom edge of the front, trace the back onto the front blank. For the top edge cuts, first mark the top edge of the board ¾ in. from each end. Draw a line 2¼ in. down from the top across the length of the board. Connect the marks at ¾ in. with the 2¼-in. line at a 50-degree angle using a template cut with your miter saw.

8 CUT THE FRONT

Make all your angled cuts as you did previously, making sure not to cut past the horizontal lines.

Then cut the two horizontal lines as you did before, making plunge cuts, stopping before the angle cuts, and finishing with a handsaw or jigsaw.

9 ADD THE CLEATS

Attach the cleats to the inside bottom edge of each side, back and front, using 1¼-in. nails and wood glue.

10 ASSEMBLE THE FRAME

Put all the frame pieces together using wood glue and 1½-in. nails. Apply wood glue on the ends of the right and left sides, and attach them to the back leg with 1½-in. nails as shown.

11 INSTALL THE BOTTOM

Apply wood glue to the top of all four cleats. Place the bottom on top of the cleats and attach it with 1¼-in. nails. Fill the nail holes with wood filler, then sand and paint.

JOE CRUZ *CONTRIBUTING EDITOR*

FIGURE C BACK

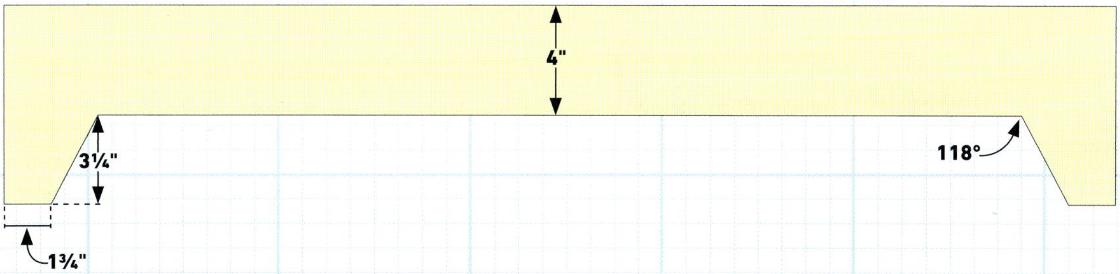

FIGURE D FRONT

RAISED PET FEEDER

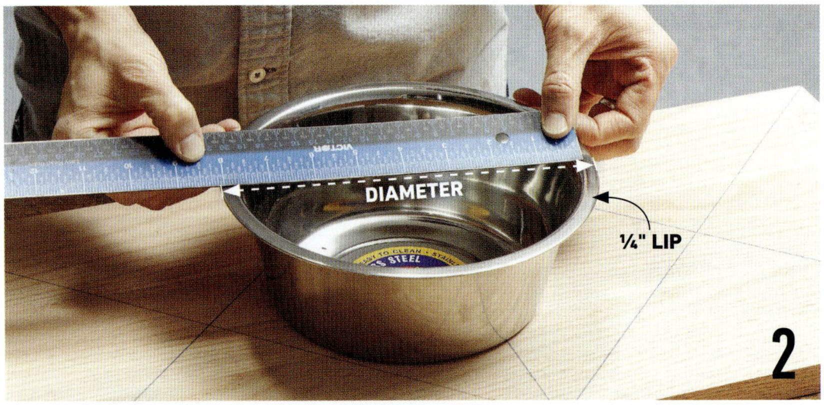

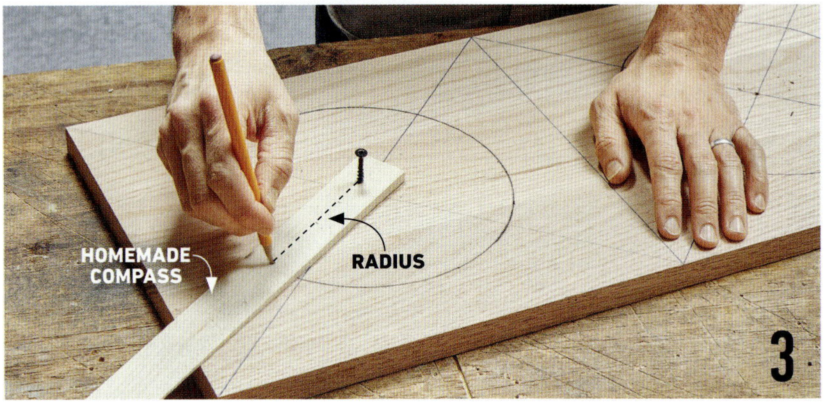

This raised pet feeder will put your best friend's chow at a custom, comfortable height. You can build it in just a few hours, and the materials will cost about $30. You'll need a 1x12 board, two 8-in. food bowls, 1½-in. screws and glue. For tools, round up a circular saw, a drill, a jigsaw and a random orbital sander.

1 LAY OUT THE TOP

After cutting the top, bottom and sides from a 1x12 board, draw a line across the middle of what will be the top (A), dividing it in half lengthwise. Find the center of each half by making an "X" from the corners.

2 MEASURE THE BOWLS

Measure the diameter of your bowls. We found it easiest to measure the diameter including the lip, divide that by two and subtract the size of the lip. This bowl has an 8½-in. diameter. The total radius is 4¼ in. Subtracting ¼ in. for the lip gives me a radius of 4 in.

3 DRAW THE CIRCLES

Drive a screw or nail through one end of a piece of scrap wood (we used a shim). Measure and mark the radius of the bowl from the tip of the screw, and drill a hole just big enough so that a pencil's point pokes through the other side. Place the tip of the screw on the center of each X and rotate your pencil to draw a perfect circle.

MATH REFRESHER

The diameter of a circle is a line through the center between two points on the outside. The radius runs from the center to a point on the outside.

4 CUT THE HOLES

Drill a ⅜-in. hole inside the circle for a jigsaw blade to slip through, then cut out the holes.

5 MARK THE SIDES

Sand all the boards up to 180 grit. Then use one of the sides (C) to trace its width on the top and bottom (B). This shows you where to drill pilot holes for the screws that fasten the top and bottom to the sides.

6 ASSEMBLE THE FEEDER

Drill pilot holes with a countersink bit through the top and bottom. Apply glue to the ends of the sides, then make the boards flush and fasten them together with screws. We used black decorative screws to blend in with the black finish.

7 FINISH THE FEEDER

After sanding the outside of the assembled pet feeder smooth, apply your finish. You can use a stain top-coated with polyurethane, or just the poly. We stained this pet feeder with India ink, which is available at craft stores. The result is a black finish with visible wood grain.

MIKE BERNER *SENIOR PROJECT EDITOR*

FIGURE A RAISED PET FEEDER

OVERALL DIMENSIONS: 24" L x 11¼" W x 8" H

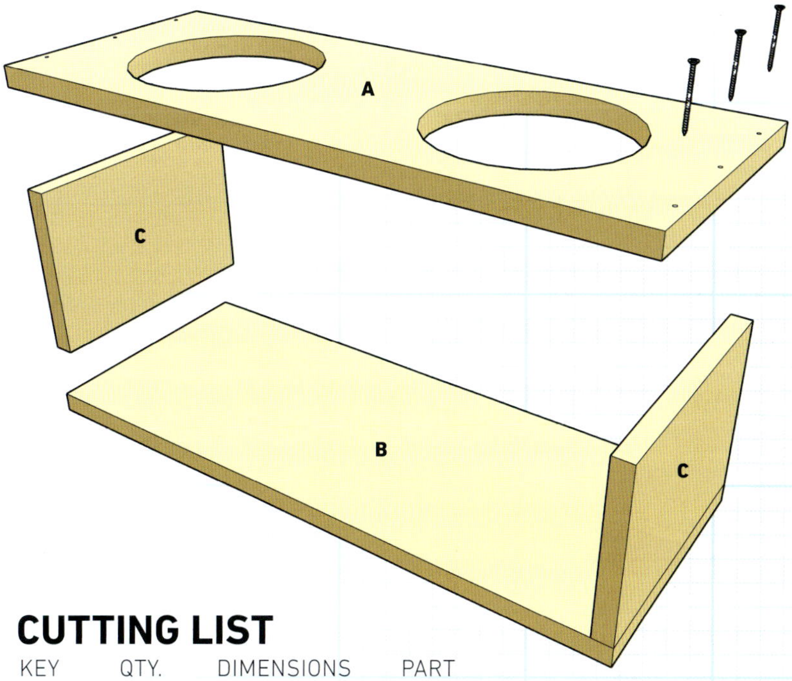

CUTTING LIST

KEY	QTY.	DIMENSIONS	PART
A	1	11¼" x 24"	Top
B	1	11¼" x 24"	Bottom
C	2	11¼" x 6½"	Sides

DOGHOUSE

Here's a simply designed, low-cost doghouse that you can build in an afternoon.

1 BUILD THE FLOOR

Cut the floor frame parts (A and B) and join them as shown with 3-in. deck screws. Attach the floor platform (C) to the frame with 1½-in. deck screws.

2 MAKE THE FRONT AND BACK

Cut 36 in. from one end of a sheet of plywood using a table saw or circular saw. Cut the front and back (D) from this piece. Lay out the roof angles and door as shown. To cut the door opening, drill a hole just inside the line for your jigsaw blade, then cut along the lines. Round over the sharp edges of the opening with 150-grit sandpaper.

3 ADD THE FRAMES

Cut the parts for the frames (E-G) using a miter saw. All the angled cuts are 45 degrees. Note that the dimensions given in the Cutting List are taken from the part's longest point.

Attach the side frames (E) to the inside of the front and back, ¾ in. from the edge, using glue and 2-in. screws. Be sure the 45-degree angle is flush with the top and follows the angle of the roof. Attach the roof frames (F) along the top edge of the inside of the front and back, using glue and 2-in. screws. These pieces should be flush with the angled edge of the front and back.

4 ATTACH THE FRONT AND BACK

Clamp the front assembly on an end of the floor assembly, making sure the side frames are flush with the floor edges. Attach the front and back to the floor assembly with 2-in. screws. Apply glue to the ends

CUTTING LIST

OVERALL DIMENSIONS: 48" L x 23¾" W x 37" H

KEY	QTY.	DIMENSIONS	PART
A	2	1½" x 3½" x 34½"	Floor frame sides
B	3	1½" x 3½" x 19¼"	Floor frame joists
C	1	¾" x 22¼" x 34½"	Floor platform
D	2	¾" x 23¾" x 35⅞"	Front and back
E	4	1½" x 1½" x 22"	Side frame
F	4	1½" x 1½" x 13⅝"	Roof frame
G	1	1½" x 1½" x 34½"	Roof ridge
H	2	¾" x 23¾" x 34½"	Sides
J	1	¾" x 20¾" x 48"	Right roof panel
K	1	¾" x 21½" x 48"	Left roof panel

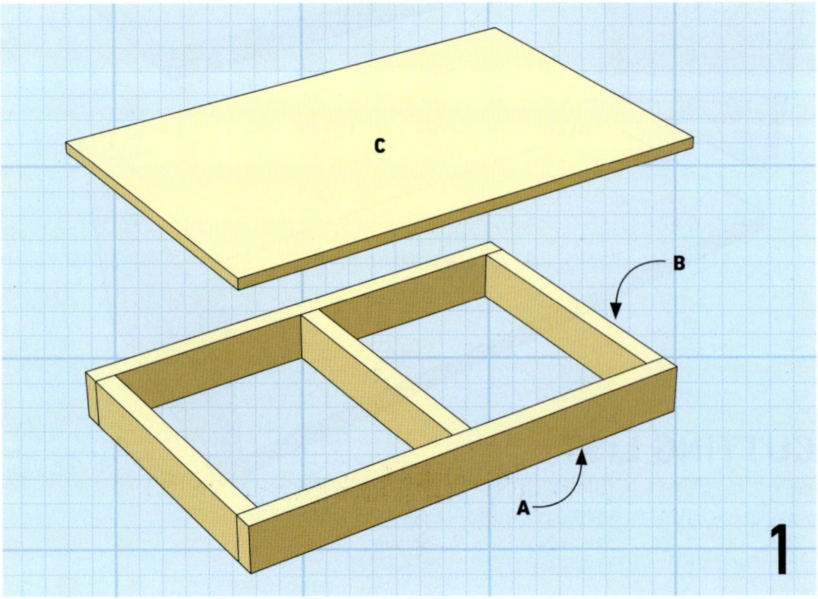

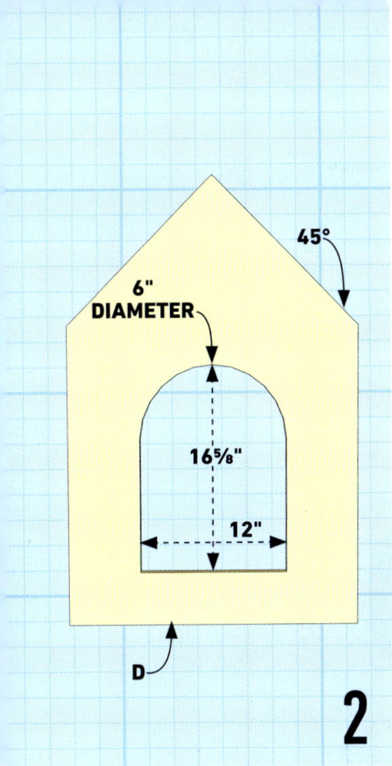

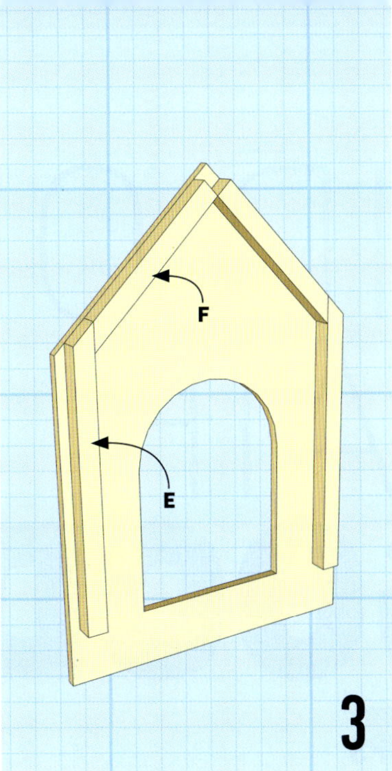

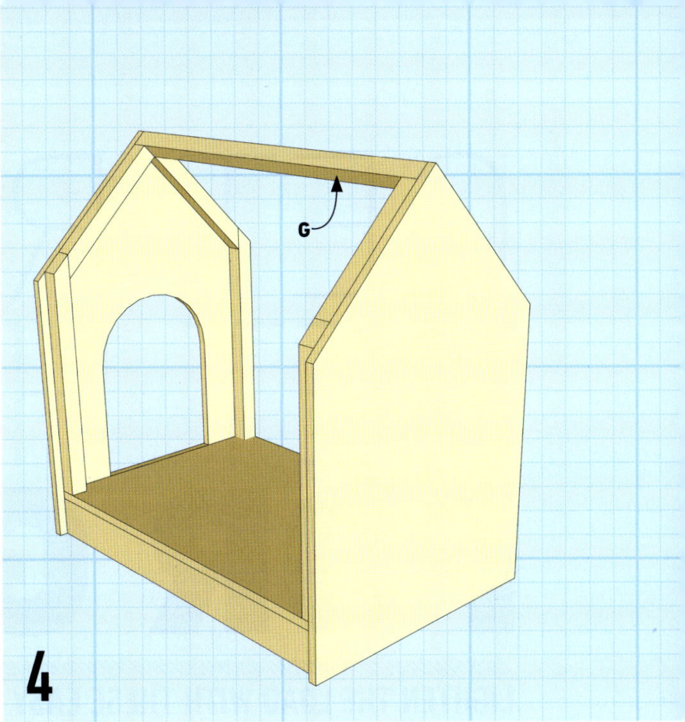

of the roof ridge (G), then set it in the notch created by the roof frames. Secure it from the outside of the front and back assemblies with 1½-in. screws.

5 ADD THE SIDES

Cut two sides (H) with a 45-degree bevel along their top edges. Set one side in place, lining up the beveled top flush with the roof angles on the front and back. Fasten the side to the frame with 1½-in. screws. Be sure to predrill the screw holes. Repeat to attach the other side.

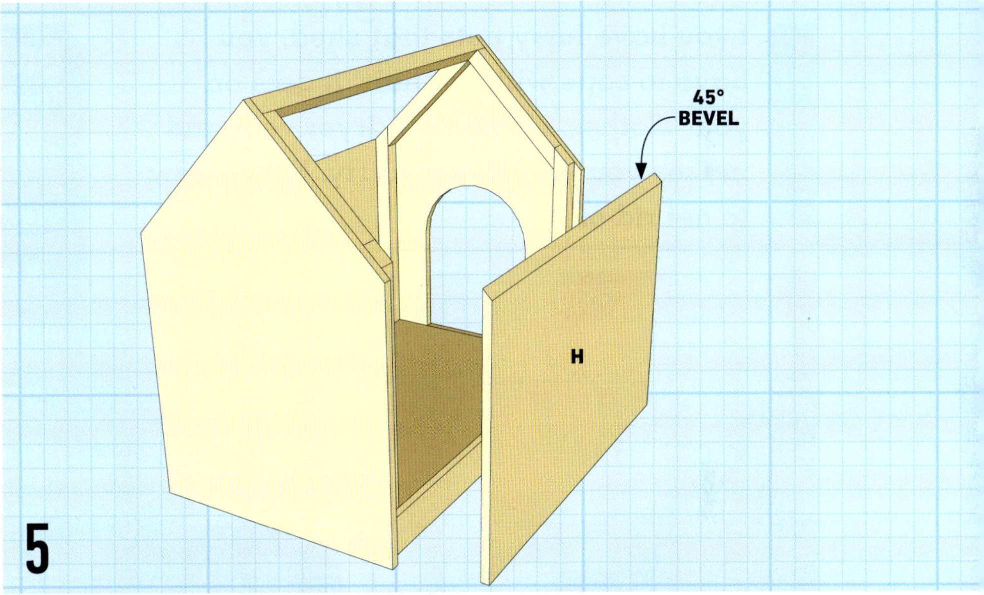

6 ADD THE ROOF PANELS

Cut the roof panel pieces (J and K). From the top front corners of each panel, draw an 80-degree line down to the bottom edge. Cut on the lines with a circular saw. Predrill ⅛-in. pilot holes to line up with the frames and ridge.

Clamp the right roof panel (J) to the roof ridge, overhanging it 3 in. off the back, and attach it with 1¼-in. finish screws. Add a bead of silicone caulk along the top edge of this panel. Place the left roof panel (K) so it overlaps the right. Secure the panel to the roof ridge and frames with 1¼-in. screws. To finish up, ease the sharp edges of the roof panels with 150-grit sandpaper. Fill the screw holes on the roof with caulk. Then prime and paint.

JOE CRUZ *CONTRIBUTING EDITOR*

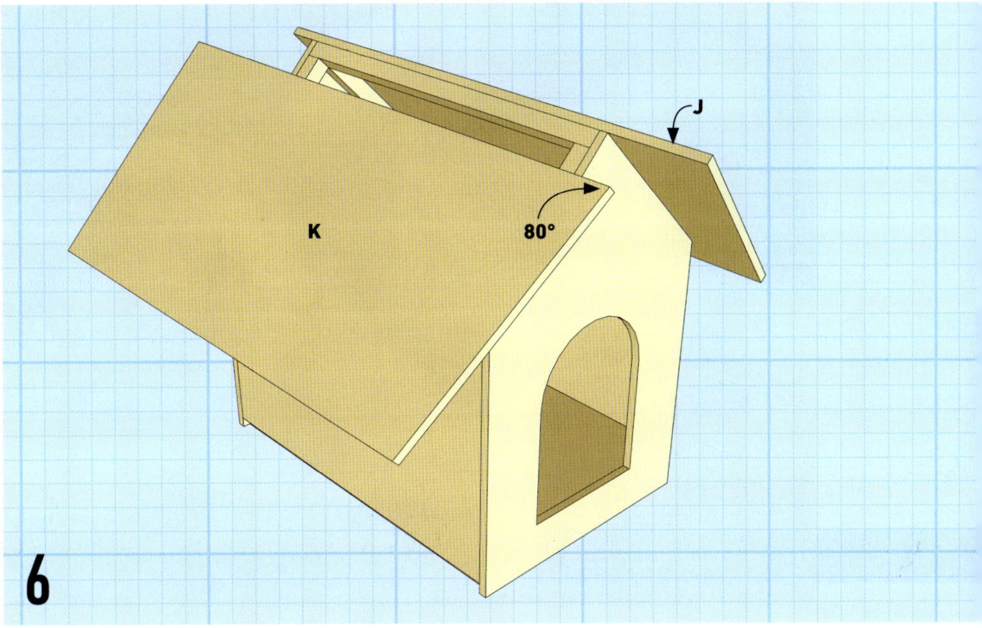

GET RID OF PET HAIR FOR GOOD

LIGHTEN THE LOAD WITH THESE EASY TIPS

If you have furry pets that shed, you have to cope with pet hair. It gets on your clothes, clogs your dryer vent and makes your house look dirty. Here's how to get rid of it!

BRUSH YOUR PET

The best way to keep pet hair from landing everywhere is to prevent it from going airborne. Grab a pet brush or silicone mitt and give your best friend a grooming session to keep shedding under control.

If your dog or cat isn't used to being groomed, take it slow and offer plenty of treats and encouragement. Some dogs love it, and others will run every time you approach with the brush. (Unfortunately, those are probably the shedders.) With a little luck, you'll reduce the pet hair you have to clean up in no time.

BY ALLY CHILDRESS

HAVE THE BASICS ON HAND

A quality vacuum cleaner with an extendable brush attachment makes quick work of finding pet hair wherever it hides. Vacuuming is the best way to get pet hair out of carpets, furniture, car seats, and any other nook and cranny, according to Dan Deonarain, owner of Galaxy Maids, a cleaning and power-wash service provider in the New York City and Boston areas.

Don't forget to empty your vacuum canister and clean the filter regularly, especially when you're dealing with pet hair. Your vacuum will last longer and run more efficiently.

BUY A GOOD LINT BRUSH

We're all familiar with lint rollers, those clever adhesive tape wands we roll all over ourselves to grab pet hair from our clothes.

Unfortunately, they create a lot of waste and they're only marginally effective. (Using several layers of tape each time you leave the house can be the norm.) Not only that, but the tape leaves a sticky residue on your clothes, making them more likely to attract hair.

Instead of reaching for the roller, try a lint brush that can be used indefinitely. Clothing and textile expert Frej Lewenhaupt says lint brushes, such as this one from Steamery (about $25 online), last forever because they have tiny polyester bristles instead of disposable tape. Just twist the handle and voila! The brush is clean and ready to go for next time.

TRY FOIL DRYER BALLS

We all want fresh, hair-free clothes when we pull them out of the dryer. We use fabric sheets and wool dryer balls and dutifully clean the lint trap, but sometimes that pet hair keeps hanging on. Patric Richardson, aka the Laundry Evangelist, says that nothing works as well as a homemade foil dryer ball—and it is reusable too. Grab a 1-yard sheet of aluminum foil, squash it into a ball and toss it in your dryer.

"The first time you do it, you'll end up with enough pet hair in the lint trap that you could knit another pet," Richardson says. "It's a really great trick."

DRY FIRST

Have you ever tossed a clean-but-slightly-hairy garment into the dryer for a few minutes? That's actually a good idea for laundry day too. "The best time to tackle pet hair on your clothes is before they go into the wash," says Matt Connelly, founder and CEO of ihateironing, a leading network of dry cleaning experts in New York City and the UK. "During the wash, pet fur gets wet and sticks more stubbornly to your clothes, making it harder to remove."

Before washing, set your dryer on a low setting and toss in your clothes, Connelly says. The tumbling action separates the hair before it has a chance to get really embedded in the wash. And make sure to clean your dryer filter regularly.

SWEEP THE RUG

Do you have a rug with strings hanging off the ends? Those are called warps, and it's irritating when they get caught in the vacuum cleaner all the time. (It's not great for the vacuum, either.) It's easy to avoid the hassle, though: Grab a broom and start sweeping! Use short strokes and work your way down the rug. Just as when using a clothing brush, friction from the bristles collects pet hair. When you have a big pile, just grab it and throw it in the trash.

BRUSH CLOTHING AND MUCH MORE

Jeans, outerwear and cotton twill can handle a heavy-duty pet hair remover, and a good, sturdy clothing brush can work wonders. "With just a few strokes, dust, dirt and hair will easily come off," Lewenhaupt says. "It's a great tool to have close at hand to give the outfit a quick sweep before leaving the house."

Use a clothing brush on upholstery and in your car too. Couches, throw pillows and other home textiles can handle the bristles. Sometimes you just don't want to haul out the vacuum cleaner.

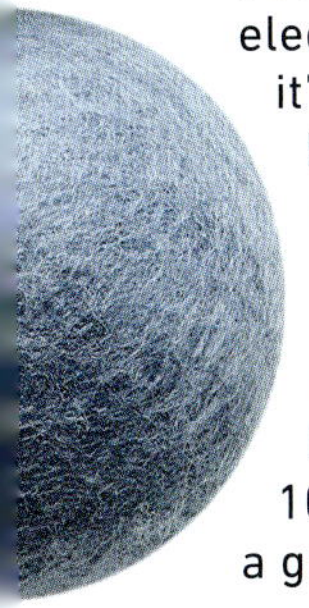

USE DRYER SHEETS AND DRYER BALLS

Pet hair clings to clothing because of static electricity. If you ever rubbed a balloon on your hair in grade school, it's the same concept. Connelly says dryer sheets and dryer balls help. "They work by decreasing the static on your clothes during the [drying] cycle, making it easier for the fur to separate from the fibers of your garments."

Lewenhaupt also recommends wool dryer balls and says they have an added benefit: "Wool dryer balls make the air circulate more evenly in the dryer, which reduces the drying time by 10% to 30% and prevents static cling. Tumble dryer balls are also a great alternative to fabric softener."

GRAB YOUR RUBBER GLOVES

Those gloves you have under the sink can be part of your pet hair removal tool kit. "When your standard vacuum doesn't seem to get the job done, rubber gloves can be a huge help," according to Leanne Stapf, COO of The Cleaning Authority.

"Put on a pair and rub down any areas that need a bit of an extra cleaning." Try this on carpet and fabric upholstery. It works because the rubber on the fabric creates static electricity—a magnet for pet hair. When you're done, simply rinse the gloves, preferably outdoors. The hair falls right off!

HUMIDIFY THE AIR

Air purifiers capture airborne pet hair and dander, but they're expensive and you'll still have to mechanically remove hair on carpets, couches and other materials in your home.

Humidifying the air can help reduce the static electricity that causes pet hair to stick to everything, and humidifiers are usually more affordable than purifiers. Humidifiers keep your skin and sinuses hydrated, but can encourage molds and allergens if the air gets too moist. Aim for 30% to 50% humidity, according to the Mayo Clinic. Bonus: Because humidifiers reduce static electricity, no more shocking yourself and your pet after walking across the carpet!

5 WAYS PETS CAN DAMAGE YOUR HOME

WE SHOW YOU THE BEST FIXES!

Even well-trained pets can leave your home looking scruffy. You can't always avoid cat or dog damage, but you can repair it.

YARD HOLES

When dogs dig holes, they don't neatly pile the dirt next to the hole as if they had shoveled it out. Instead, it gets kicked out behind them and you can't just put it back. If you don't have ready access to extra dirt on your property, you'll need to buy it. You can repair the damage by reseeding or laying in a sod patch. You will need a straight-blade shovel, black dirt or topsoil, and grass seed or sod.

RESEEDING

1 FILL THE HOLE
Fill in dirt up to the level of the surrounding soil. Wet the soil down so it settles, then top it off as needed.

2 SEED THE NEW SOIL
Add grass seed and cover it with a thin layer of dirt. Water as directed.

1

2

3

4

PATCHING WITH SOD

1 *FILL THE HOLE, ALMOST*

Fill the hole with dirt, stopping below the level of the surrounding soil by the thickness of the sod. Cover the filled hole with a patch of sod.

2 *TRACE THE PATCH*

Cut around the sod patch using a straight-blade shovel or any cutting tool. You don't need to cut very deep, just the thickness of the sod patch.

3 *CLEAR THE PATCH AREA*

Lift the sod patch and shovel out the cut area so that the sod will be flush with the surrounding turf when it's set in place.

4 *ROLL THE PATCH IN*

Carefully lay the sod patch in the cut area. Pat the patch down, feeling for any high or low spots. Peel the patch back, and add or remove dirt to flatten as needed. Then water the patch daily for a couple of weeks until the new sod has taken root.

BRAD HOLDEN *DEPUTY PROJECT EDITOR*

PET STAINS IN CARPET

Pets are bound to have some accidents on the carpet. Here's how to remove them. You'll need a funnel, a soft-bristle brush, a spray bottle and a vacuum, as well as baking soda, dish soap, hydrogen peroxide and white vinegar.

IMMEDIATE ACTION

Act immediately after discovering an accident. Remove vomit or feces using a plastic bag. Be careful not to embed anything farther into the carpet fibers. Note: Never use hot water or a steam cleaner on pet odors and stains! The heat will set the stain in the carpet permanently.

Lay three or four paper towels over the soiled area. Blot, don't rub, putting pressure on the towels and pulling the moisture out of the carpet. Repeat this until the dry towels no longer absorb moisture. You may have to stand on the towels to get all the moisture out.

HOMEMADE CLEANERS

Mix a 50/50 solution of white vinegar and cold water in a spray bottle. Or, mix ½ cup of hydrogen peroxide with 2 cups of water. You can also add a few drops of unscented dishwashing detergent to the hydrogen peroxide solution for more cleaning power.

LIFTING THE STAIN

- Spray a liberal amount of the cleaning solution on the stain so it soaks into the carpet and pad.
- Lay paper towels over the area and blot. Repeat until the towels no longer absorb moisture.
- Sprinkle baking soda directly on the stain. Spray more cleaning solution on the baking soda.
- Use a soft-bristle brush to work the baking soda into the fibers of the carpet.
- Let dry overnight and vacuum up the dried baking soda.

Tip: If the soiled area is dry, wet it with cold water and let it sit for 15 minutes before blotting.

Enzyme cleaners also work well for pet stains and odor elimination. One choice is Nature's Miracle Advanced Stain and Odor Eliminator, but many options are available.

For dried and set stains, consider renting a wet vac carpet cleaner or a carpet spot cleaner and stair detailer from a hardware store or rental center—a grocery store may have them too. These machines deep clean carpet fibers, drawing out particles and dirty water.

JOE CRUZ *CONTRIBUTING EDITOR*

PET SCRATCHES ON A WOOD DOOR

Cats and dogs still haven't figured out how to open doors, but that's never stopped them from trying. Painted doors can be spackled and repainted to hide the damage, but natural wood doors can be more of a problem. However, if the scratches aren't too deep, you can usually mask the damage with stain and varnish. You'll need a fine-grit sanding sponge and a stain brush, clear spray finish and gel stain.

Sand the damaged area lightly (Photo 1), feathering the sanding into the surrounding undamaged area. Wipe off all dust.

If you don't have the original stain or finish, buy a matching gel stain. If you have a small piece of matching wood, experiment with it first, or take a photo of the door to the paint store for help. Start with a lighter stain—it can always be darkened. You can also buy a few colors and blend them or streak them together.

Wipe the scratched area with a rag dipped in thinner to keep the stain from looking blotchy. Put a small amount of the gel stain on a rag, then dab a little on a dry brush. Wipe excess stain on the rag. Drag the brush lightly along one edge and quickly wipe it dry to see how the color looks. Leave the stain on longer, apply additional coats or blend in other colors to darken it (Photo 2).

If the stained area looks too dull after it dries, lightly spray the area with clear finish, feathering it into the surrounding area.

1 *SAND* Lightly sand the scratches and the area around them.

2 *THEN STAIN* Brush the stain over the sanded area with a dry brush, mixing colors to match the existing finish.

ERIC SMITH *CONTRIBUTING EDITOR*

A CHEWED POWER CORD

Discovering that your pet chewed a power cord to an appliance or lamp can be frustrating. Here's an easy way to repair the cord. You'll need a heat gun and a wire stripper/cutter, as well as heat shrinkable tubing and solder seal wire connectors.

MAKING A PLAN

If the cord is old, brittle and easily cracks, it's time to replace the whole cord. This may entail taking the appliance apart. If you're not comfortable with replacing the entire cord, you may want to get help from a pro. When you see bare wires, you know it's time to replace or fix the cord.

If your pet chewed near the end of the cord close to the plug, cut the cord and replace the plug. If your pet chewed in the middle of the cord, cut out the chewed section and splice the two cords together. If the cord is chewed closer to the appliance, replace the old with a new cord. To replace a plug or an entire cord, go to *familyhandyman.com* and search "replace a lamp cord."

REPAIRING THE CORD

1 CUT OUT THE DAMAGED SECTION

Cut the chewed section out of the cord with a wire cutter. Slip a 4-in. piece of heat shrink tube over one of the cord sections (Photo 1). Separate the wires about 2 in. down. Strip about 1 in. off the ends of all four wires using a wire stripper.

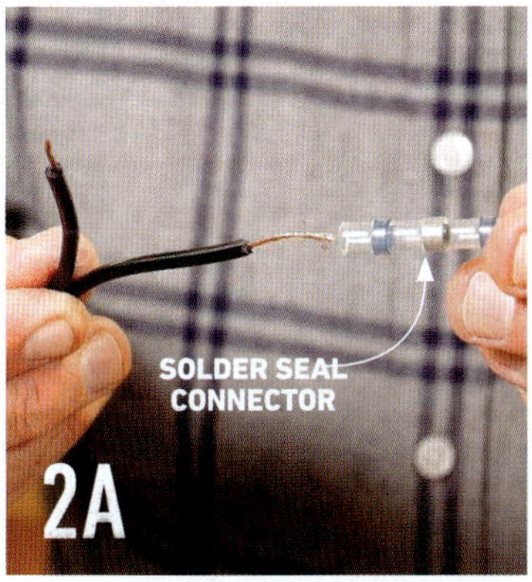

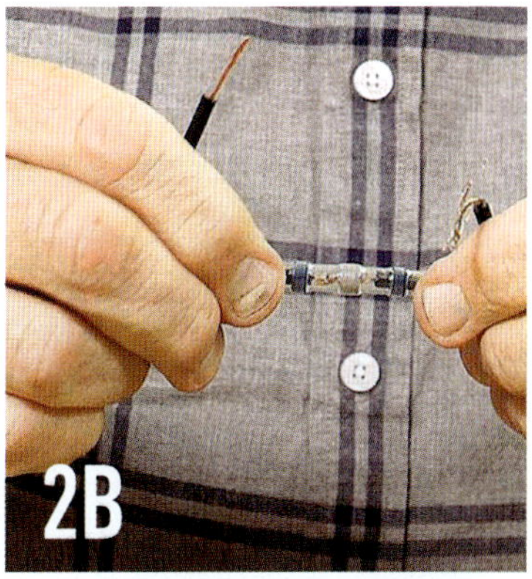

2 SOLDER THE WIRES

Slip a solder seal wire connector over one of the wires (Photo 2A). Twist the two matching wires together. Move the connector so the middle solder ring aligns with the middle of the splice (2B).

3 HEAT THE SOLDER RING

Using a heat gun, heat the middle solder ring so it melts first (Photo 3A), then heat the other two rings so they melt. Rotate the connector so the heat is applied evenly. Repeat on the other wire.

Move the heat shrink tube over the connectors and use the heat gun to apply heat to the tube until it shrinks (3B). Rotate the cord so the heat is applied evenly.

JOE CRUZ *CONTRIBUTING EDITOR*

TORN DOOR OR WINDOW SCREEN

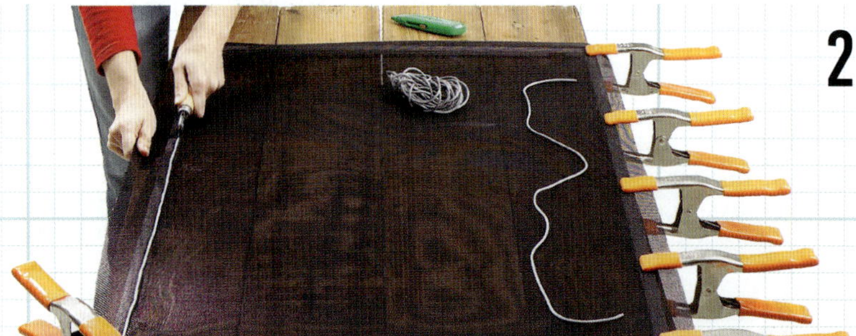

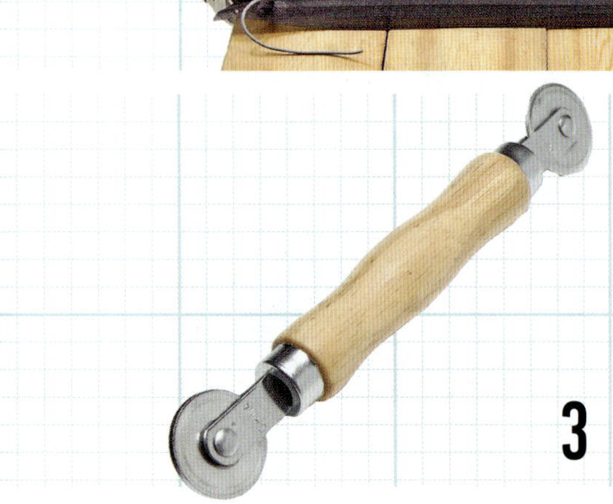

You could try to train your pet to stop pushing and clawing at the door or window, but it is a lot easier to install heavy-duty screen. The toughest screen we know of is PetScreen, which is sold at home centers and online. However, heavy screen does have one drawback: It blocks sunlight and your view more than standard screen.

Heavy-duty screen is installed just like any other. If your screen is in a wooden frame, you'll have to carefully remove moldings and pry out staples to remove the old screen. Then staple the new screen into place, stretching it tightly as you go. Replacing screen in a metal frame may look more complex, but it's actually faster and easier.

All you need are scissors, a utility knife, clamps, a nail set, a spline roller and spline. Spline comes in three sizes; take a piece of the old spline to the home center to match the thickness. These replacement steps take about 15 minutes:

1 REMOVE THE OLD MATERIALS

Pull out the old spline and remove the screen. Cut a new piece of screen about 4 in. wider and longer than the old one. Also cut four pieces of new spline, making each a couple of inches longer than the sides of the frame.

2 ADD THE NEW SCREENING

Clamp the screen to one long side of the frame. On the opposite side, roll the spline into the groove, stretching the screen as you go. Remove the clamps and add spline on the other side. Repeat the process on the short sides.

3 ROLL THE SPLINES

A spline roller has a concave wheel and a convex wheel. Use the concave end first. When all four splines are in place, roll them again, this time with the convex wheel.

4 TRIM THE EXCESS

Trim off the excess screen with a utility knife. Put a sharp new blade in the knife and pull it carefully along the spline.

GARY WENTZ *CONTRIBUTING EDITOR*

HOW TO BUILD A CHICKEN COOP

GET FRESH EGGS, RIGHT OUTSIDE YOUR DOOR

BY JOE CRUZ

There's no doubt that fresh eggs are the best eggs, which is why backyard chicken coops have become popular whether you live on small acreage or in the city. This chicken coop includes both the coop and the run. You can easily build it in a couple of days with minimal skills and a few power tools.

WHAT IT TAKES

TIME	COST	SKILL LEVEL
2 days	$400-$600	Intermediate

TOOLS
Circular saw or table saw, miter saw, drill/driver, crown stapler, painting tools, pocket hole jig, quick clamps, Speed square, tape measure

FIGURE A
COOP FRAME

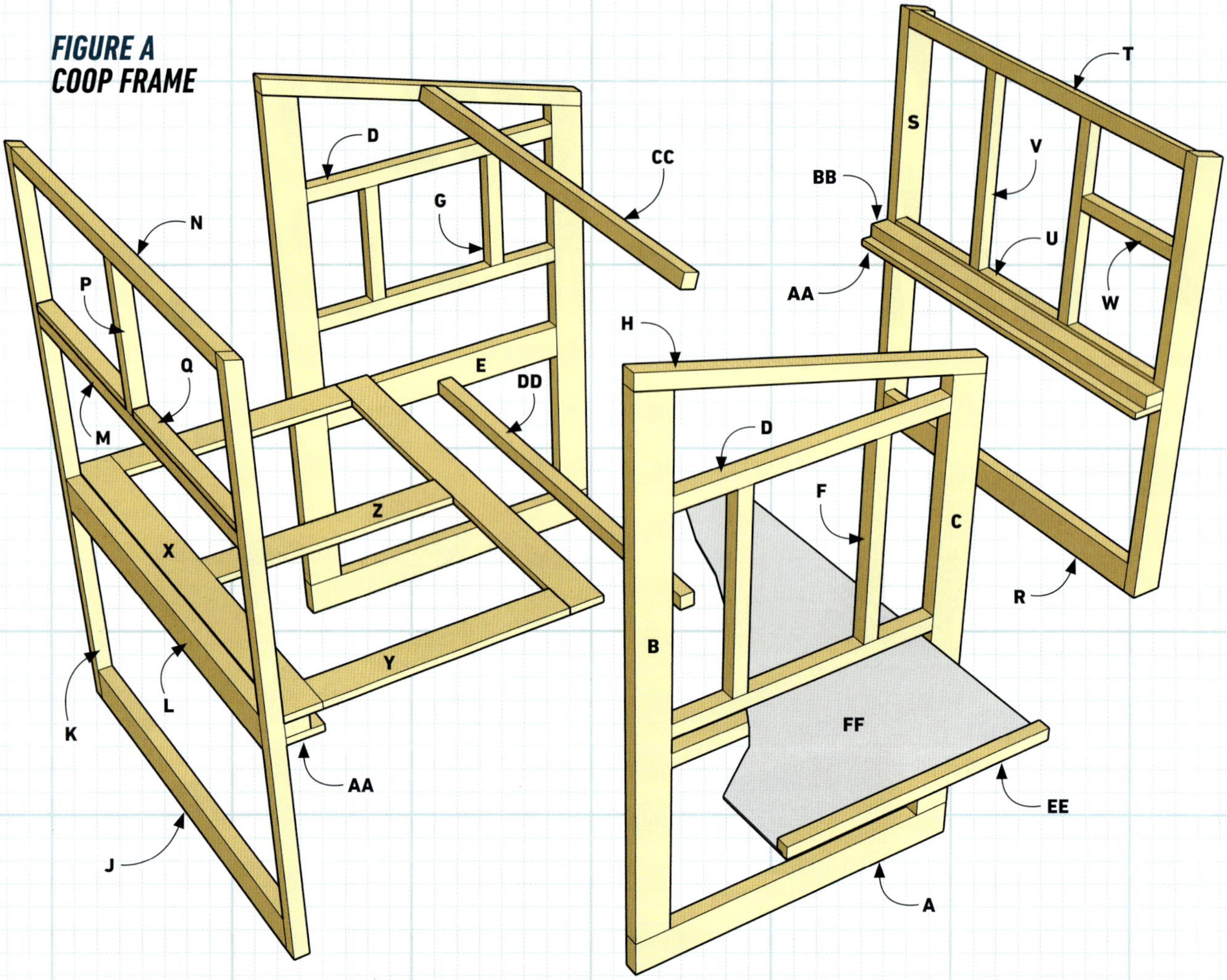

FIGURE B
RUN FRAME

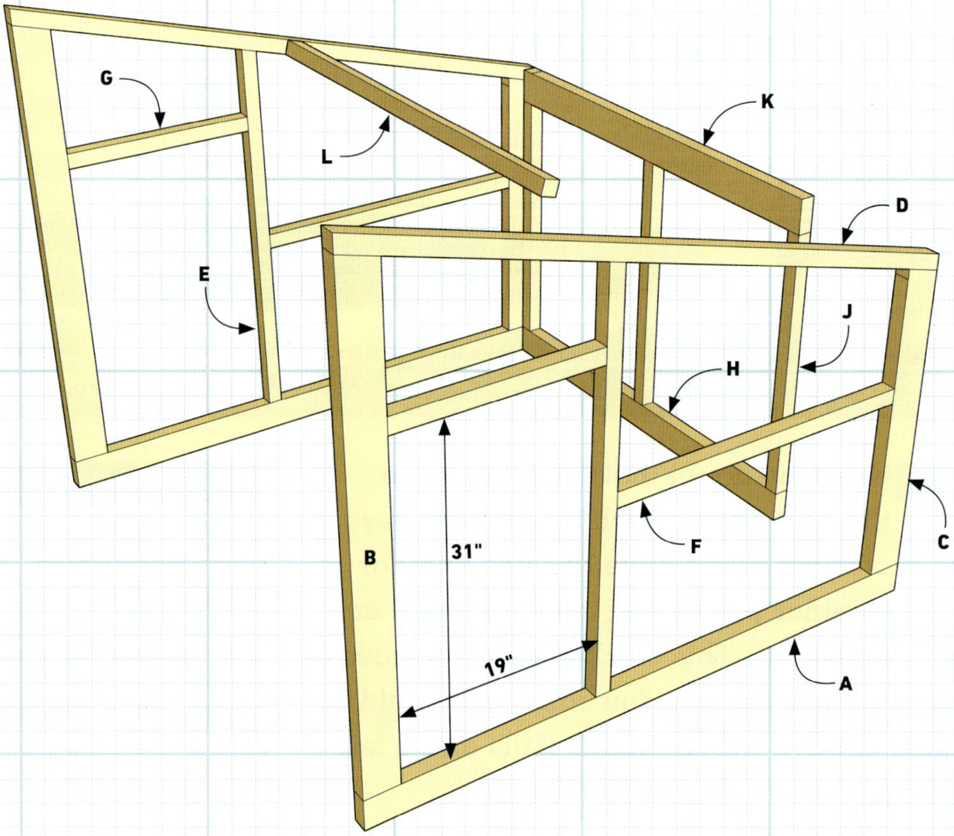

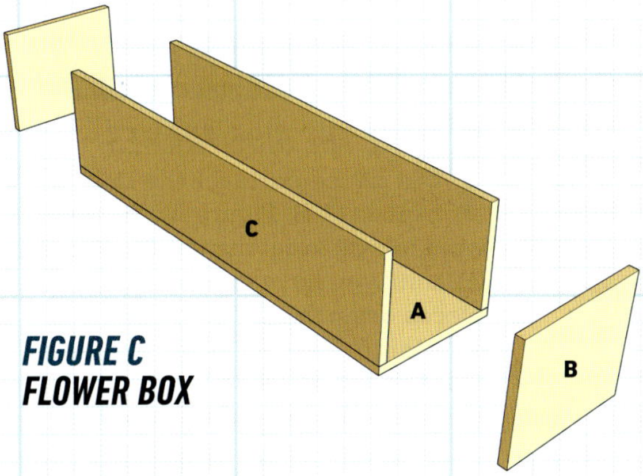

FIGURE C
FLOWER BOX

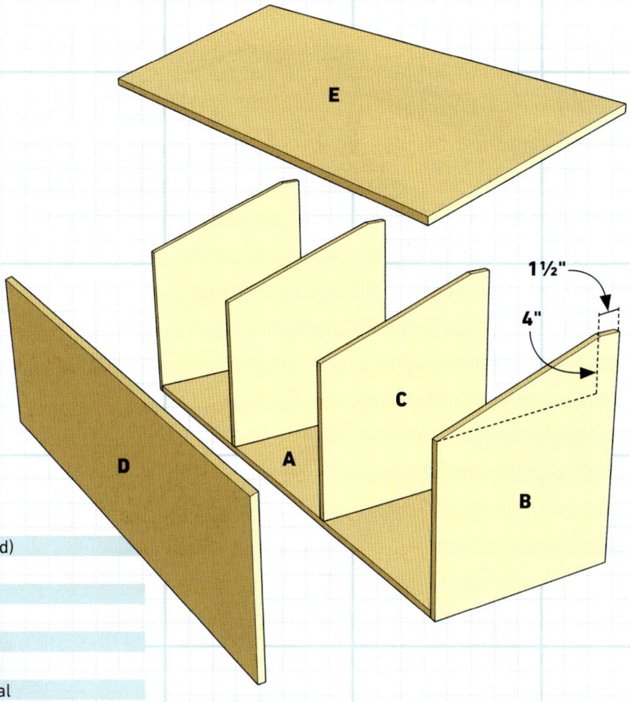

FIGURE D
NESTING BOX

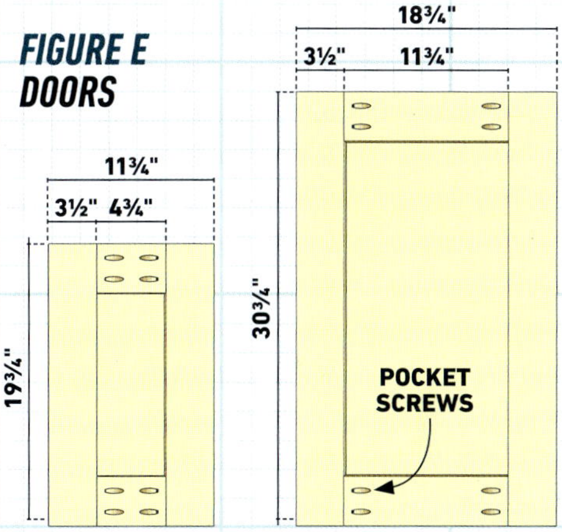

FIGURE E
DOORS

CUTTING LIST

KEY	QTY.	DIMENSIONS	PART
THE COOP			
A	2	1½" x 3½" x 34"	Side frame bottom (treated)
B	2	1½" x 3½" x 53 9/16"	Side frame back
C	2	1½" x 3½" x 45 7/16"	Side frame front
D	5	1½" x 1½" x 27"	Side frame horizontal
E	1	1½" x 3½" x 27"	Side frame mid support
F	2	1½" x 1½" x 20"	Side frame door vertical
G	2	1½" x 1½" x 12"	Side frame window vertical
H	2	1½" x 1½" x 35 3/16"	Side frame top
J	1	1½" x 3½" x 42"	Back frame bottom (treated)
K	2	1½" x 1½" x 58⅝"	Back frame vertical
L	1	1½" x 3½" x 42"	Back frame mid support
M	1	1½" x 1½" x 42"	Back frame upper support
N	1	1½" x 1½" x 42"	Back frame top
P	1	1½" x 1½" x 14⅛"	Back frame partition
Q	1	¾" x 1½" x 20¼"	Hinge build-up
R	1	1½" x 3½" x 42"	Front frame bottom (treated)
S	2	1½" x 3½" x 49⅞"	Front frame vertical
T	1	1½" x 1½" x 42"	Front frame top
U	1	1½" x 3½" x 42"	Front frame horizontal
V	2	1½" x 1½" x 22½"	Front frame upper vertical
W	1	1½" x 1½" x 13"	Front frame upper horizontal
X	2	¾" x 3½" x 45"	Floor frame side
Y	2	¾" x 3½" x 24"	Front frame end
Z	1	¾" x 3½" x 24"	Floor frame mid
AA	2	¾" x 3½" x 45"	Tray supports
BB	2	1½" x 2¼" x 45"	Floor supports
CC	1	1½" x 1½" x 45"	Roof supports
DD	1	1½" x 1½" x 45"	Cross member
EE	1	1¼" x 1¼" x 26½"	Tray front
FF	1	¼" x 45" x 26¼"	Waste tray (acrylic)
THE RUN			
A	2	1½" x 3½" x 57¾"	Side bottom (treated)
B	2	1½" x 3½" x 45"	Side back vertical
C	2	1½" x 3½" x 30½"	Side front vertical
D	2	1½" x 1½" x 59 13/16"	Side top
E	2	1½" x 1½" x 39"	Side mid support
F	2	1½" x 1½" x 30⅜"	Side horizontal support
G	2	1½" x 1½" x 18⅞"	Side door support
H	1	1½" x 3½" x 45"	Front bottom (treated)
J	3	1½" x 1½" x 27½"	Front vertical
K	1	1½" x 3½" x 45"	Front top
L	1	1½" x 1½" x 45"	Roof support
NESTING BOX			
A	1	½" x 13½" x 41"	Bottom
B	2	½" x 13½" x 16"	End
C	2	½" x 13½" x 15½"	Partition
D	1	½" x 12" x 42"	Front
E	1	½" x 14¼" x 44"	Lid
FLOWER BOX			
A	1	½" x 7½" x 26"	Bottom
B	2	½" x 7½" x 6½"	End
C	2	½" x 6" x 26"	Front and back

MATERIALS LIST

ITEM	QTY.
No. 14 x 2½" pocket hole screws	
No. 9 x 3" construction screws	
½" x 2' x 25' galvanized hardware cloth	1
½" x 4' x 8' exterior or marine plywood	1
CoverLite plastic closure strips	6 pieces
4' x 4' acrylic or polycarbonate glass	1
Exterior paint	1 qt.
1½" construction screws	
1½" roofing screws with rubber washers	
1" MultiLite screws	
2x2 x 8' furring strip	15
26" x 8' clear polycarbonate roof panel	2
⅜ x 4' x 8' beaded plywood panel siding	2
Galvanized hinge sets	2
Slide bolt latch	2
2x4 x 8' premium construction/ framing lumber	8
1x4 x 8' select pine board	4
2x4 x 8' ground-contact green pressure-treated lumber	4
4" strap hinges	

1

4

BUILD THE FRAMES

1 MAKE THE SIDE FRAMES

Cut all the parts for the side frames (A-H, Figure A). You may want to wait to cut the two top boards (H) until you have the rest of the pieces assembled. Lay out the parts on a large flat work surface. Mark the verticals (B and C) where you'll attach the horizontals (D and E).

Drill pocket holes, and attach the back and front (B and C) to the edge of the bottom (A) using pocket screws. Attach one horizontal (D) to the right-side frame and the other (E) to the left-side frame. Next, build the right-side door frame (D and F) and the left-side window frame (D and G).

Use pocket screws to attach the door and window frame parts between the verticals. Now measure and cut the two top boards (H), and attach them to the top of the side frames.

2 MAKE THE FRONT AND BACK FRAMES *(NOT SHOWN)*

Measure the height of the side frames (Figure A) at their tall end. Cut the verticals (K) to length for the back wall. Do the same for the front frame, taking your measurement from the lower end of the side frame, then cut the two front frame verticals (S) to length. Cut the remaining frame parts.

Use a circular saw or table saw to rip a 2x4 down the middle at a 15-degree angle for both top boards (N and T). Mark the front and back frame verticals where you'll attach the horizontals. Attach the verticals to the bottoms, tops and horizontal supports, then attach the remaining vertical supports with No. 10 x 3-in. exterior construction screws.

3 BUILD THE RUN FRAMES *(NOT SHOWN)*

Construct the frames (A-L, Figure B) for the run just as you did the coop frames. To get the angle of the roof line from the coop continuing into the run, measure the height on the coop front frame from the bottom to the short point of the angle on the top (R). This gives you the height of the run's side frames at the long point of the angle. Cut the components, drill the pocket holes and assemble the frames as before.

MEET THE BUILDER

JOE CRUZ IS A CONTRIBUTING EDITOR, ALL-AROUND HANDYMAN AND BUILDER OF ALL THINGS.

ASSEMBLE THE FRAMES

4 PREASSEMBLE THE COOP

Clamp the frames together to make sure they all fit perfectly, starting with the coop frames. Start by clamping the back frame between the two side frames, aligning the angles at the top of each frame. Predrill pilot holes through the side frames and secure the side frames to the back frame with No. 10 x 3-in. screws. Attach the front frame in the same manner.

5 PREASSEMBLE THE RUN *(NOT SHOWN)*

Clamp the run's side frames to the coop front frame vertical (S), keeping them tight against the side frame front vertical (C). Again, predrill holes and secure the frames together with lag screws. Attach the run's front frame between the two sides of the run.

6 CUT THE BEADED PANELS

Measure and cut the beaded plywood panels for the inside of the coop. For each side of the coop, cut large panels, then mark and cut with a jigsaw for the roof angle, door, window, nesting box and flower box locations.

To keep the vertical direction of the beads on the panels, you will need two 4 x 8-ft. sheets to get all six pieces. Alternatively, cut individual panels for each framed section out of a single 4 x 8-ft. sheet.

7 PAINT THE COOP AND RUN

Disassemble the frames in reverse order of assembly. Paint all surfaces of the frames. Paint the beaded coop panels an accent color if you choose. Once the paint dries, attach the beaded plywood panels to the backs of the frames with construction screws.

8 INSTALL CHICKEN WIRE

Cut and attach chicken wire or hardware cloth to the coop and run frames, as well as to the coop floor frame, using crown staples.

6

7

8

9 ADD THE FLOOR SUPPORTS

Measure, cut and install the floor and tray supports (AA and BB) onto the front and back frames.

10 ASSEMBLE THE COOP AND THE RUN

Clamp all the finished parts together and secure them with construction screws.

11 ADD THE FLOOR AND WASTE TRAY

Install the assembled coop floor (X, Y, Z), including chicken wire, by lowering it through the roof opening or raising it from the bottom and placing it on the floor supports. After that, slide the waste tray in its slot under the floor.

The waste tray (FF) is simply a piece of 1/4-in. polycarbonate or plexiglass attached to the tray front (EE) with a 1/4-in. by 3/4-in. rabbet joint and a couple of screws. Add a knob for easy tray removal.

ADD THE DOORS AND WINDOWS

12 MAKE THE DOORS

Cut the beaded plywood panels for the coop and run doors. Build the door frames as shown in Figure E out of 1x4 boards, and then glue and nail them to the back of the door panels. Attach the doors by flat-mounting hinges and install a sliding bolt latch to keep them secure.

13 ADD THE WINDOW (NOT SHOWN)

Cover the window opening with a piece of polycarbonate or plexiglass left over from the waste tray, cut to a 13 1/4-in. square. Predrill pilot holes in all four corners and secure the piece inside the window opening with 1-in. pan-head screws.

14 ATTACH THE ROOF

Attach a cross support between the two run side frames. Then install plastic closure strips for corrugated roofing on the top of the front and back coop frames, and another on the run's front frame and cross support.

Place the roof panels on top of the coop and run frames, letting them overhang a minimum of 1 in. on each side. Secure the panels using roofing screws with rubber washers.

BUILD THE NESTING BOX

15 BUILD THE NESTING BOX

Cut all nesting box parts listed in Figure D. Using a circular saw, cut the top angles on the ends (B) and partitions (C). Assemble the nesting box as shown, remembering to leave the top free since it will be hinged.

After painting, install the nesting box into its opening by driving screws into the framing around it from the inside.

16 INSTALL THE LID

Cut the angle on the top edge of the nesting box lid (E); it should be about 18½ degrees. Place the lid on the nesting box so the overhang is uniform on all sides, and attach it with strap hinges.

BUILD THE FLOWER BOX

17 BUILD THE FLOWER BOX

Cut the five pieces from the Cutting List on p. 147 (also see Figure C). Construct the box as shown here, using crown staples and wood glue. Drill a handful of $\frac{3}{16}$-in. weep holes along the center of the bottom (A) to allow rainwater to escape. Paint the flower box and install it into its opening by driving construction screws into the framing around it from the inside.

GET YOUR CHICKENS!
Now it's time to get some chickens, plant flowers in the box and add a simple ramp from the coop into the run so the chickens can move back and forth. Check local regulations. In urban areas, you likely won't be able to keep roosters.

12

14

15

16

17

INVISIBLE FENCES

LEARN ABOUT THE PROS AND CONS OF THREE DIFFERENT TYPES

Even the best invisible fence for dogs isn't as good as a real fence, according to dog trainer Ali Smith, founder of Rebarkable, but sometimes you don't have a choice. Some communities don't allow physical fences, some terrain isn't suitable and some properties are too large. Besides, invisible fences can be convenient (for you, not really for your dog). Here's a look at the options.

TRADITIONAL BURIED-WIRE INVISIBLE FENCE

This comes as a kit with thin 20-gauge boundary wire that you bury a few inches deep, a transmitter that broadcasts a signal through the wire, and a collar with a receiver that administers a warning to the dog as it approaches the boundary.

- Installation calls for digging a shallow trench to bury the wire, locating the transmitter in a safe place and connecting it to the wire. Marker flags are usually supplied with the kit to remind you where the wire is buried.
- You can establish boundaries within boundaries to protect flower gardens and other sensitive areas.
- This type won't work during a power outage.
- The wire can be damaged when you dig or do other yard work, and it can corrode too.

WIRELESS INVISIBLE FENCE WITH TRANSMITTER

The transmitter broadcasts a signal through the air that the receiver in the collar picks up.

- The signal is omnidirectional and can only establish a circular fenced area.
- The boundary can extend through all kinds of terrain—even water.
- It won't work during a power outage.
- The transmitter must be in the center of the fenced area.
- The transmitter has a limited range. More transmitters may be required for properties larger than three-fourths of an acre.

BY CHRIS DEZIEL

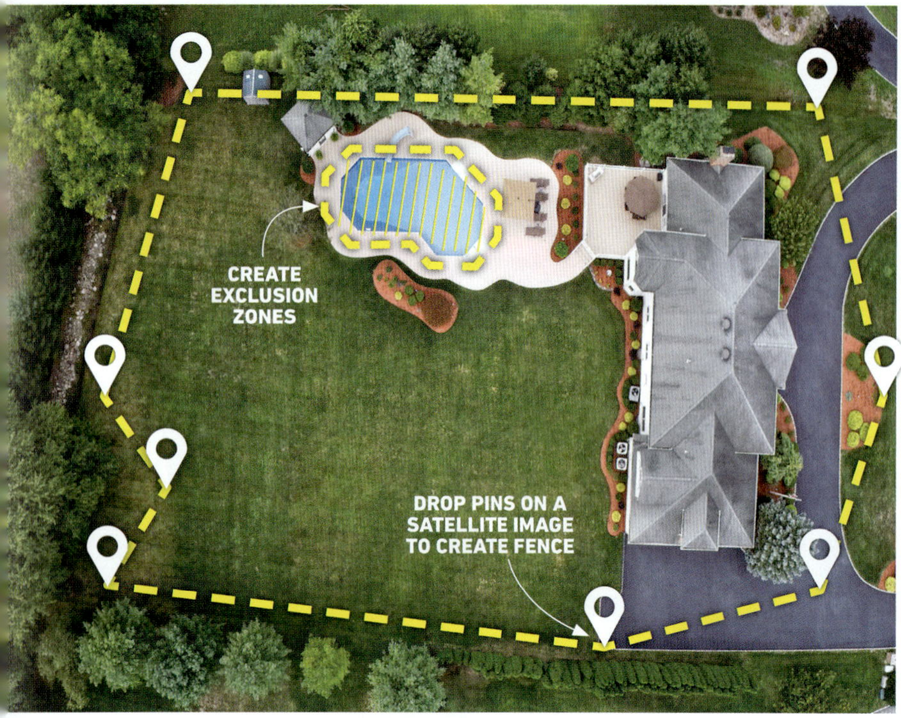

All invisible fences require training because the dog has to learn to recognize the signal and respond to it appropriately. "Training is pretty rough on the dog, as it works by aversion," warns Smith. Beside this, invisible fences have other drawbacks, not the least of which is that a dog who muscles through the signal produced by the collar to chase a rabbit or squirrel can't get back into the yard without experiencing the signal again.

Before buying an invisible fence, consider that the collars require a battery. The battery adds weight that could be uncomfortable for small dogs, and the fence obviously won't work if the battery dies. With all that in mind, here are the best invisible fence options for different situations.

HOW MUCH DOES AN INVISIBLE FENCE COST?

Fences with in-ground wires are the cheapest, costing about $200, more if you need more wire than comes with the kit. Fences controlled by a wireless transmitter are only slightly more expensive, ranging from $250 to $350.

App-based geofences are considerably more expensive, costing from $650 to $1,300. Most also include a monthly subscription fee for the app.

GPS INVISIBLE FENCE

The newest type of wireless fence relies on a GPS receiver in the collar. You create the boundaries using an app on your smartphone, either by setting the boundary on the screen of your device or walking the boundary while the app is in programming mode.

- This is the most expensive type of invisible fence.
- Boundaries can be programmed remotely from anywhere in the world.
- The collars tend to be large and may not suit smaller dogs.
- Boundaries for your dog can be set up anywhere—for example, at a friend's house or a campsite.

BEST FOR SMALL PROPERTIES

GPS dog fences will work in small yards, but they're overkill and not recommended. A wireless transmitter will also work, but the wireless signal tends to get picked up by other devices, so it isn't an ideal choice in a crowded neighborhood.

A buried wire invisible fence, such as the **PetSafe In-Ground Dog Fence Kit**, is the best choice for a small property and is also the least expensive option. Digging is minimal on a small property, and the transmitter can easily be located in the basement or garage.

BEST FOR LARGE PROPERTIES

The GPS dog fence wins this one hands down. Although it's possible to bury a wire around the boundary of a multi-acre property, it's a lot of work. You need a lot of wire, and the more wire you bury, the greater the chances of an accidental break. Wireless transmitters, for their part, don't have the range to cover a lot of ground.

Sung Vivathana, co-founder and vice president of **SpotOn Fence**, says his product allows you to "create and save up to 20 fences of any shape and size nearly anywhere in the world using just your smartphone and the SpotOn collar." Case closed.

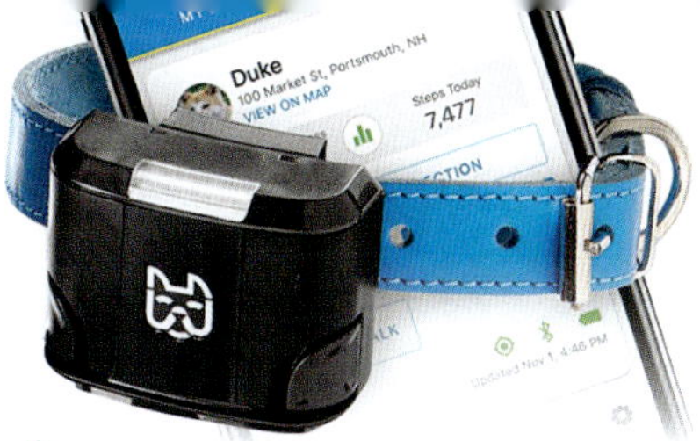

BEST FOR ROUGH TERRAIN

You don't want to do any digging in uneven or rocky ground, so a buried wire isn't the best choice for rough terrain. If the ground is severely sloped to the point that some areas are out of range of the signal, a wireless transmitter would also be a poor choice.

A GPS fence gets its signal from a satellite, just like a cell phone, so it will work no matter how steeply sloped the ground is, and installation involves no digging. In addition, if your property has hazards, such as a pond, you can program a GPS fence "with keep-out zones to avoid any potential dangers," according to Terry Anderton, founder and CEO of **Wagz**.

BEST FOR CAMPING

The choice here is easy. If you like to take your dog on camping trips and you don't want them to go running off into the forest, you need a GPS fence. Use the app to establish the boundary around your campsite, then enjoy the scenery without having to keep a constant eye on your dog.

There's one caveat: You need a cell signal for GPS devices to work, so if you're planning a trip to remote locations where your phone doesn't work, don't forget to pack a dog leash.

BEST FOR CATS

We know training a cat to stay within a boundary is a tall order, but the makers of **Invisible Fence Brand** claim it can be done. If it's true, the collar they make is one of the few that can do it. It weighs only 1 oz., so it's perfect for cats as well as small dogs.

The Invisible Fence is available as a wired system or as a GPS collar. If you have both a dog and a cat, you can give each of them a collar and control both collars with a single system.

BEST FOR LARGE, ACTIVE DOGS AND MULTIPLE DOGS

Large dogs need a lot of space to roam and the best way to give it to them is with a GPS fence such as **Halo**. It's designed for dogs that weigh 20 lbs. or more, and like all GPS fences, it's controlled by an app on your smartphone.

The app tracks your dog's activity, so you'll know its favorite places, and you'll be able to customize the boundary to keep your dog out of hazardous areas. The app works with multiple collars, so if you have more than one dog, this system is for you.

BEST FOR SMALL DOGS

Small dogs tend to be sensitive, and a harsh vibration or shock can cause them considerable distress. Moreover, they can't support a large collar intended for bigger dogs. The **PetSafe Stubborn In-Ground Fence** is designed for dogs that weigh as little as 8 lbs., and it has a tone plus vibration mode as well as four customizable static levels.

It comes with enough wire to enclose a third of an acre, and you can enclose up to 25 acres by purchasing extra wire.

BEST FOR BOUNDARIES WITHIN BOUNDARIES

If you have a garden, swimming pool or other landscape feature you don't want your dog to encounter, a wireless transmitter won't help because it can establish only a single boundary. You can establish multiple boundaries with buried wire, but the extra wire has to be routed to the transmitter, which can create logistical difficulties.

A GPS fence is your best bet. Not only does it allow you to establish boundaries within boundaries, but it lets you move them as the landscape develops or your pet's habits change.

BEST FOR RENTERS

If a renter gets the landlord's permission to bury a wire, and they go to the trouble to do it, that wire will probably stay in the ground when the renter leaves. Renters want a fence they can take with them, and either a GPS fence or wireless transmitter qualify.

Because it can be used anywhere, a GPS fence is a great choice for someone renting a sizable property, but compared with a wireless transmitter, it is a big investment. If you're on a budget and don't live in a crowded neighborhood, go for the wireless transmitter.

5 EXTERIOR REPAIRS & IMPROVEMENTS

BY MIKE BERNER

INSTALL AN EGRESS WINDOW

RECEIVE A BIG PAYOFF: A BRIGHTER, SAFER BASEMENT

One of the best investments you can make in your home is to add finished square footage, and for many homes, the basement is the best place to do that. What many people don't know is that the new habitable space in your basement requires an egress window to provide an exit in case of an emergency. Installing one is a big job, but the larger window will flood your basement with natural light and make it code compliant.

WHAT IT TAKES

TIME	COST	SKILL LEVEL
5-7 days	$5,000+	Advanced

TOOLS
Mini excavator (rental), shovels, rakes, hand tamper, concrete saw, 8-lb. maul, drill, impact driver, circular saw/miter saw, table saw, oscillating multi-tool, hand seamer, basic carpentry tools

BEFORE YOU START

Adding an egress window is a big job, and it is important to plan your project to meet the building requirements in your location. Here are the steps we took before starting to excavate.

- **APPLY FOR A PERMIT.** This process could take a few weeks. Our city required detailed plans of the well, the dimensions of the window and rough opening, the size of the header and a drawing of the property, including the house.
- **GET AN ENGINEERED DRAWING.** The retaining walls that made up our well were tall enough to require an engineer's approval. We sent our plans to a local engineer who gave us a new drawing with a stamp of approval to include with our permit application. If you buy a manufactured well, this step is likely unnecessary, but the final call is with your city's building department.
- **CALL THE DIGGING HOTLINE.** Even if you're digging just a few inches deep, call to have underground utilities located and marked. Digging is dangerous if you don't know where utilities are.

  If you skip this step and hit a gas, water or power line underground, you'll risk the lives of yourself and others, *and* you'll be on the hook for costly repairs. So be sure to call 811 before you start working on your project. The process varies by state, so call a few days ahead.

FIGURE A
PLAN VIEW

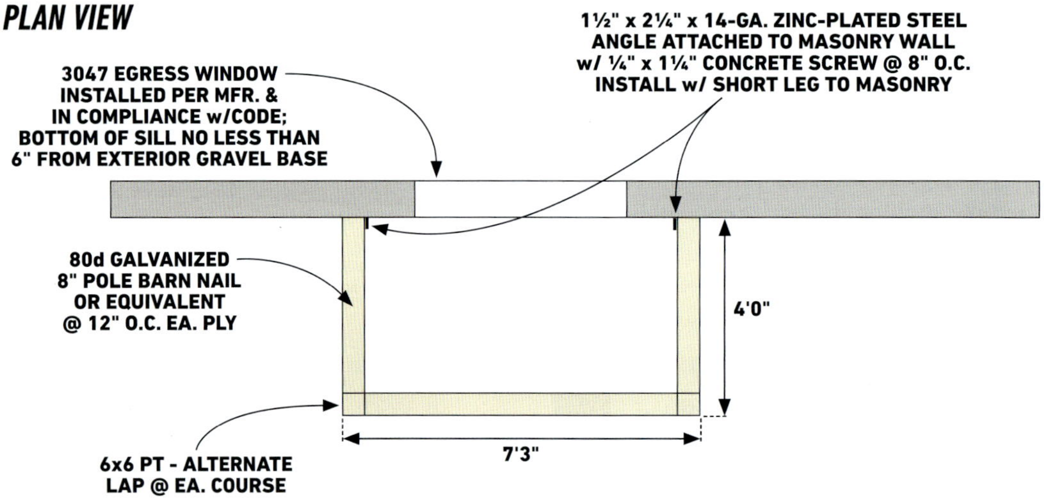

FIGURE B
ELEVATION VIEW

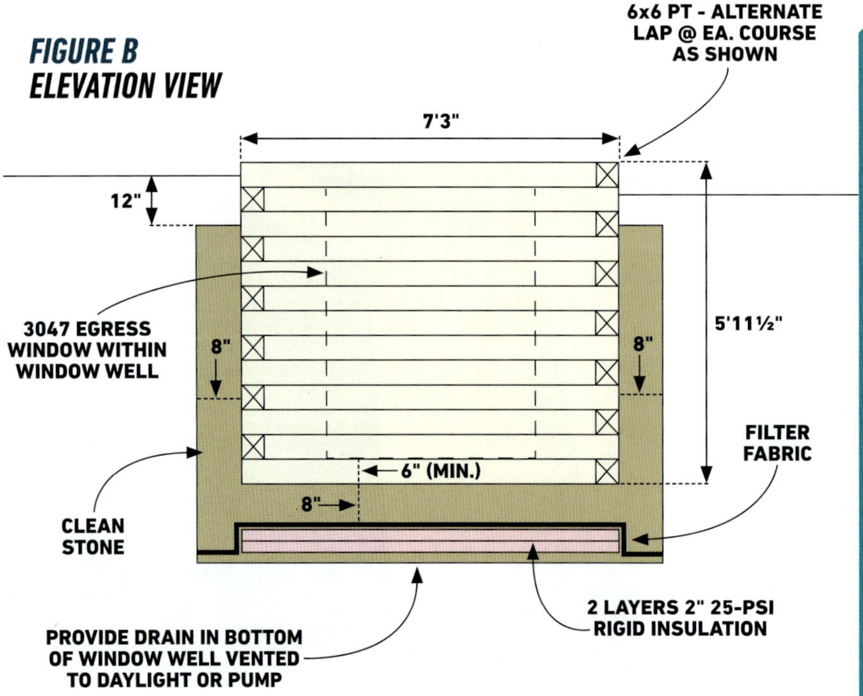

RULES FOR EGRESS WINDOWS

There are several requirements for installing an egress window. Here are the minimum requirements identified by the building code:

- The opening needs to be 5.7 sq. ft.
- The minimum width is 20 in.
- The minimum height is 24 in.
- The well needs to provide a clear space of 3 ft. x 3 ft. when the window is open.
- From the inside the sill height cannot exceed 44 in.

1 DIG THE WINDOW WELL

Heeding our plans, we tagged the window well location with marking paint. We rented a mini excavator to make the digging much easier and to avoid hand digging. Have a plan for the dirt being removed; we took nearly 10 cubic yards of dirt to a compost site. A trench 5 ft. deep or greater requires a protective shoring system to keep the soil from caving in. Consult the building department in your area.

2 ADD A DRAIN

Once the well was dug and free of loose dirt, we dug a trench underneath the house and fed a drainpipe to meet the drain tile system. This was required by the city to prevent water from pooling and freezing against the house, perhaps harming the foundation. The drain provides a path to the sump pump for water collecting in the well. With the drainpipe set, fill well with clean rock.

3 LEVEL THE BASE

Use any remaining loose dirt to create a slope toward the drain. Then cover the bottom surface with geotextile fabric and a 2-in. layer of clean rock, leveled and tamped. The fabric keeps the rock from settling into the dirt and causing the entire base to shift.

4 INSULATE THE FOOTING

Our window is 55 in. tall; to make room for the installation, we dug down closer to the footing than we normally would. Because we live in an area that experiences freeze/thaw cycles, the footing needed frost protection. So, we added two layers of 2-in. rigid insulation rated to 25 psi. (That rating ensures the rock won't crush the insulation.) We cut a hole to feed the drain through and positioned the insulation in the bottom of the well.

MEET THE BUILDER

MIKE BERNER
LIKES BEING IN THE TRENCHES AND TACKLING COMPLICATED PROJECTS.

PRO TIP

The rock we're using isn't "gravel" or "class V." When you call to order it, ask for "¾-in. clean rock." It's an angular rock that's free of silt that could clog the drain. It compacts well, creating a solid base for the retaining wall and a drainage field.

MATERIALS LIST

ITEM	QTY.
Clean ¾" rock	7 tons
6x6 critical-structure treated timbers	30
2x4 x 8' pressure-treated lumber	4
2x6 x 8' cedar lumber	45
2x10 x 8' lumber	1
2x12 x 8' lumber	2
5/4x6 x 8' cedar decking	45
4" x 10' perforated drainpipe	1
2" x 4' x 8' 25-psi rigid insulation	5
12½' x 27½' geotextile fabric roll	2
1" x 8' Z-flashing	1
3" sidewall flashing	8'
Flexible flashing tape	1 roll
Seam tape	1 roll
48" x 25' fiberglass screen	1 roll
2¼" x 1½" x 72" steel angle	2
6" timber/lag screws	8
8" timber screws	200
1¼" concrete anchors	25-ct.
2½" concrete anchors	25-ct.
Composite deck screws	250-ct.
1¼" roofing nails	1-lb. box
Silicone	

5 ADD ROCK FOR THE TIMBER WALL BASE

We covered the insulation with another layer of fabric, then added 8 in. of clean rock on top. The extra layer of fabric will keep the sharp rock from puncturing the insulation. Make sure the rock is level and compact it with a hand tamper.

6 LINE THE WELL

Before laying the timbers, we lined the well with geotextile fabric. We unrolled the fabric along the dirt walls and folded it over the edges of the hole. The fabric will keep dirt from entering and clogging the drainage space behind the timbers.

7 BUILD THE RETAINING WALL

After you've established a level base of clean rock, start building the retaining wall. The first course of timbers must be level along the length and width of the well. You might have to tamp and move rocks to position this first course.

Each consecutive course will be placed by alternating the overlapped corners. As the timbers are stacked, check that they are plumb or leaning out slightly, and fasten each course to the previous one with 8-in. coated timber screws every 12 in.

8 BRACE THE END WALLS

To keep the ends of the retaining wall from being forced in during backfilling, we added a length of steel angle against the foundation on the inside of the well. We drilled pilot holes with a hammer drill and fastened the angle to the block wall with construction adhesive and 1¼-in. concrete screws. The retaining wall needs to be able to shift a bit, so don't fasten it to the steel angle.

9 BACKFILL THE WELL

Fill the space outside the well with clean rock. The rock allows water to drain away from the wall and gives it space to dry, adding longevity to the treated lumber. Leave about 4 in. of grade at the top to be filled with topsoil.

10 COVER THE BACKFILL

Fold the rest of the fabric over the rock and tack it to the retaining wall. Then cover the fabric with topsoil, maintaining a slight slope away from the well. The fabric prevents dirt and silt from clogging the drainage space.

11 INSTALL A HEADER

Before cutting the hole in the wall, we reinforced the rim joist with a header to span the new opening. We used the header span tables in the International Residential Building Code to determine how many 2x10s we needed to add to support the larger opening. We used construction adhesive and lag bolts to fasten two 2x10s, one at a time, to the existing rim joist. We cut each new ply 8 in. longer than the opening to ensure there was enough bearing on each side of the opening.

REMODELING CHALLENGES AND SOLUTIONS

We ran into a challenge where our new well transitions to stucco siding. Our solution was to add a drip ledge above the well. This creates an eave over the window, allowing water to shed in front of the window instead of onto it. It also makes a smooth transition from the existing stucco to the thicker insulation and cladding.

12 *ADD FLASHING*

The flashing behind the existing siding and water-resistant barrier is vital. To fit the flashing behind the stucco and felt paper, we lightly pried the layers from the house and cut any nails that were in the way with an oscillating multi-tool. Once the flashing was tucked behind the stucco, we pressed down on it to slope it away from the house.

13 *FASTEN THE LEDGE*

We ripped a cedar 2x6 to 4 in. wide and gave it an 8-degree bevel. Then we drilled evenly spaced pilot holes on its edge. We secured the ledge to the rim joist with 6-in. timber screws.

14 CUT THE WINDOW OPENING

With the well structure built and the drip ledge and header installed, we were ready to cut the new opening. We measured our window and added 4¼ in. to the total height and width to determine the rough opening size. We transferred the measurements to the block wall.

Then, donning rain ponchos, ear and eye protection, and respirators, we carefully cut the block. To keep the chain or blade from binding, we cut the bottom first, then the sides.

15 INSTALL THE WINDOW BUCKS

Once cut blocks were removed, we filled the cores of the bottom wall blocks with concrete and fit window bucks around the opening. We cut 2x12 pressure-treated wood bucks to fit the width of the opening and fastened the top buck to the bottom of the sill plate with screws. Then we leveled the bottom buck with shims, gave it a slight pitch outside and fastened it to the core-filled blocks with concrete anchors.

Note: As shown in the next photos, we set the bucks proud of the block wall by 2 in. to line up with rigid insulation that will be added to the wall outside.

PICK A CONCRETE SAW

Typically, a window opening is cut with a **circular concrete saw**—a large gas-powered tool equipped with a diamond blade and a hose connection. These saws need a constant flow of water to keep the blade cool and require you to make cuts on both sides of the wall. But making the cut on the inside fills the house with gas fumes and floods the floor.

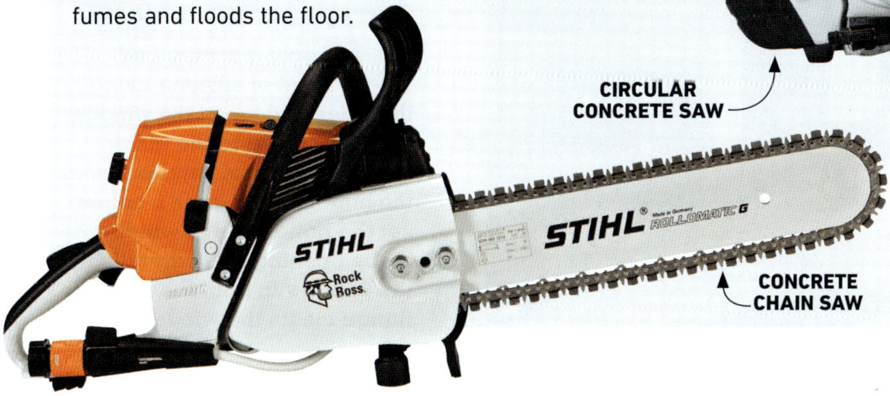

We used a **concrete chain saw** instead. The chain saw made a clean cut all the way through the 12-in. block from the outside, keeping fumes and puddles out of the house.

16 FLASH THE OPENING

We used 6-in.-wide flexible flashing tape to create a window pan. We started by covering the front of the sill, wrapping tape up the sides about 6 in., then stretched the tape around the corners and the front of the bucks. Next, we applied the tape to each side, overlapping the tape on the sill. Finally, we covered the top of the bucks, making sure to adhere the tape up the block wall, sealing any entry points where water could get inside framing.

Note: On a normal window, the flashing tape folds around the window buck and adheres flat to the block. That seals the gap between the block and the buck. In this application, you seal the gap with caulk and protect the wood with tape.

17 PLACE THE WINDOW

Apply a continuous bead of silicone along the sides and top of the window bucks as close to the inside edges as you can get. Don't seal the bottom. Then, with a helper, set the bottom of the window in the opening and carefully tip the window in until the nailing flange meets the window bucks.

18 LEVEL AND PLUMB THE WINDOW

With your helper outside holding the window, head inside to position it. First, raise the window ½ in. off the sill and level it with a few shims. Then center the window and have your helper drive one roofing nail in each bottom corner of the window's nailing flange. Next, place a level against the hinge side and adjust it plumb. Use a few shims to keep it in place and check the other side.

Check the window to make sure it's level and plumb, and also check that the measurements from opposite corners are equidistant. Then drive a nail in each top corner of the nailing flange. Before nailing the rest of the window, place the level back on the sides. If there are gaps between the frame and the level, use shims to straighten the frame, then have your helper nail the sides and the top of the window's flange.

19 INSULATE THE WALL

Believe it or not, the soil we removed from against the house was insulating the basement, so we needed to replace the soil with a 2-in. layer of rigid insulation. We ripped a pressure-treated cleat to match the depth of the insulation and fastened it with concrete screws a few inches from the retaining wall. Then we pressed the insulation between the cleat and the wood bucks. We pressure-fit insulation all the way around the window and sealed all the seams with sheathing tape.

20 ADD A DRIP CAP

We cut a piece of 1-in. Z-flashing to ½ in. wider than the window. Then we used a hand seamer to fold the ends down to cover the sides of the window. After nailing on the drip cap, we covered the flange with flashing tape to keep out water.

PRO TIP
We covered the blue rigid insulation with leftover landscape fabric to keep it from showing through the cladding.

21 ADD FURRING STRIPS

Before dressing up the inside of the well with cedar, we ripped a pressure-treated 2x4 into ¼-in.-thick strips and fastened them inside the well every 2 ft. This will allow water to drain away to keep the cedar cladding and the timbers free of rot.

22 INSTALL PEST SCREEN

To prevent pests from finding a home behind the cedar cladding, we lined the inside of the well with a roll of fiberglass screen mesh. We made sure the mesh was taut, stapling it to each furring strip.

23 CLAD THE WALLS

We used cedar deck boards to clad the inside of the well. We cut each piece to length and fastened the boards to the timber wall with composite deck screws through each furring strip. We made sure each board was level so each course would line up at the corners.

PRO TIP

We purchased our window at a builders' reuse center for just over $200. We didn't mind that it didn't match the other windows, but we didn't like the center piece of trim. We removed the piece after the window was installed.

24 BUILD THE STAIRS

We glued and screwed two 2x4s together. Then we cut one end at 60 degrees and the other at 30. Starting with the bottom stair, we fitted each one into the corner, shortening each step as we worked our way up the wall. In our city, each step is required to be 12 in. wide and at least 3 in. away from the wall, with no more than 18 in. of rise between them. We added deck boards to the tops and faces to match the rest of the well.

25 TRIM THE WINDOW

To trim the window, we used Boral TruExterior boards. We ripped them to 1¼ in. wide and fastened them on edge with composite decking screws.

26 SEAL THE WINDOW

Caulk the trim to the window at the sides and bottom. We used a door-and-window sealant that remains flexible after curing. The caulk prevents water from getting trapped between the window and the trim. We capped the top of the retaining wall with cedar decking and finished the well with a few coats of tung oil.

HOW TO FIX SIDEWALKS

ROLL DOWN YOUR SLEEVES AND PUT ON A DUST MASK—PATCHING IS A DUSTY, GRIMY JOB

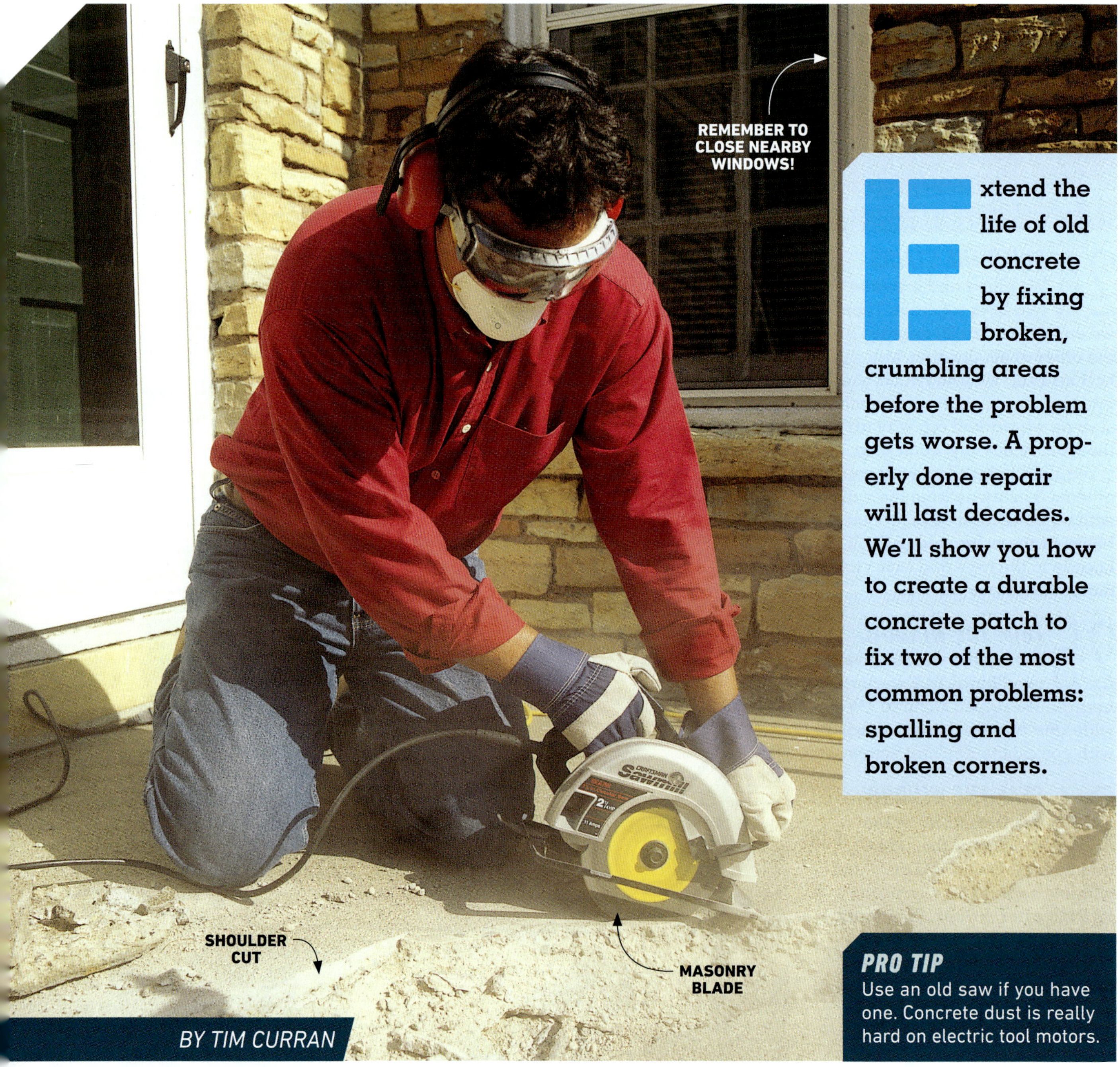

Extend the life of old concrete by fixing broken, crumbling areas before the problem gets worse. A properly done repair will last decades. We'll show you how to create a durable concrete patch to fix two of the most common problems: spalling and broken corners.

PRO TIP

Use an old saw if you have one. Concrete dust is really hard on electric tool motors.

BY TIM CURRAN

A corundum masonry blade grinds through concrete, but slowly. A diamond blade costs a lot more but cuts much faster.

CONCRETE PATCH: SIZE UP THE JOB

Concrete can be intimidating, but with the proper tools and techniques shown here, even a novice can make a durable patch on the first try. Sawing concrete with a special masonry blade may be new to you, but if you've handled a circular saw, you'll quickly get the hang of it. It's less hazardous than sawing wood. However, the blade kicks up an incredibly thick cloud of abrasive dust, so be sure to wear goggles to protect your eyes, hearing protection, gloves, a dust mask and old clothes.

Size up the job first. Before you begin any repair, assess the general condition of the concrete slab. (See "Patch or Replace?") Sometimes the best strategy is to break out an entire section and repour it with new concrete rather than patch it. Patching works best for local damage in otherwise sound concrete.

We won't deal with the other common problem: cracks. You can repair them exactly as we show here, but they'll most likely return unless you can stabilize the concrete slab to prevent the movement that caused the cracks in the first place.

If this is your first concrete repair project, allow about a half day to pick up materials and complete two to three patches. It took us about four hours from start to finish to complete the two repairs we show here.

Do this job in comfortable working conditions, ideally in dry weather with a temperature between 50 and 80 degrees. Both you and fresh concrete happen to agree on this one. Fresh concrete is easiest to handle and hardens best (a process called "setting" and "curing") in this temperature range. Colder weather lengthens the setting time; freezing temperatures can ruin the concrete. Hotter weather causes faster setting and drying—the slab may harden before you can smooth it—or the surface can dry too fast and not harden properly, eventually causing it to spall. In hot weather, work in the cooler mornings or in the shade.

WHAT IT TAKES

TIME	SKILL LEVEL
A full day	Beginner

TOOLS
Circular saw, cold chisel, 2 lb. maul, hammer, wood float, sponge float, edging tool, broom, masonry blade, shop vacuum. You'll also need a dust mask, hearing protection and safety glasses.

MATERIALS
Acrylic fortifer, concrete or sand mix

PATCH OR REPLACE?

Should you patch your old concrete or completely tear it out and repour it? While there's no hard and fast rule, here are some tips to guide your decision:

1. ASSESS THE SEVERITY OF THE DAMAGE. If your driveway is full of spalled areas and broken edges, the surface is probably severely weakened. It'll continue to deteriorate, and chances are the patches won't last.

2. CALL IN A CONCRETE CONTRACTOR (search online for "concrete contractors"). Contractors will help assess the situation and can quote a price on complete replacement. But keep in mind that contractors are in the business of selling concrete. With their labor costs, it's usually cheaper for them to replace than repair. We had trouble finding a contractor who would even do patching.

3. IS APPEARANCE IMPORTANT? A patch will be lighter-colored than the old concrete. Even after weathering for a few years, the new patch will probably still stand out. One way to hide the patch is to stain the entire surface. But you'll have to renew the stain periodically.

4. HOW MUCH ARE YOU WILLING TO SPEND? Material costs for a repair are low. Professionals will probably want to completely replace the slab to ensure a high-quality result. The cost would be substantial.

1

PRO TIP
You'll raise an impressive dust cloud when sawing, so close nearby windows and doors. Otherwise, you'll be doing housecleaning too!

2

3

REPAIR SPALLED AREAS: CUT OUT THE DAMAGE

"Spalling" is the mason's term for concrete that's pitted or chipped. The key to a lasting repair is to make a saw cut around the perimeter of the damaged area, cutting back to solid concrete (Photo 1). The cut should be at least 3/8 in. deep: Most repairs that fail do so because the patch is too thin at the edges and breaks off. Set a masonry blade at a 5-degree angle so the cutout is slightly wider at the bottom than at the top. This helps to"lock in" a patch.

Slowly guide the saw through the concrete. The masonry blade grinds a groove, so don't put a lot of pressure on the saw; let the blade do the work. Cut about ¼ in. on each pass. A diamond grit blade can cut the concrete about five times faster than a masonry blade, and it won't wear out as fast. But it also costs much more. The extra cost is worth it if you have more than about 10 ft. of concrete to cut. Or save money—and time—by renting a diamond blade or a concrete saw with a diamond blade.

Once you've cut and thoroughly cleaned loose concrete from the repair area (Photos 2 and 3), moisten it with a wet sponge before packing in the concrete mix. Don't leave standing water in the patch area; use enough just to dampen the old concrete to help it bond to the new.

1 CUT AROUND THE CHIPPED AREA

Cut a ⅜-in.-to-½-in.-deep "shoulder" around the edge of the spalled area with a saw and masonry blade. Move the saw slowly as you cut. Make sure you cut back into solid concrete to ensure a strong bonding surface.

2 CHISEL OUT WEAK AREAS

Break out all weak and loose concrete with a maul and cold chisel. Sharp concrete chips will come flying out, so wear safety goggles.

3 BRUSH AWAY DEBRIS

Clean the chips and dust from the repair area with a broom or shop vacuum. Be thorough. Then mix the patching material.

REPAIR SPALLED AREAS: PACK IN THE REPAIR MIX

For your patching mix, use either a prepackaged sand mix or a concrete mix, depending on the depth of the patch. (See "Use the Correct Patching Mix.") Each 60-lb. bag makes about ½ cu. ft. of concrete, enough for a 2-in.-thick patch about 1 ft. wide by 3 ft. long. Estimate the volume of patching material by multiplying approximate length, width and thickness (in feet) to arrive at cubic feet, and buy a bit more than you think you'll need. Better to have too much than to fall a few scoops short!

Mix patching mix with water and acrylic fortifier, following the directions on the package. The fortifier strengthens the new concrete and helps it bond better to the old concrete. The mix should be just wet enough to hold together when it's troweled into the repair. Don't add too much water as it'll result in weaker concrete.

We used a normal sand mix, which sets hard enough to walk on in about a day or two. It continues to cure and harden for weeks. If you have to use the area right away, you can buy a special fast-setting concrete, which hardens in about an hour. It costs about twice as much and you won't have as long to spread and smooth it, so stick to the regular mix when possible. Most building supply dealers that carry regular concrete also carry the fast-setting type.

After mixing the concrete, pack it firmly into the repair area, the tighter the better, using a wood float (Photo 4). Mound the mix so it's slightly higher than the old concrete. Then immediately level it even with the old concrete using a straight board (Photo 5).

CAUTION

Wet concrete is highly alkaline and can cause severe burns to bare skin. Immediately wash off with cool water any that gets on your skin.

4 MOISTEN AND FILL

Moisten the patch area with a wet sponge. Then pack in the patch mix with a wood float. Leave the mix slightly higher than the surface of the old concrete.

5 SCREED OFF THE EXCESS

Screed off excess material by sliding a board side to side in a sawing motion while pushing it forward. If you find low spots, pack in more mix and screed off again.

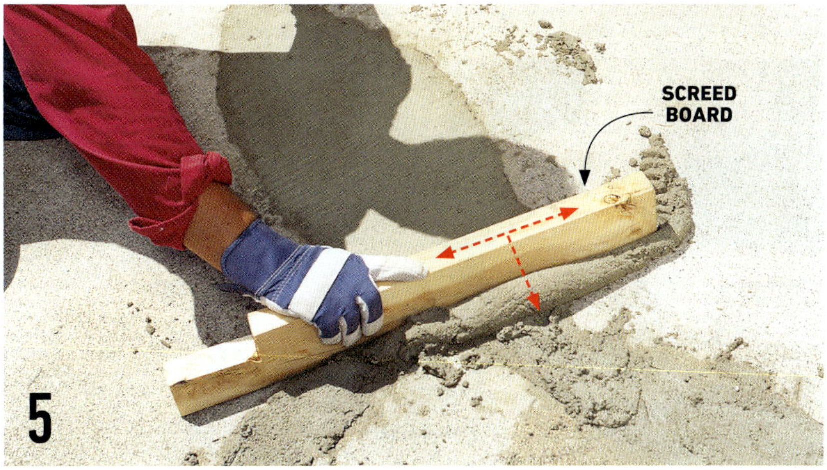

USE THE CORRECT PATCHING MIX

In a nutshell: Use a sand mix for repairs less than 2 in. deep. Use a concrete mix for repairs deeper than 2 in. Replace 50% to 80% of the water with the acrylic fortifier in either mix to improve the patch's bonding strength.

Concrete mix *consists of sand, gravel and Portland cement. The gravel reduces shrinkage, so it won't crack as readily when laid in thick. However, it may not bond well in thin layers.*

Sand mix *(sometimes called topping mix) consists of sand and Portland cement. It's easier to trowel in thinner layers (to about ¼ in. minimum) for thinner patches or patches with thinner edges. However, if you apply it thicker than 2 in., its natural shrinkage might cause it to crack or break the bond with the old concrete.*

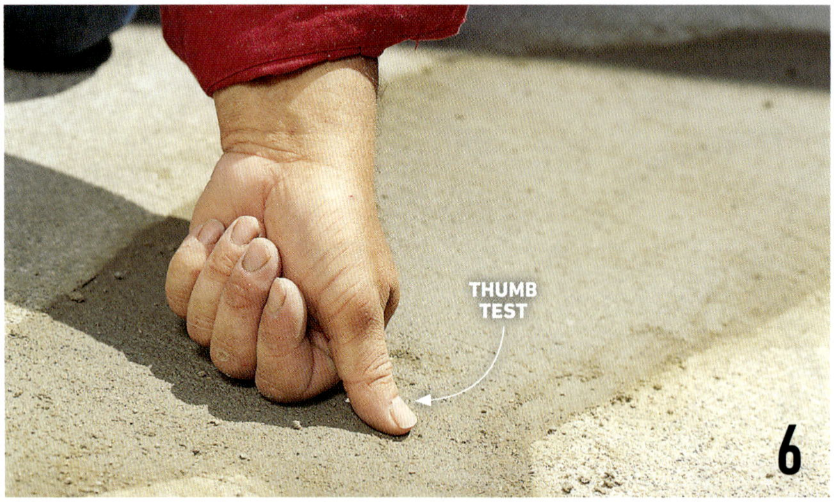

Begin finish-trowel work when the surface moisture starts to evaporate and the patch begins to harden. It may be only 10 minutes on a warm day or perhaps an hour on a cool day. One sign of evaporation is the loss of some of the surface gloss. When the patch appears to be getting stiff, test it with your thumb (Photo 6). Once the surface is about as stiff as the skin of a grapefruit, begin the finish work. We used a sponge float (Photo 7) to match the slightly rough texture of the old concrete. A sponge float has a rough rubber surface. If you want a smooth surface, use a steel trowel; for a lightly grooved appearance, drag a stiff-bristle broom across the surface.

After using a float on the surface, cover the patch with plastic for two days (Photo 8). The plastic helps the concrete retain moisture, which the concrete needs to cure and strengthen.

6 *LET THE CONCRETE STIFFEN* **Test the firmness of the patch by lightly pressing your thumb on the surface. When your thumb no longer leaves an indentation, go ahead and finish the surface.**

7 *FLOAT THE SURFACE* **Match the texture of the old, rough concrete by rubbing the surface of the patch with a sponge float. Use a steel trowel for a smooth finish or a stiff-bristle brush for a lightly grooved finish.**

8 *COVER WITH PLASTIC* **Cover the patch with plastic to retain moisture. Weigh down the edges to keep the plastic from blowing off. Concrete requires moisture to cure properly.**

PRO TIP
Coat the wood form with vegetable oil or WD-40 to keep the concrete from sticking to the wood.

REPAIR BROKEN CORNERS: CREATE A LEDGE

Use the same basic patching technique for a broken corner as for spalled areas, but add three key steps.

1. Create a ledge for the patch to make a stronger bond with the old concrete (Photos 9 and 10). Don't be afraid to make the cutout well beyond the edges of the original damaged area. Smaller patches simply won't hold as well as larger ones.
2. Prop a wood form tightly against the vertical portion of the step to hold the concrete patch in place (Photo 10). Block the form against the step with bricks or other heavy objects.
3. When the concrete begins to set, use the edging tool to create a slightly rounded edge to match the step (Photo 11). Then remove the form board (carefully, because the concrete is still soft) and finish all the exposed surfaces with a float or trowel to match the texture of the old concrete. Cover the patch with plastic and let the concrete cure for at least two days before walking on it.

9 CUT AROUND THE STEP DAMAGE

Square off the edges of the broken step with a masonry blade. Chip out loose and weak concrete with a cold chisel.

CAUTION
Cut the underside of the break as well to make a firm ledge.

10 FORM THE REPAIR AND PACK IN PATCHING MIX

Anchor a form board against the side of the step, moisten the area and pack in the repair mix. Screed off the excess patching material.

11 ROUND THE EDGE

Slide an edging tool along the step edge to round it. Use the edging tool only if the old step portion has a rounded edge.

BY SAM ROSENMAYER

PRESSURE-WASHING SURFACES

Once you find out that a pressure washer is able to serve a valuable role in home maintenance, you'll want to use it all the time. But don't get carried away! Here's a guide to surfaces that can—and shouldn't—be pressure-washed.

DO'S

There's nothing quite like pressure-washing a grimy surface and uncovering the beauty beneath. Here are suitable surfaces to pressure-wash:

◀ **CONCRETE.** Pressure-washing concrete and stone surfaces such as sidewalks, patios and driveways boosts curb appeal. To clean these surfaces, a 25-degree nozzle works well; if you have a tough area, use a 15-degree nozzle. Cleaning concrete calls for a high psi of 3,000. Pressure washers from 1,300 to 2,300 psi can handle a concrete driveway, but it'll take longer. Start at the high end of your driveway or sidewalk and work your way down.

0° SPRAY TIP

15° SPRAY TIP

25° SPRAY TIP

40° SPRAY TIP

BRICKWORK. Brick paths, driveways, patios and steps tend to grow mold, algae and moss over time, so it's important to keep them clean. The recommended psi range for brick is 1,250 to 1,500. A 25-degree nozzle works well for this job.

If you are cleaning a path, be sure to park the pressure washer near the high spot so you're dragging the hose behind you, rather than constantly kicking it out of your way.

SIDING. Grime and mildew tend to accumulate on vinyl and aluminum siding. The recommended psi level for pressure-washing vinyl is 2,500 to 3,000 and for aluminum, 1,200 to 1,500. Use either a 25-degree or 40-degree nozzle, and test in an inconspicuous area. Avoid spraying your windows, painted surfaces, air conditioners and screens.

FENCE. Pressure-washing your wooden fence gives it an instant face-lift. Wood fences, especially those made of redwood, cedar and pressure-treated lumber, are safe to power wash. An appropriate psi for a softwood fence is 500 to 800 psi; for harder woods use a psi of 1,200 to 1,500. The nozzle size for a fence would be a 25-degree or 40-degree tip. Test a small portion of the fence to see what psi setting works best. Spray one board at a time, using a gentle sweeping motion, and avoid sudden stops.

DECK. It is no surprise that decks get dirty extremely quickly. Wood decks, including redwood, cedar and pressure-treated lumber (but not composite decks) are good candidates for pressure-washing.

A 25-degree nozzle and a psi of 1,200 to 1,500 would be appropriate, as if you were pressure-washing a wooden fence. This allows enough pressure to clean the surface without damaging the wood. Spray one deck board at a time, using a gentle sweeping motion. Be sure to avoid sudden stops.

DON'TS

Sometimes pressure-washing can do more harm than good. Avoid pressure-washing these surfaces:

WOOD SIDING. If water gets under the siding, it can damage insulation and electrical wiring, and even spur mold growth.

AIR CONDITIONERS. The intense flow of water can bend or crush the delicate fins and restrict airflow, which in turn shortens the life of the unit.

LEAD PAINT. Lead paint should be carefully contained when removed, not blasted into the air and surrounding surfaces.

ELECTRICAL PANELS AND METERS. Though panels and meters are built to withstand a rainstorm, pressure-washing can force water into cracks and crevices, causing damage and costly repairs.

ASPHALT SHINGLES. The water pressure strips away the granules that protect your roof.

VEHICLES. Using a high-pressure wash to clean your vehicle can cause small dents and even chip the paint, leaving it vulnerable to rust.

OUTDOOR LIGHT FIXTURES. Outdoor lighting can withstand rain and other weather elements, but you should not pressure-wash these fixtures. You'll risk forcing water inside the fixture, causing damage.

GUTTERS. Gutters can withstand rainstorms, but not the extreme power of a pressure washer.

WINDOWS. The high pressure can break them, giving you a major headache and an expensive window to replace.

PAINTED SURFACES. Unless you're pressure-washing to help remove paint, avoid using the washer on painted surfaces. A pressure-wash will easily chip paint off most surfaces, so use only a low-pressure flow of water to wash painted items such as a porch floor or painted outdoor furniture.

OLD MORTAR. Any loose mortar, especially on older structures, will be blasted away by pressure-washing on a high setting.

LIVING THINGS. We hope this one is a no-brainer. Never pressure-wash humans, pets or plants.

CREATE A MORE SUSTAINABLE HOME

SAVE MONEY & REDUCE YOUR CARBON FOOTPRINT WITH THESE 12 TIPS

BY ALLY CHILDRESS

1 BUILD A CLOTHESLINE

People have been drying their clothes outside for millennia. (Sunshine is the best disinfectant, after all.) Tumble drying your clothes, especially on a high heat setting, is rough on fabrics. It also takes energy. Why not reduce your footprint by building a clothesline? Jhánneu Roberts, sustainability expert for "Opendoor's 2023 Eco-Forward Cities," says using a clothesline is a great way to save energy and extend the life span of your clothes. "It's also a great way to enjoy some fresh air while doing your laundry." Many space-saving options are available.

While you're in laundry mode, think about switching to cold water. "Washing clothes in cold water uses less energy than hot water," Roberts says. Bonus: "Many detergents today are formulated to work just as effectively in cold water."

2 REDUCE VAMPIRE LOADS

Many of today's appliances and electronics aren't really off when we turn them off. Smart TVs, coffee makers, toaster ovens and other appliances draw small amounts of energy just waiting for the signal to come alive when we need them. These "vampire loads" account for 5% to 10% of your home's energy use and can cost about $100 a year.

Greg Fasullo, CEO of Elevation, a residential clean technology company, says vampire loads add up, but there's an easy solution: Just unplug the appliance when it's not in use. To make it easier, plug your electronics and computers into power strips so you can cut the power with one switch. And Energy Star appliances are designed to use less vampire power, so always look for that blue sticker when you shop.

3 HARVEST RAINWATER

Watering the lawn and other outdoor irrigation processes use massive amounts of water—about 8 billion gallons a day. In fact, most households use more water outside than for showering and doing the laundry combined! Joe Raboine, vice president of design at Belgard, says rainwater harvesting reduces water use and can be accomplished in a couple of ways.

"At a simple level, you can do this with rain barrels," Raboine says. Rain barrels capture water from your downspouts, storing it for later use, and can be purchased or made yourself. With a larger investment, you can include permeable pavers with an underground capture system in your patio and outdoor landscaping for a less visible method.

4 AIR-SEAL YOUR HOME

When you put your hand to your windows, do you feel a breeze? Drafty windows can account for 25% to 30% of heating and cooling costs, but doors, electrical outlets, attic hatches and ductwork are prime culprits for air leakage too. Caulking and weatherstripping are easy DIY fixes that can pay dividends when it comes to reducing your energy usage and costs.

Walk around your house and look for cracks in the facade and gaps around windows and exterior penetrations (like pipes). Inside your home, use rubber gaskets behind switch plates and outlet covers, and make sure your windows and doors have adequate weather-stripping. The Inflation Reduction Act provides help for homeowners wanting to upgrade to energy-efficient windows and doors.

5 CHANGE TO LED LIGHTBULBS

If you're still buying and replacing incandescent lightbulbs, it's time to switch to LEDs. After a brief delay, the Department of Energy is moving forward with a long-proposed rule that phases out inefficient lighting. Changing your home's lightbulbs and fixtures to LED saves money and reduces your carbon footprint.

"LED lights use up to 90% less energy than incandescent, and 80% less energy than halogen bulbs," according to Michael Meiser, lighting expert at Lumilum. They also last longer—a lot longer. LEDs have a typical life span of 25,000 hours, compared to a paltry 1,200 for incandescent and 2,000 for halogen.

6 INSTALL A WATER FILTER

When you want a drink of water, do you reach for a disposable plastic bottle? Thirsty Americans toss out 2.5 million plastic bottles *every hour*, and only about a quarter are recycled. Millions of tons of plastic waste end up in landfills and the oceans every year.

Drinking tap water significantly reduces our plastic trash burden, but many people simply think bottled is better. If that describes you, try a water-filtering system. Water filtration significantly reduces your household trash footprint, saves money and gives you clean, fresh-tasting water. Lots of bottled water is simply municipal tap water anyway, so why not cut out the intermediary?

7 RETHINK YOUR LANDSCAPING

Traditional turfgrass lawns need lots of water, and xeriscapes can be great sustainable alternatives. "Xeriscaping is increasing in popularity and involves using native plants, turf, gravel or other materials to reduce or eliminate the usage of grass," Raboine says. Consider planting pollinator gardens, rainwater gardens, edible landscapes such as blueberry bushes, and native prairie plants and wildflowers.

If you're not interested in gardening or maintaining plantings, try decorative gravel or artificial turf. If you opt for a straight hardscape like concrete, Raboine says to consider permeable pavers. "These pavers allow for rainwater to permeate the surface and return to the ground, replenishing natural aquifers." This will also reduce the burden on stormwater drains.

8 UPGRADE YOUR INSULATION

Is your home drafty? Do you routinely wear sweaters when your thermostat is set to 75 degrees? "Poor insulation can account for 35% to 40% of a home's heat loss," Fasullo says. Instead of staying put in the living areas, warm air ends up flowing into your attic, garage and basement. But that's not the only problem.

"Homes that lack adequate insulation don't just waste energy through lost hot and cold air," Fasullo says. "Those inefficiencies can lead to expensive damage to other parts of your home." Your HVAC in particular can suffer from a shortened life span when you're trying to make up for drafts and leaks. Luckily, 30% of the cost of new insulation can be claimed as a home energy efficiency tax credit (see *energystar.gov/about/federal_tax_credits/insulation*).

9 INSTALL A BIDET

People around the world use a staggering 42 million tons of toilet paper every year, according to Spencer Weidner, digital marketing director at Bio Bidet by Bemis. And even though toilet paper goes right down the drain, most of it is made from trees chopped down for just that purpose. One way you can reduce this heavy environmental toll is to install a bidet.

You're not just saving the trees either. Weidner says the amount of water involved with using a bidet pales in comparison to the amount used in toilet paper manufacturing, so you're reducing your home's environmental impact on two fronts. Plus, bidets clean better!

Bidets are easy to install too. "Bidet toilet seats and bidet attachments are actually designed for an easy at-home installation," Weidner says. "They connect to your existing plumbing using the provided adapter and hose in a matter of minutes." (Electric models require a nearby outlet.)

10 LOOK FOR REBATES

Upgrading old appliances, replacing windows and doors, and sealing ductwork can drastically reduce your energy consumption and save money in the long run. You can get help on the initial cost too. "Looking at rebates available for home efficiency and improvement projects, the Inflation Reduction Act offers up to $840 back on efficient appliances, $600 on new windows, $500 on new doors, and $1,600 for insulation and air duct sealing," Fasullo says.

Look for Energy Star ratings when you purchase any major appliance, and check utility company and manufacturer websites for additional promotions. The Energy Star website can also hook you up with qualified contractors. "The electrical or wiring work required to install upgraded appliances, solar or home energy storage also qualifies for rebates," Fasullo says.

11 GET A HOME ENERGY AUDIT

The first step to understanding the sources of your home energy costs and emissions is to get a home energy audit. Fasullo says these assessments can cost as little as $100 to $150 and reveal areas of your home where you're wasting the most energy and money.

Home energy auditors check for air leakage, determine your insulation levels, and inspect your fireplaces, lights and smoke detectors. They'll even do an analysis of your electrical bills. Best of all, Fasullo says the Inflation Reduction Act covers 30% of the cost of the audit (up to $150), making this step a no-brainer.

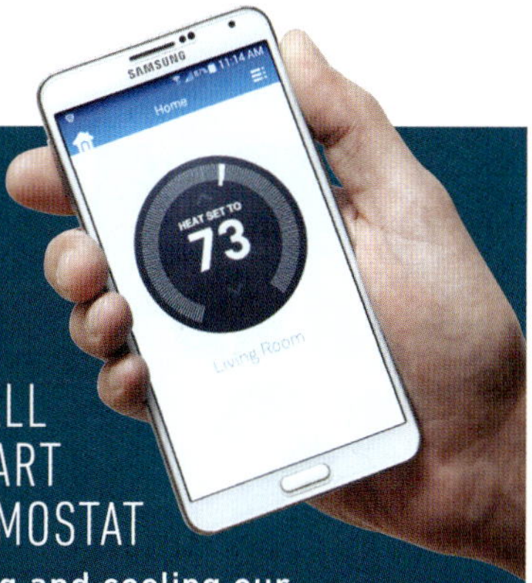

12 INSTALL A SMART THERMOSTAT

Heating and cooling our homes accounts for more than half of our total energy usage, so it's a logical place to target for reductions. Step one should be installing a smart thermostat. "Maintaining a more consistent home temperature, particularly during summer months, can drastically reduce your utility costs and keep your AC running at its best," Fasullo says.

Automating your heating and cooling system makes your life easier too—no more remembering to turn the thermostat down when you leave the house or go to bed. "Smart thermostats can be programmed with eco-friendly settings that keep a home's heating and cooling set point at a comfortable and efficient temp," Fasullo says, "and they adjust for daytime or nighttime hours automatically."

But don't stop at thermostats. "Adopting smarter, automated appliances across the board can help reduce inefficiencies and take the guesswork out of optimizing energy use," Fasullo explains.

TRADITIONAL VS. SUSTAINABLE BUILDING MATERIALS

FIND OUT THE DIFFERENCES, AND THE PROS AND CONS

We see so much about sustainability in the news, and it's becoming important to many homeowners and contractors to use more products that are environmentally friendly. These sustainable materials are becoming more readily available to DIYers, so let's look at sustainable building products and how they compare with more traditional ones.

BY MIKE BERNER

TRADITIONAL BUILDING MATERIALS

Quite simply, traditional building materials are ones we DIYers and contractors have been using for years. Although there has been an evolution in these products as the decades go by, the evolution has been more about health and safety, or efficiency, rather than a move toward eco-friendly materials. Because of the long-standing use of traditional materials, they are familiar, and they are often less expensive.

SUSTAINABLE MATERIALS

In general, sustainable materials are produced, used and disposed of in a way that keeps the environment in mind. The sustainable materials we've used have been manufactured using waste products, come from properly managed forests, and have characteristics that will ensure their longevity. These materials are often more expensive than traditional ones, and sometimes require new installation methods.

FIBERGLASS INSULATION

For many years, fiberglass insulation has been the gold standard to insulate our homes.

PROS:

- It has a relatively high resistance to heat transfer; a 2x4 wall is rated an R-11.
- It is easily accessible and comes in batts of many widths and as loose-fill, making it easy to install in any wall or attic space.
- It can come faced in kraft paper for a built-in vapor barrier.
- It's very affordable.

CONS:

- It contains only 20% to 30% recycled material.
- When it's compressed or it becomes wet, its R-value is significantly decreased.
- It's noncombustible but won't provide the best fire block.

MINERAL WOOL INSULATION

Mineral wool is made by heating and spinning slag, a byproduct in steel production, into a fibrous, wool-like material.

PROS:

- It has a higher R-value; a 2x4 wall will have an R-value of up to R-15.
- It's very dense, making it great for isolating sound.
- It will not absorb water and is very fire resistant.
- It contains 70% recycled material.

CONS:

- It's higher in cost.
- It is heavier than other insulation options.
- Although mineral wool is made with recycled material, the manufacturing process is energy intensive. This is not uncommon with insulation products.

SMART VAPOR RETARDER VS. 6-MIL POLY SHEETING

One new-to-us product we included in our "sustainable retreat" is referred to as a smart vapor retarder. We chose MemBrain vapor retarder by CertainTeed over the 6-mil poly sheeting type because it allows moisture to escape the wall cavity while keeping moisture out.

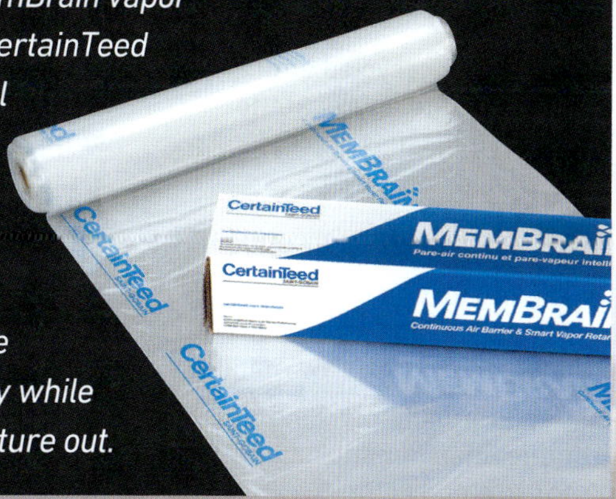

SUSTAINABLE CLADDING: A TOSS-UP

During a walk around the block in many neighborhoods, you can observe several different types of siding: stucco, vinyl, wood, masonry and even the newer engineered wood choices. Most houses are donning their original siding, which attests to their sustainability. Here are the pros and cons of a few popular cladding choices.

STUCCO

Stucco is a popular cladding in the western half of the U.S., but it can be found across the country. It's made with a mixture of cement, sand and water.

PROS:

- It is durable. When properly installed, stucco can last many decades.
- Stucco has insulating properties and can help regulate the temperature inside a building, helping with energy costs.
- It is low maintenance. Once installed, stucco doesn't need to be painted and requires only occasional cleaning.
- It is easily recycled and crushed into aggregate to be used for new stucco.

CONS:

- It's not a DIY-friendly option.
- The production of stucco requires a high amount of energy to extract raw materials.
- Repairing and patching pose difficulties in matching both texture and color.

VINYL

Because vinyl is a type of plastic, not everyone considers it to be sustainable, but it is reusable. It is used nationwide and is popular in new construction and renovations.

PROS:

- It is very tough and will look good for decades as cladding.
- Its manufacturing process produces nearly zero waste; any trimmings or scraps are processed into even more siding.
- It is recyclable. If it makes it to a recycling center, it will be shredded and reused to produce other usable items.
- It is very inexpensive.

CONS:

- The color fades over time.
- It can crack or break.
- If it doesn't get recycled, this material will sit in the landfill forever.

ENGINEERED WOOD

Engineered wood siding, like OSB sheathing, is made with wood chips that are compressed and glued to form different siding products.

PROS:

- It comes in many styles: lap, board and batten, panels or trim boards.
- Cutting it does not require special blades.
- It uses waste from lumber processing, keeping the waste from entering the landfill.
- It is long lasting and maintenance free (no painting, up to a 30-year warranty).

CONS:

- It is more expensive.
- It requires careful adjustment of pneumatic nail guns to prevent overdriven nails.
- Each cut needs to be sealed before installation.

What constitutes a sustainable deck material is a matter of debate. Two top options are cedar and composite boards. Look over their pros and cons to see which one would make more sense for your application.

VS.

CEDAR DECKING

A very popular real-wood option for long-lasting decks.

PROS:

- This material is an all-natural renewable resource.
- It is resistant to insects, weather and rot.
- It can be stained or left raw.
- It is easy to recycle at the end of its life.
- It is easy to work with and to install using deck screws or hidden fasteners.

CONS:

- It is prone to cracks, splinters and splits.
- It needs yearly maintenance, and sanding and refinishing every few years.

COMPOSITE DECKING

Composite decking is made of recycled plastic and wood pulp.

PROS:

- It's made of up to 95% recycled plastic.
- It will last a very long time. Some decking manufacturers offer up to 20-year warranties against fading.
- It has zero maintenance outside of occasional cleaning.

CONS:

- It's not recyclable at the end of its life cycle because it is combined with wood pulp.
- It needs a special composite cutting blade to cut boards to size.
- It is much heavier and more expensive than wood options.
- It may require additional framing for support.

SOLID WOOD TRIM VS. FINGER-JOINTED TRIM

You may not have thought about trim in terms of its sustainability, but more sustainable choices do exist.

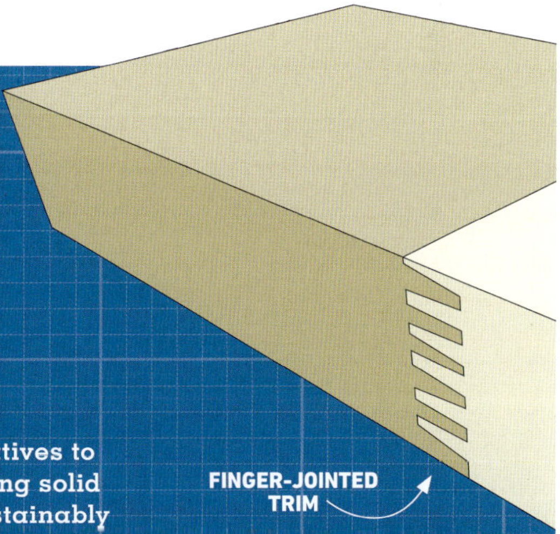

STAINED AND FINISHED SOLID WOOD

If you're seeking the look of hardwood, there are few alternatives to solid wood trim, and none pass the eye test for us. When using solid lumber, look for the FSC stamp, which verifies it is being sustainably sourced by the Forest Stewardship Council.

PAINTED

Most trim we see in new homes now is painted. We've installed miles of "primed for paint" trim, and we always use finger-jointed trim. As its name indicates, this trim consists of many small cutoffs that are finger-jointed together. This process takes pieces of wood that were unusable and joins them to create the straightest trim in the lumberyard.

6 OUTDOOR STRUCTURES, LANDSCAPING & GARDENING

BRICK PIZZA OVEN

MAKE WOOD-FIRED PIZZAS AND MORE, RIGHT IN YOUR BACKYARD

BY BRAD HOLDEN

If you crave wood-fired pizza and would love to make it in a brick oven in your own backyard, these plans prepared with the help of pro Dick DeGrood are just for you. With advanced skills, attention to detail and a helper, you can build this brick pizza oven for a fraction of what it'd cost to have a professional mason build it for you. And once you have mastered the skill of controlling the temperature, you can bake anything that you'd normally make in a conventional oven.

WHAT IT TAKES

TIME	COST	SKILL LEVEL
About one week	$3,000 to $5,000	Advanced

TOOLS
Table saw, drill/driver, masonry tools, wet saw, concrete tools

MEET THE EXPERT

DICK DEGROOD, PRESIDENT OF TWIN CITY BRICK & STONE, HAS SPENT OVER 46 YEARS IN THE MASONRY SUPPLY INDUSTRY. "I BUILT MY OWN WOOD-FIRED OVEN OVER 20 YEARS AGO, AND IT'S STILL WORKING AS IT DID THE DAY IT WAS BUILT."

1 DIG AND PREP THE PAD SITE

Build a form for the concrete pad using 2x10s. Our pad is 8 in. thick, so we spread Class V gravel in the form, leaving 8 in. to the top of the form. Tamp down the base to compact it. Make sure your form is braced and sloped to shed water.

2 POUR THE PAD

Pour concrete mix into the form, and then screed off the top. Once the concrete begins to set, trowel the surface and tool the edges. Allow the concrete to cure for a day before removing the form.

3 CAST THE CAPSTONE

Build a form for the capstone using melamine. Set the form on sturdy sawhorses with 2x4s underneath for full support. Apply a bead of silicone at each bottom corner of the form. Once the silicone is dry, fill the form with lightweight countertop concrete mix. We used fiberglass rebar to reduce the weight and avoid rust stains. We set the rebar grid and then pressed it into the concrete. When the concrete begins to harden, trowel the surface and tool the corners. The capstone is only 3 in. thick, so we allowed it to cure for several days before removing the form.

4 LAY THE FIRST COURSE OF BLOCK

Before setting our first course of blocks, we drilled the pad and added rebar. This way, after filling the cores in Step 6, the base is firmly attached to the pad.

Lay the outline of the base on the pad and set the first course of concrete blocks. Because our pad is sloped, we set the first course of block in mortar. That way we could build up the back enough to make our base level.

5 FINISH THE BASE

Set the rest of the block for the base using landscape adhesive. This is much easier and faster than using mortar. Pay close attention to keeping the whole thing square, plumb and level as you build.

6 FILL THE CORES

When the adhesive is dry, fill all the cores of the block with concrete mix and rebar.

7 PLACE THE CAPSTONE

Remove the form from the capstone. Clean off any silicone that's stuck to the corners and smooth any sharp edges with a rub block. Apply landscape adhesive to the top of the base, and then set the capstone in place. This thing is very heavy—find a few friends to help you!

8 SET THE PERIMETER

Set bricks around the perimeter of the capstone. Mix your mortar according to the directions on the bag. Use a grout bag to apply a ½-in. bed of mortar under each brick and about a ½-in. layer between bricks. We didn't want the hollow sides of the bricks to show, so we cut ends off extra bricks to cover the hollow faces. Let the mortar cure for 24 hours.

9 ADD FIRE BRICK BASE

To bring the fire bricks up to the height of the perimeter bricks, we set them on a thick-bed floor-mix mortar. We set PVC pipe in place as a temporary guide to screed the mortar to the height we wanted.

10 SET THE BASE FIRE BRICKS

Set the fire bricks in place using refractory mortar to bring them to final level on top of the floor-mix base. Use a level or straightedge to keep them flush with the tops of the perimeter bricks. Traditionally, mortar isn't used between the fire bricks in the oven base.

FIGURE A
WOOD-FIRED OVEN

OVERALL DIMENSIONS:
44" W x 48" D x APPROX. 72" H
INCLUDING THE CHIMNEY

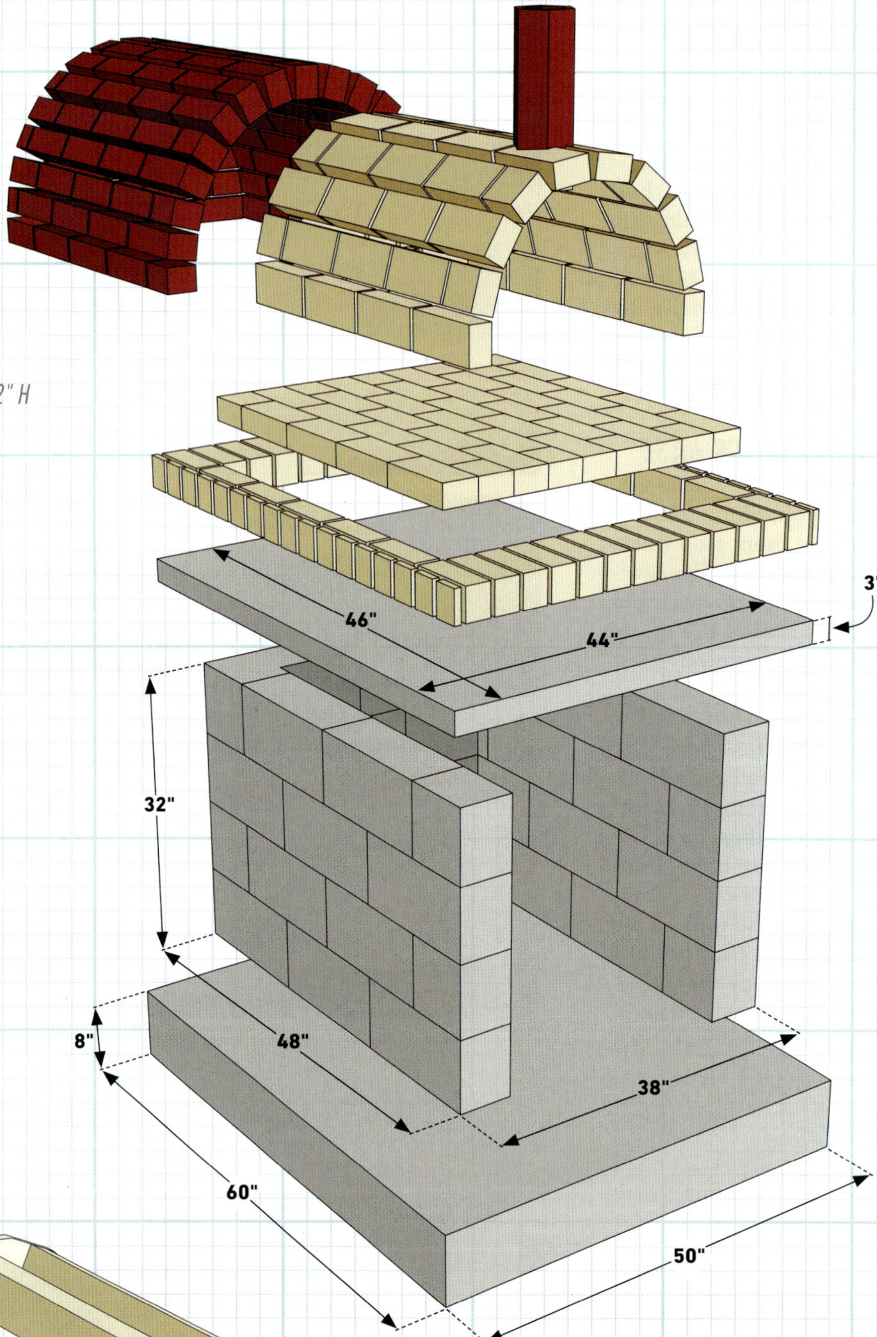

FIGURE B
ARCH FRAME

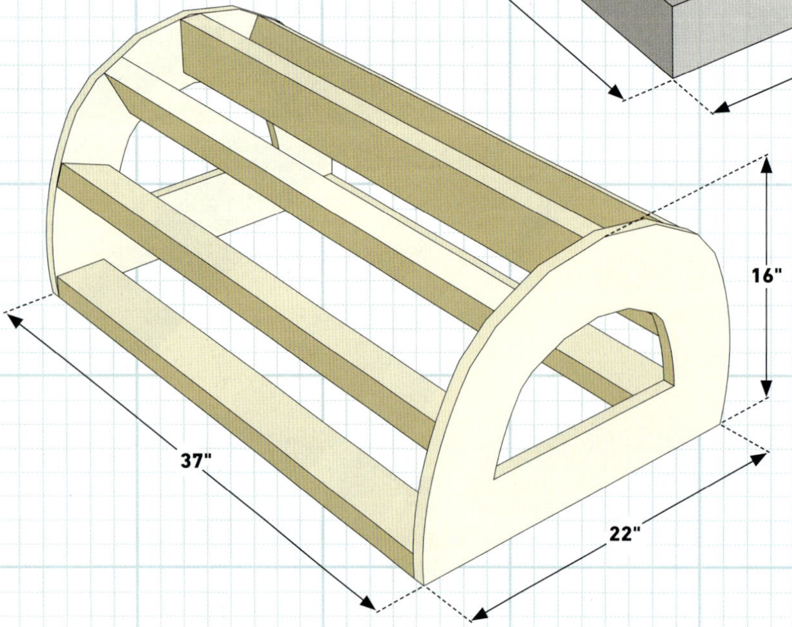

11 CUT THE ARCH ENDS

Cut the ends for the arch form as shown in Figure B. These can be made from any scrap plywood or MDF.

12 ATTACH THE RIBS

Connect the arches using straight 2x4s and construction screws. Don't add glue; you want the form to be easy to take apart later.

13 FINISH THE ARCH FORM

Attach the tempered hardboard skin to the arch framework with roofing nails. Cut a large hole in the center of each arch. This makes removing the form much easier.

14 START THE FIRE BRICK ARCH

Center the arch form on the oven base and start setting fire brick from both sides of the form. Determine the width of the mortar by setting the fire bricks in place, making adjustments to avoid using partial bricks. Use refractory mortar to set the fire bricks.

MATERIALS LIST

ITEM	QTY.
Concrete block	36
Bricks	
Fire bricks	80
60-lb. bags concrete countertop mix	9
½" x 10' rebar	15
½" x 10' fiberglass rebar	10
Cultured stone	30 sq. ft.
Class V base	1 yd.
Refractory mortar	
Type S mortar	
50-lb. floor-mix thick-base mortar	2
Concrete mix	1 yd.
¾" x 4' x 4' plywood	1
8' 2x4s	4
3⁄16" x 4' x 8' tempered hardboard	1
3½" I.D. chimney	1

15 FINISH THE ARCH

Continue working up the arch, staggering the fire brick joints on each consecutive course. We left the fire bricks loose in the flue area for the time being.

16 APPLY THE BRICK VENEER

After setting all the fire bricks, we applied a parge coat of mortar to the whole arch. This thin coat of mortar provides a smooth, continuous surface for setting the outer bricks. Add the outer brick veneer once the mortar has set on the fire brick arch. We applied mortar to each brick, then filled in as necessary with a grout bag. Once the mortar begins to set, tool the mortar joints.

17 SET THE FLUE

Using a diamond wheel on an angle grinder, cut out an area in the two top front fire bricks to accommodate the opening in the flue. Set those fire bricks, and then mortar the flue into place. When the mortar is firm, continue setting the remaining outer bricks, cutting them to fit around the flue.

18 REMOVE THE FORM

Let the arch cure for a day or two, then carefully remove the arch form. Start by unscrewing the ends. Then—as gently as possible—pull the ribs free of the hardboard. Avoid any prying or pounding. You don't want to crack the mortar.

19 FILL THE BACK

Fill in the back of the oven with fire brick followed by a parge coat. Cover the back using slices of the outer brick mortared to the parge coat. Use a grout bag to fill in the joints.

20 VENEER THE FLUE

We used brick slices to veneer the flue. We staggered the corner joints and filled in mortar around the flue as we built up the veneer. At the top, we capped the bricks with a coat of mortar sloped to shed water. You can skip veneering the flue if you like.

21 VENEER THE FRONT CORNER

To cover the concrete block base, we used landscape adhesive to apply cultured stone. We started on the inside and wrapped around the front corner, then worked around the whole base. Cardboard shims hold the stone up off the slab for water drainage.

22 FINISH THE BASE

Continue applying the cultured stone all the way around and inside, working your way up. At the corners and the top, you'll need to trim the stones. They are easy to cut with a diamond wheel on an angle grinder.

THE HEAT IS ON

BUILD THIS SAUNA IN YOUR GARAGE AND ASSEMBLE IT WHEREVER YOU LIKE

BY JOE CRUZ

EASY TO TRANSPORT THEN REBUILD!

Last fall we built this compact four-person sauna with materials we picked up at a local home center. Using the modular design, we were able to easily construct the walls, floor, roof and benches in a garage. Then we strapped the sections to a trailer and transported them to the site shown here. You can build it on site or take it to your cabin or other remote site for assembly. Our sauna is 5 ft. x 4 ft. x 7 ft. 8 in., but you can change the size for your needs.

WHAT IT TAKES

TIME	COST	SKILL LEVEL
Multiple days	More than $1,000	Intermediate

TOOLS

Miter saw, circular saw, table saw, 18-gauge finish nailer, router, flush-trim router bit, cordless drill/driver, eye and hearing protection, bar clamps, Speed square, staple gun, tin snips

Before you start cutting parts, make a flat work surface such as a 4 x 8-ft. sheet of plywood on sawhorses. This makes assembling the components much easier. And you'll want a helper once you're ready to lift the walls and roof components.

1 BUILD THE BASE

Assemble the outer base frame (A and B) using pressure-treated 2x4s. Then measure the inside of the outer frame to get the dimensions for the inner frame (C and D). Cut and assemble the inner frame parts as shown in Figure A. Attach the inner frame in the outer frame, raising the inner frame 1½ in. from the bottom of the outer frame.

2 INSTALL THE FLOOR

Cut the floor (E) and attach it to the inner frame with No. 8 x 2-in. exterior screws. Flip the base over and glue 1½-in. foam insulation between the floor joists.

3 CUT FRONT WALL PARTS

Cut all the front wall parts to length (Figure B). Rip a 15-degree angle down the center of a 2x4 for your top plate (G). Save the offcut for the top plate of the back wall (GG). To lay out the stud placement on the wall, hold the top and bottom boards together and mark where each stud will be attached.

4 ASSEMBLE THE FRONT WALL

Lay all the front wall parts (F-K) down on a flat surface. Using No. 9 x 3-in. deck screws, attach all the studs to the top and bottom plates. Attach the door header as shown in Figure B.

MEET THE BUILDER

JOE CRUZ IS A CONTRIBUTING EDITOR, ALL-AROUND HANDYMAN AND BUILDER OF ALL THINGS.

CUTTING LIST

KEY	QTY.	DIMENSIONS	PART
SAUNA			
A	2	1½" x 3½" x 60"	Floor base outer frame front & back (pressure treated)
B	2	1½" x 3½" x 45"	Floor base outer frame sides (pressure treated)
C	2	1½" x 3½" x 57"	Floor base inner frame front & back
D	5	1½" x 3½" x 42"	Floor base inner frame stringers
E	1	¾" x 45" x 57"	Floor base plywood floor
F	2	1½" x 1½" x 57"	Front & back walls bottom plate
G	2	1½" x 1⅞" x 57"	Front & back walls top plate
H	2	1½" x 1½" x 84 9/16"	Front wall 2x2 stud
J	2	1½" x 3½" x 84 9/16"	Front wall 2x4 stud
K	1	1½" x 3½" x 22¼"	Doorway header
L	4	1½" x 3½" x 12¾"	Back wall bench blocking
M	5	1½" x 1½" x 72 3/16"	Back wall studs
N	2	1½" x 1½" x 48"	Side wall bottom plate
P	2	1½" x 1½" x 49 11/16"	Side walls top plate
Q	2	1½" x 3½" x 85"	Side walls front stud
R	2	1½" x 1½" x 81¾"	Side walls stud
S	2	1½" x 1½" x 78¾"	Side walls stud
T	2	1½" x 1½" x 75¾"	Side walls stud
U	2	1½" x 3½" x 73 1/16"	Side walls back stud
V	4	1½" x 3½" x 9¾"	Side wall bench blocking
W	2	1½" x 3½" x 17"	Heater mount blocking
X	2	1½" x 1⅞" x 60"	Roof frame front & back
Y	5	1½" x 1½" x 46 9/16"	Roof frame studs
Z	1	¾" x 73" x 63"	Roof deck
AA	13	¼" x 3½" x 55⅞"	Roof cedar shiplap
BB	46	¼" x 3½" x 57"	Front & back walls cedar shiplap
CC	50	¼" x 3½" x 44 9/16"	Side walls cedar shiplap
DD	2	¾" x 2½" x 74½"	Front & back roof trim
EE	2	¾" x 2½" x 63"	Side roof trim
FF	2	9/16" x 48" x 89¾"	Side wall panel
GG	1	9/16" x 61⅛" x 76¾"	Back wall panel
HH	1	9/16" x 61⅛" x 89¾"	Front wall panel
JJ	4	¾" x 2½" x 89¾"	Front wall corner trim
KK	4	¾" x 2½" x 76 9/16"	Back wall corner trim
LL	2	¾" x 3½" x 73½"	Door trim sides
MM	1	¾" x 3½" x 30"	Door trim top
BENCHES			
NN	4	1½" x 3½" x 56"	Front & back frame boards
PP	2	1½" x 3½" x 12"	Upper bench frame sides
QQ	5	1½" x 1½" x 53"	Nailing cleats
RR	2	1½" x 3½" x 23"	Lower bench frame sides
SS	2	1" x 5½" x 12"	Upper bench decking
TT	5	1" x 5½" x 23"	Lower bench decking
GLASS PANEL DOOR			
UU	2	1½" x 3½" x 70¼"	Stile
VV	1	1½" x 10¼" x 14¼"	Bottom rail
WW	4	1½" x 4½" x 14¼"	Rail
XX	8	¼" x 1½" x 3¾"	Short spline
YY	2	¼" x 1½" x 9½"	Long spline

FIGURE A *EXPLODED VIEW*

SAUNA OVERALL DIMENSIONS:
62⅝" W x 50" D x 103" H

UPPER BENCH DIMENSIONS:
56" W x 15" D x 3½" H

LOWER BENCH DIMENSIONS:
56" W x 26" D x 3½" H

CHOOSE THE HEATER

You can heat your sauna with natural gas, propane, electricity or wood. Natural gas or propane heaters are efficient and work well for larger saunas. You'll need to plumb and vent the heater just the same as a gas furnace. Electric heaters are the most common and affordable. They're also convenient, providing heat with the flip of a switch. You can find them in different kilowatt sizes to fit any size sauna. Depending on the heater, you may need a 220-volt circuit. If no gas or electricity is available for your sauna, use a wood-burning heater. Vent it just the same as a wood stove. Infrared panels and infrared lightbulbs are other options if electricity is nearby.

BUILD A PANEL DOOR

You can build your door using the same method as the walls if you like. Your sauna door should always open out and never have a lock. We made our door using tempered glass cutting boards, which are inexpensive and come in many sizes. The other components of the door will vary in size depending on the glass you buy.

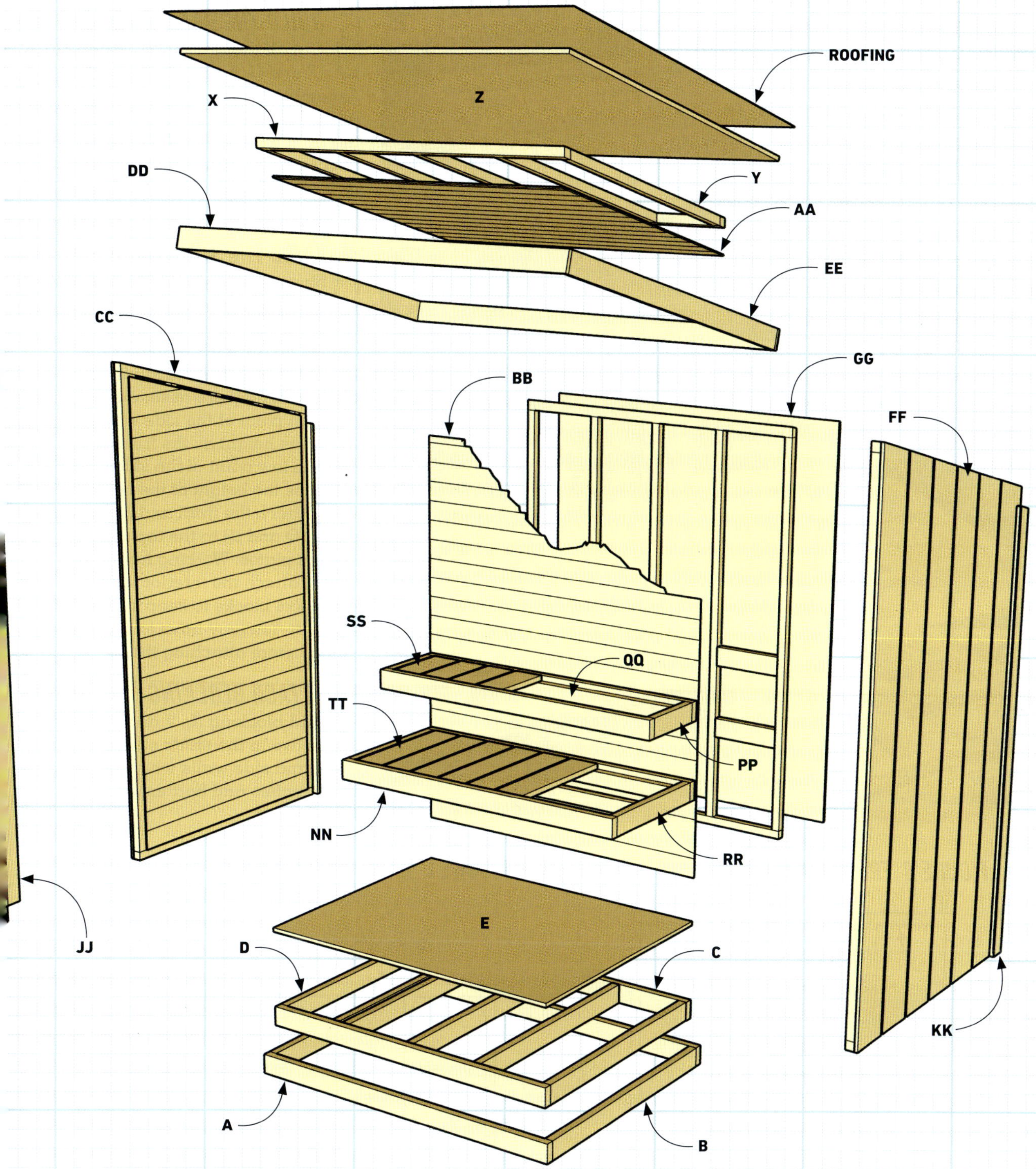

MATERIALS LIST

ITEM	QTY.
No. 11½ x 2" galvanized siding nails	
No. 13 x 2" galvanized finish nails	
No. 8 x 2" finish screws	
No. 8 x 2" exterior screws	
No. 9 x 3" deck screws	
1x4 x 8' cedar trim	14
¼" x 3½" cedar shiplap	123 sq. ft.
26" x 8' corrugated metal roof panels	3
2x4 x 8' cedar	7
3½" hinges	#
⅜" staples	#
4' x 8' x 1½" foam insulation	4
4' x 8' T1-11 plywood (wall sheathing)	5
4' x 8' x ¾" plywood	3
5⁄16" x 4" structural screws	
5⁄4" x 6" x 8' cedar deck boards	4
8' 2x2s	24
8' 2x4s	14
8' 2x4s, pressure treated	3
Drive-in ball catch for door	1
Foil vapor barrier	123 sq. ft.
Horizontal plastic closure strips	2
¼" x 1½" x 8' furring strips	18
Ice and water shield	40 sq. ft.
Rubber gasket roofing screws	
Aluminum foil tape	
Butyl sealant tape	
Door handle	1
Glass cutting boards	4
2x12 x 3'	1
2x6 x 8'	1
2x4 x 8'	2

5 BUILD THE BACK WALL

Cut all the back wall parts (F and G, L and M) to length. Assemble the back wall frame (Figure C) the same way you did the front wall, using the angled offcut from the front wall top plate for the back wall top plate and No. 9 x 3-in. deck screws.

6 BUILD THE SIDE WALLS

Since the side walls (Figure D) are identical, cut all the parts (N-W) for both. Cut 15-degree angles on the ends of all 2x2 and 2x4 studs and trim the studs so that when they are assembled, the high point of the side wall is the same height as the front wall and the low point of the side wall matches the height of the back wall. Attach the front and back studs (Q and U) to the top and bottom plates. Working from right to left, attach the interior studs using 2x4 blocks to keep spaces uniform. You may have to trim the studs before attaching them.

7 ATTACH BLOCKING

Add blocking (L, V and W) between the studs on the back and side walls where the benches and heater will be attached.

FIGURE B FRONT WALL FRAME

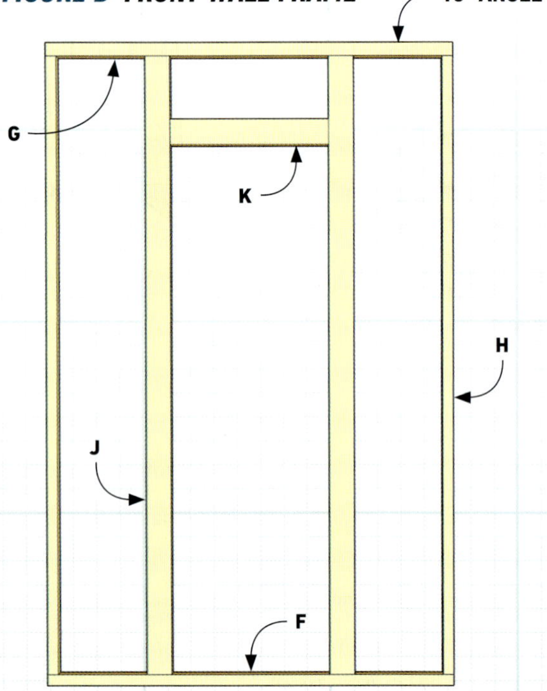

FIGURE C BACK WALL FRAME

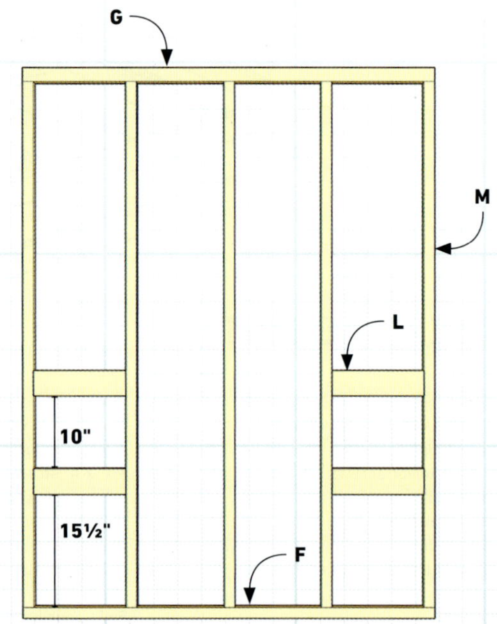

8 SKIN THE WALLS

Place a sheet of siding (FF-HH) on top of each wall frame, keeping it flush with the bottom of the frame. Hold it in place with some clamps or drive a few nails along the bottom edge. Once the wall frame is square with the long edge of the siding, finish nailing it to all the studs with No. 11½ x 2-in. galvanized siding nails.

For the front and back walls, you'll need to cut an extra strip to span the width. To install, cut the top edges flush with the frames. Let the front and back wall siding hang 2¼ in. over both edges.

9 TRIM THE SIDING

Cut the angle along the top edge of the side walls using a router with a flush-trim bit. Use the router and flush-trim bit to cut out the door opening on the front wall as well.

10 INSULATE THE WALLS

Measure the spaces between the studs. Using a table saw or a long-blade utility knife, cut pieces of 1½-in. foam insulation for each stud cavity. The foam insulation simply friction-fits into each space.

11 ADD A VAPOR BARRIER

Staple radiant foil vapor barrier to the interior of all four walls. Seal the edges and seams with foil tape.

FIGURE D SIDE WALL FRAMES

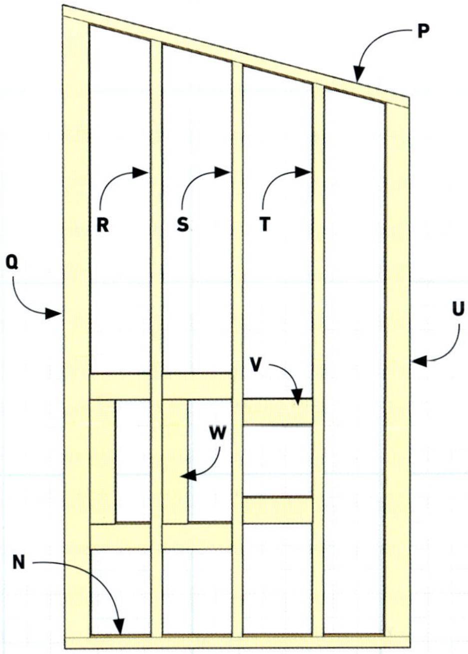

12 FINISH THE INTERIOR

Nail 1/4 x 1 1/2-in. wood vapor gap strips onto each stud, the full length of all four walls. This creates a gap between the interior siding and the vapor barrier, allowing moisture to evaporate. For the side walls, start the first row of shiplap siding (CC) 2 1/4 in. from the bottom and 1 1/2 in. from each edge, using 1 1/4-in. nails into each stud. When you reach the top of the wall, let the shiplap hang over the angle, then trim off the pieces using a router with a flush-trim bit. For the front and back wall shiplap (BB), start your first row 2 1/4 in. from the bottom but run it out to 1/2 in. from each edge.

13 ASSEMBLE WALLS

Set the back wall on the base. If you don't have a helper to hold it in place, attach a 2x4 from the edge of the wall to the base. Set one of the side walls on the base and clamp it to the back wall. Check to see if the tops of the walls line up, then join the two walls with 5/16 x 4-in. structural screws. Attach the other side wall to the back wall in the same manner. Set the front wall on the base and clamp all four walls together, checking to see if the tops of the walls line up. Then secure both side walls to the front wall with 5/16 x 4-in. structural screws.

14 CUT THE DOOR PARTS

Straight-line your boards with a track saw or on a jointer, then cut all pieces (UU-WW) to length.

15 CUT SPLINES AND GROOVES

Using a table saw with a dado blade or a router with a slot-cutting bit, cut a groove the thickness of your glass (and a minimum of 1/4 in. deep) on the edges of the boards as follows: one long edge on both stiles, three edges on the rails and all four edges of the mullions. Rip splines (XX and YY) the thickness of your glass and the width of two slots put together. Cut the spline pieces to length.

16 CHECK THE FIT

Set one stile on its edge with the groove facing up. Dry-fit all the pieces starting with the bottom rail, adding a piece of glass and one mullion at a time until you get to the top rail, then add the second stile.

17 ASSEMBLE THE DOOR

Add glue to each spline joint. Be sure to wipe away any glue that squeezes out. Clamp the door together. Use scrap pieces of wood between the clamp jaws and the door edge to prevent dents. When the glue is dry, sand the door up to 220-grit and apply spar varnish or exterior paint.

18 MAKE THE ROOF FRAME

To cut the roof frame front and back (X), rip a 2x4 in half at a 15-degree angle just like the top plates of the front and back walls. Clamp those two boards along the top of the front and back walls, each aligned with the 15-degree angle. Measure the distance between the two boards, then cut the five roof studs (Y) to that length. Attach the studs to the front and back roof frames with 3-in. screws.

Cut ¾-in. plywood for the roof deck (Z). Center the roof frame on the deck and attach it with No. 8 x 2-in. exterior screws. To finish the roof interior, insulate each stud cavity and attach a vapor barrier and vapor gap strips to the frame as you did for the walls. Apply the shiplap siding (AA), keeping it flush on all four edges of the frame.

16

17

18

19 TRIM THE ROOF EDGES

Install roof trim (DD and EE) along all four sides of the roof deck with No. 13 x 2-in. galvanized finish nails.

20 INSTALL THE ROOF

Starting at the bottom of the roof, staple ice and water shield to the roof deck, overlapping the seam 3 in. as you work your way up the roof.

Cut corrugated metal roof panels so they overhang the roof deck at least 2 in. on all four sides. Attach horizontal plastic closure strips at the top and bottom edges of the roof deck to seal the gaps between the corrugated roof panel and the ice and water shield.

Attach the roof panels with roofing screws. Overlap the panels at least 3 in., sealing the seams with butyl tape. With a helper, lift the roof assembly and set it into place. Secure it with 5⁄16 x 4-in. structural screws along the top rim of the walls.

21 PAINT THE EXTERIOR

Protect the siding with an exterior paint or deck stain.

22 APPLY TRIM

Attach 1x4 cedar trim (JJ and KK) to the four exterior corners. Use No. 8 x 2-in. finish screws to attach the trim so it can be removed later if you disassemble the sauna for transport. Add trim around the exterior of the door (LL and MM) if desired.

23 BUILD BENCHES

In a sauna, you typically have two benches: an upper bench about 30 in. from the floor, and a cool-down bench no more than 18 in. from the floor. These benches are simply 2x4 cedar frames (NN, PP and RR) with 1x6 cedar (SS and TT) attached to nailing cleats (QQ) set inside the frames.

If your sauna is a different width than ours, measure it and adjust the front and back frame boards as necessary. Cut all the parts to length, assemble the frames and attach the nailing cleats. Attach the deck boards with No. 8 x 2-in. finish screws, with a ½-in. gap between boards.

24 INSTALL THE BENCHES

Attach the benches to the back and side walls using 5⁄16 x 4 in. structural screws through the cedar shiplap into the bracing inside the walls.

25 INSTALL A GUARDRAIL

No matter what heater you choose, always build a guardrail around it to protect you and your sauna guests from burns.

FOLD-UP HAMMOCK STAND

CREATE IT IN AN AFTERNOON, HANG OUT IN IT FOREVER

BY JOE CRUZ

If that perfect lounging spot in your yard doesn't have trees to hold your hammock, this stand is the ticket. It's foldable, portable and easily storable, and it will take only a few hours to build.

FIGURE A
FOLD-UP FRAME

OVERALL DIMENSIONS: 84" W x 49¾" D x 7" H

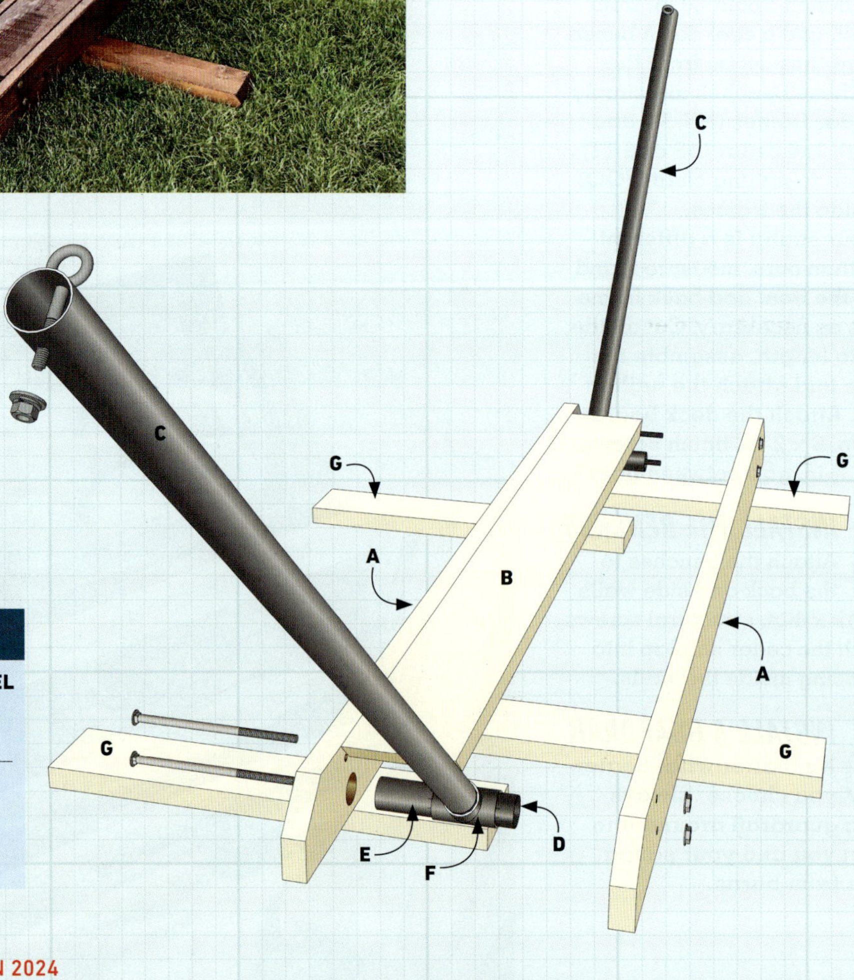

WHAT IT TAKES

TIME	COST	SKILL LEVEL
Half day	$150 to $200	Beginner

TOOLS
Circular saw, hacksaw, drill/driver, Forstner bit, basic hand tools

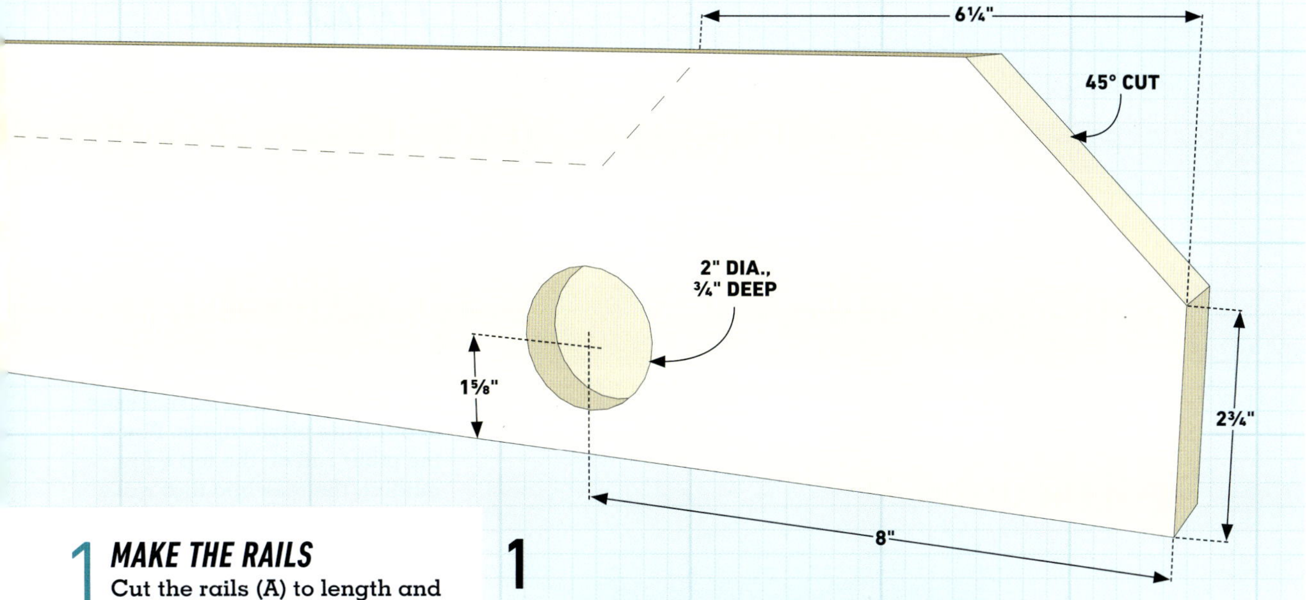

1

1 *MAKE THE RAILS*

Cut the rails (A) to length and cut each of the top corners at 45 degrees. Use a 2-in. diameter Forstner bit to drill ¾-in. deep recesses on the inside face, and then mark the position of the top (B) on the ends of each rail.

2 *CUT THE TOP*

Using a miter saw or circular saw with a Speed square as a guide, cut the top (B) to length with a 45-degree bevel at each end.

NOT SHOWN: Cut two 5-ft. arms (C) from the 10-ft. pipe. Then cut two 6-in. nipples to 4¼ in. (E). Don't discard 1¾-in. cutoffs (D). Always clamp pipes to a sturdy surface for cutting.

3 *ASSEMBLE THE TEES*

Screw the 4¼-in. and 1¾-in. pieces into the two ends of each galvanized tee (F). The assembled length of the tee should be no more than 8¾ in.

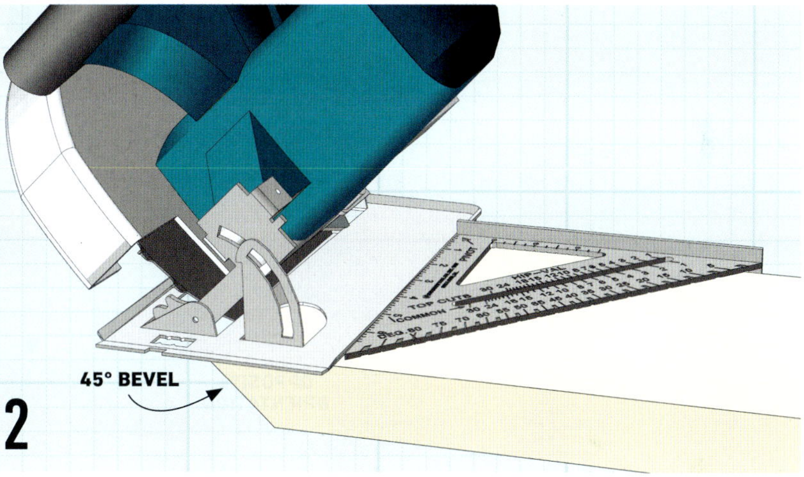

2

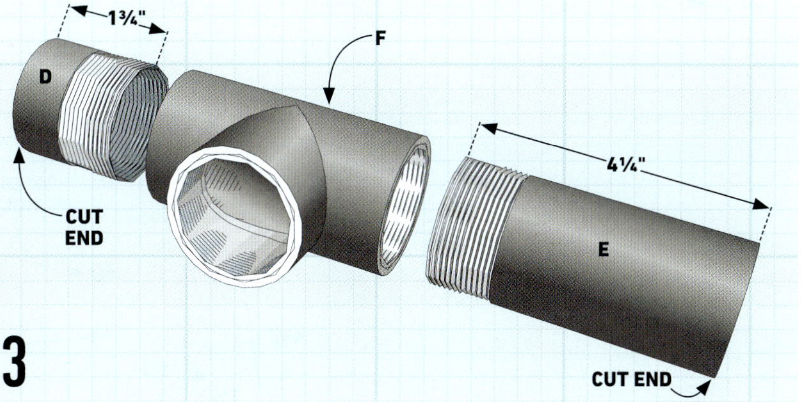

3

MATERIALS LIST

ITEM	QTY.
2x6 x 96"	5
1½" x 10' threaded pipe	1
2" x 2" x 2" tee	2
2" x 6" threaded pipe nipples	2
⅜" x 2½" eye bolts	2
½" x 12" carriage bolts	4
½" locknuts	4
½" washers	4
⅜" washers	2
⅜" lock washers	2
⅜" hex nuts	2
1½" plastic end caps	2
No. 10 x 3½" deck screws	
¼" x 3½" exterior lag screws	
Hammock	

CUTTING LIST

KEY	QTY.	DIMENSIONS	PART
A	2	1½" x 5½" x 84"	Rails
B	1	1½" x 5½" x 71½"	Top
C	2	2" x 60"	Arms (galvanized pipe)
D	2	2" x 1¾"	Short pivot pipe
E	2	2" x 4¼"	Long pivot pipe
F	2	2" x 2" x 2"	Galvanized pipe tee
G	4	1½" x 5½" x 30"	Feet

4 ATTACH THE RAIL

Attach one rail to the edge of the top, lining it up with the layout marks made in Step 1. Fasten the rail and top together using 3½-in. screws every 12 in., making sure the pipe recesses face inward.

5 COMPLETE THE RAIL/TOP ASSEMBLY

Lay the top and rail assembly on its side, then set the tee assemblies in the 2-in. recesses in opposite orientations. Place the other rail on the top edge, guiding the tees into that rail's recesses. Then attach the rail with 3½-in. screws.

6 DRILL CARRIAGE BOLT HOLES

Use a ½-in. spade or brad point bit to drill two bolt holes on the ends of each rail. The bolts hold the rails together and act as stops for the arms when they are open.

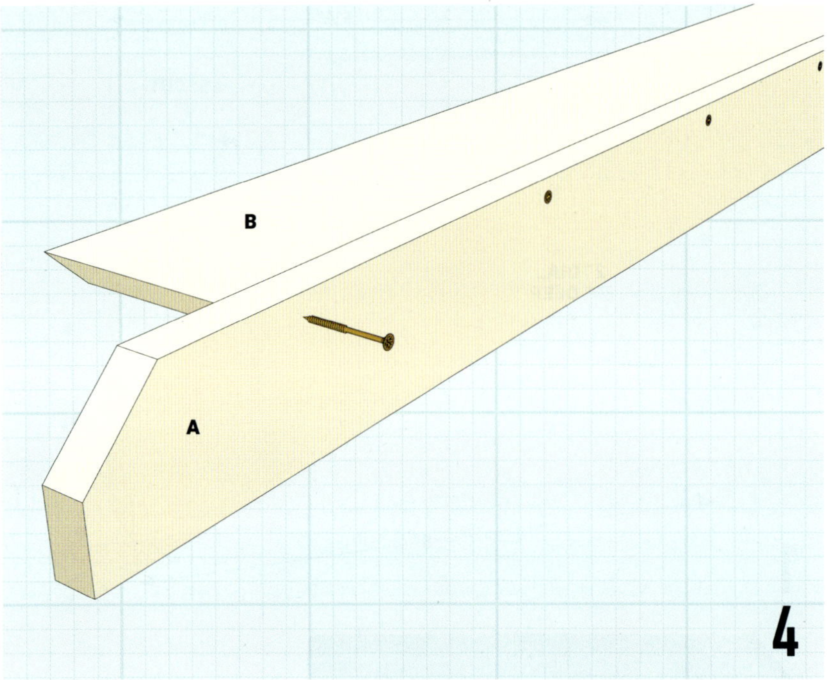

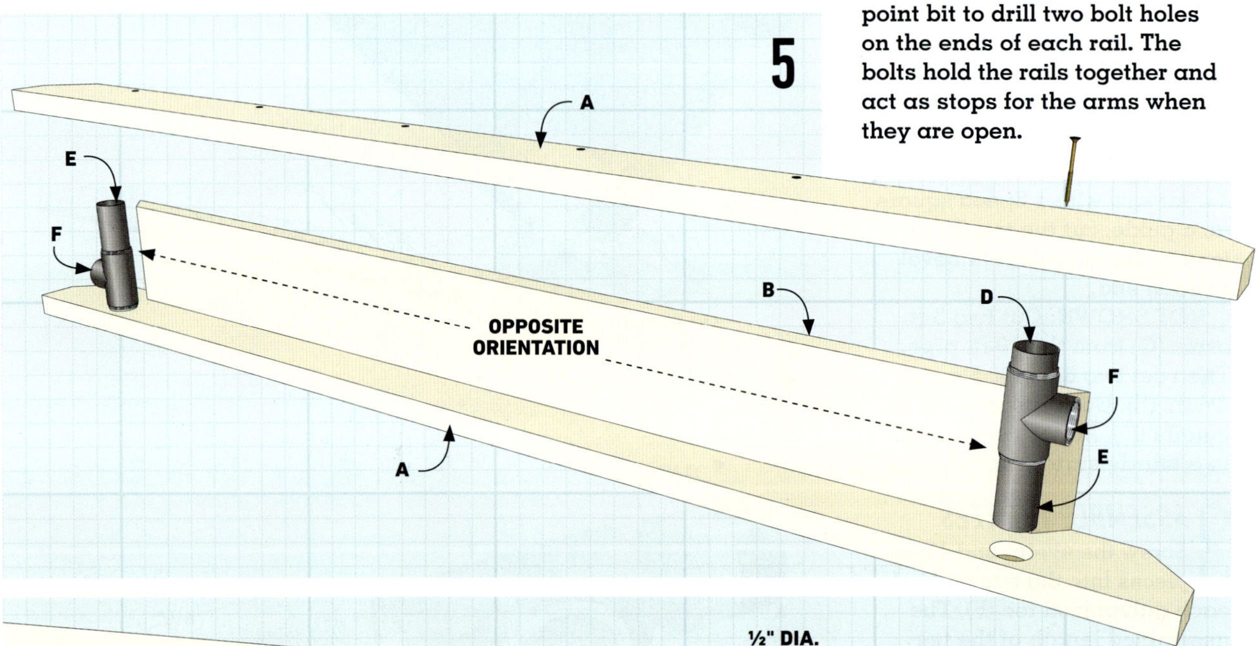

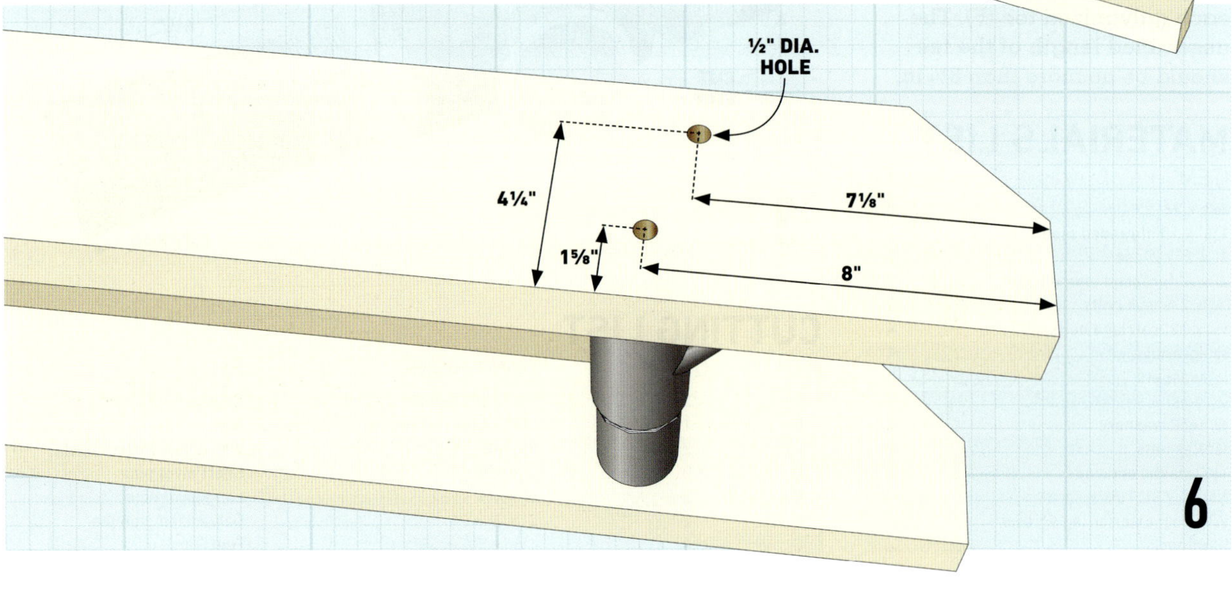

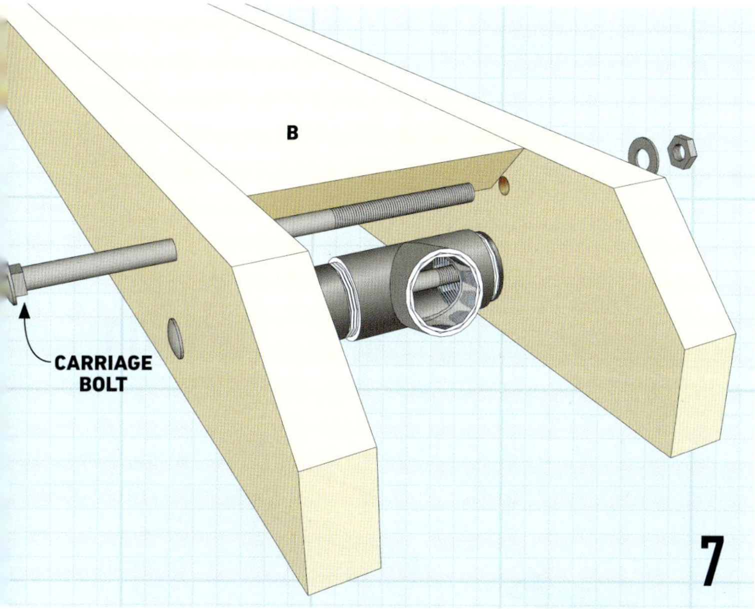

7

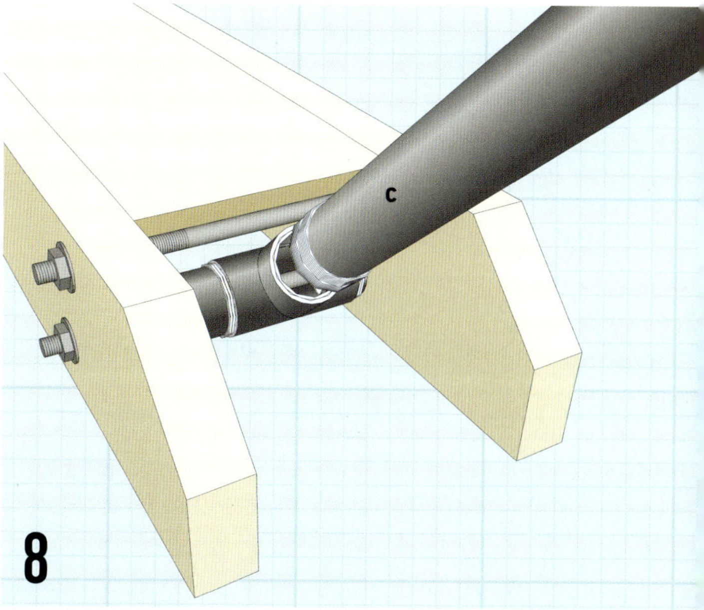

8

7 INSTALL CARRIAGE BOLTS

Insert ½ x 12-in. carriage bolts in the holes in the rails. Add a flat washer to the threaded end of each bolt and tighten the nuts.

8 INSTALL PIPE ARMS

Rotate the tees and thread the pipe arms (C) tight with a pipe wrench.

9 INSTALL EYE BOLTS

Drill a ⅜-in. hole 1 in. from the end of each pipe. Insert an eye bolt and secure it with a lock washer and nut. Then cap each end with a plastic cap.

10 LAYOUT HOLES IN THE RAILS

Make layout marks on the bottom of each rail as shown. Drill 3/16-in. pilot holes 2 in. deep at the marks.

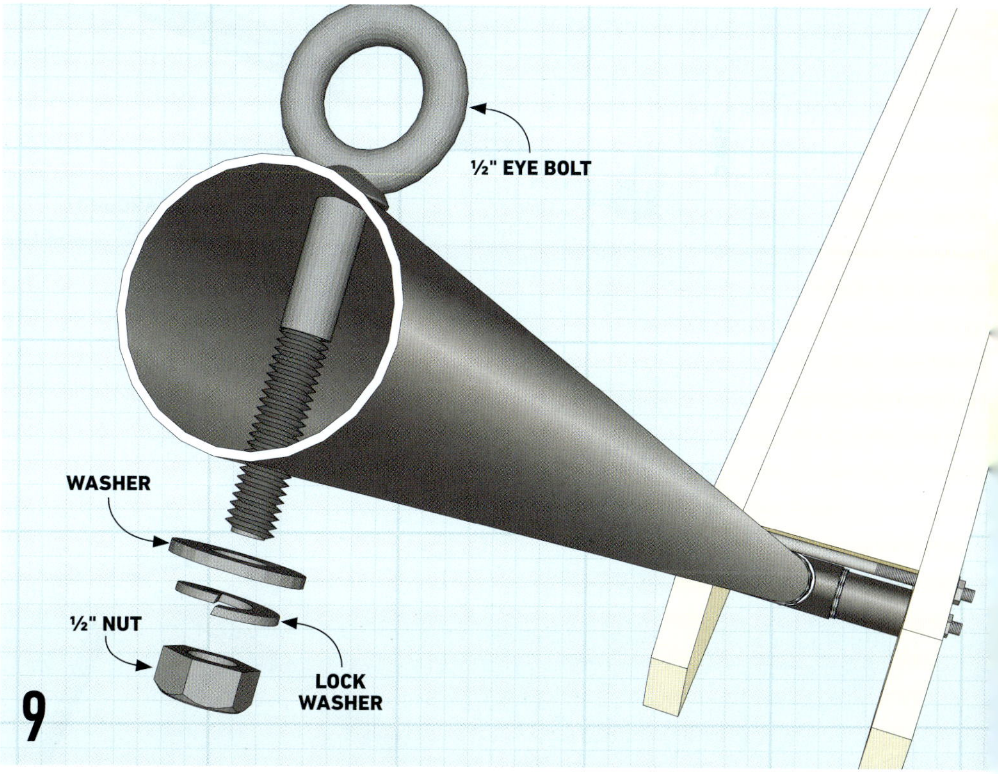

9

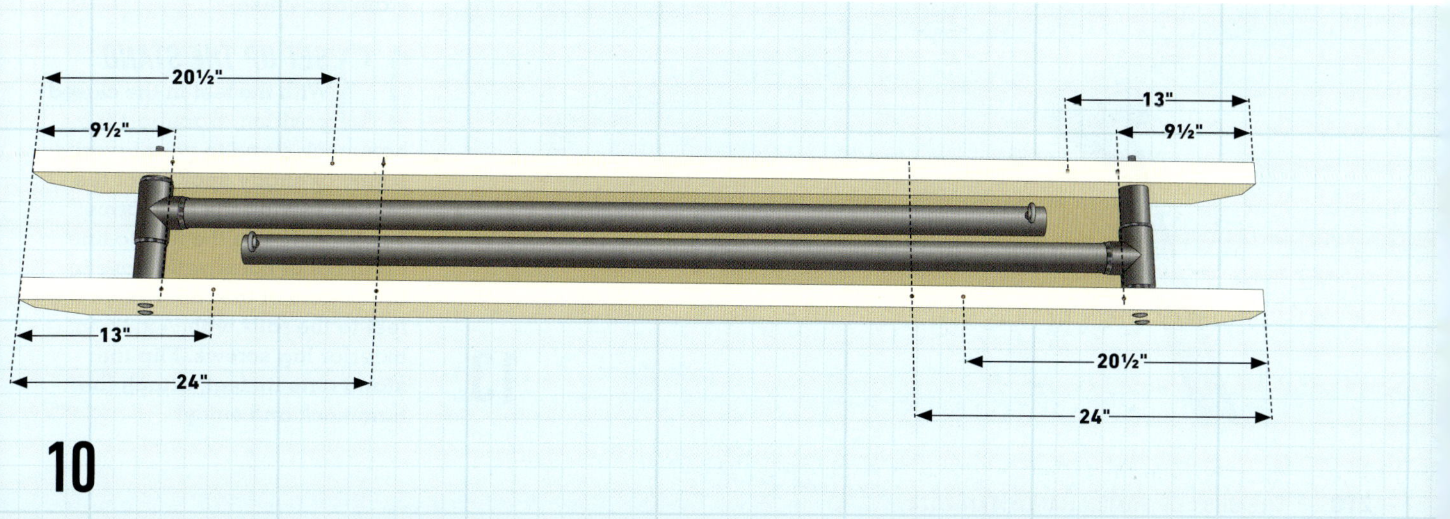

10

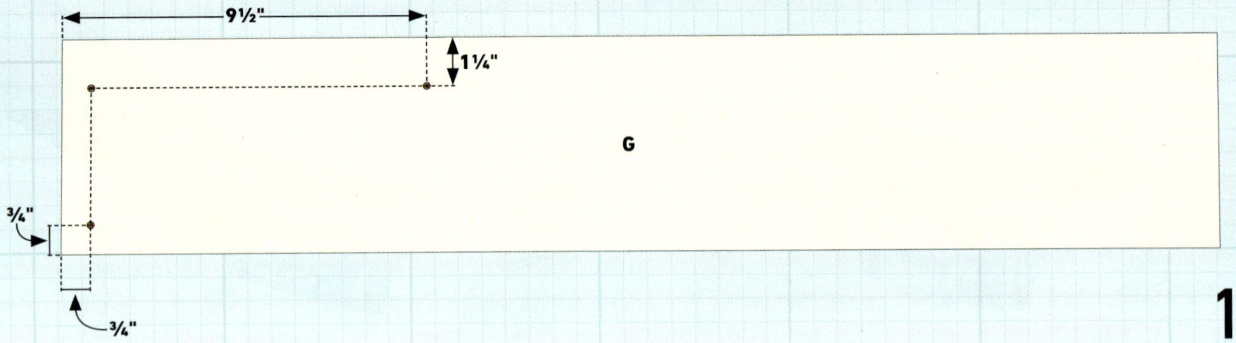

11

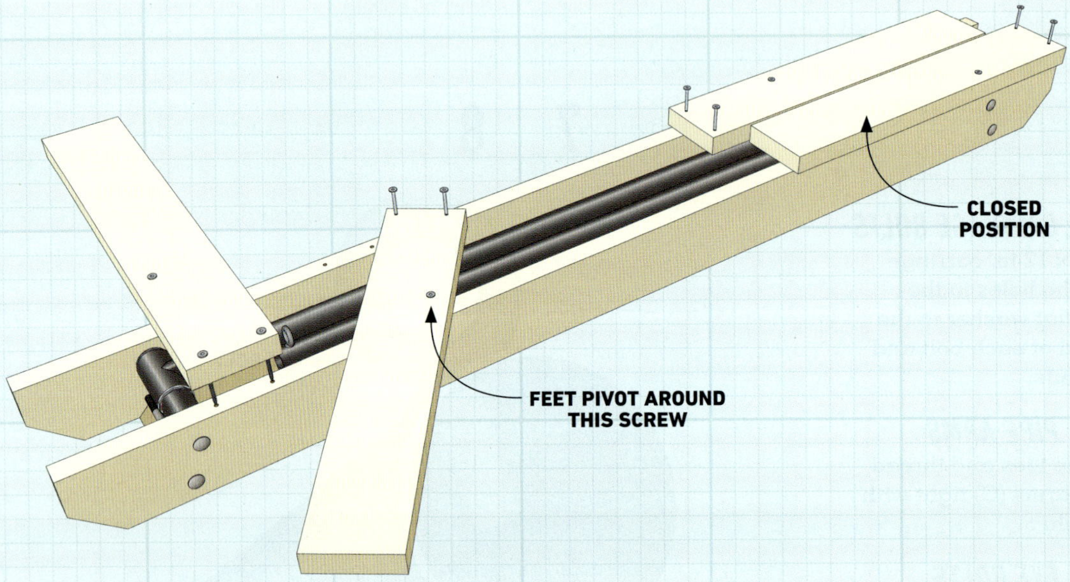

12

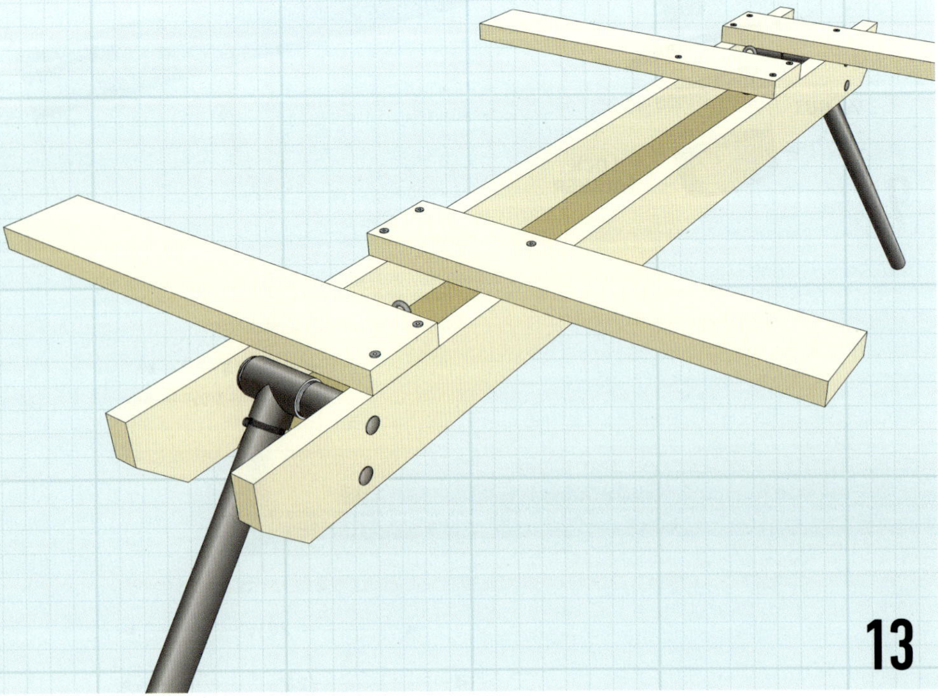

13

11 PREDRILL THE FEET

Cut the feet (G) to length and drill ¼-in. diameter holes in the feet as shown.

12 INSTALL THE FEET

Attach all four feet to bottom rails as shown. Use ¼ x 3½-in. lag screws through the pilot holes in the feet. At this point, apply your stain and finish.

13 SET UP THE STAND

With the feet in the closed position, transport the hammock stand to your favorite sunny or shady spot. Pivot the feet and swing the pipe arms out. Then rotate the feet to line up the pilot holes with those in the bottom of the rail. Fasten the feet to the rails with ¼ x 3½-in. exterior lag screws. Flip the stand onto its feet, attach the hammock and enjoy!

MODERN WATER FOUNTAIN

FIND A SPLASH OF PEACE FOR YOUR PATIO

BY MIKE BERNER

When you think of deep relaxation, does the sound of water immediately come to mind? Maybe crashing ocean waves, the trickle of a nearby brook, a cascading waterfall or light rain?

To bring this calming sound to your backyard, we've designed a sleek water feature using a simple box for a reservoir, a pump and basic plumbing parts to keep the water flowing. It can be disassembled easily and tucked away for winter or moved around your patio. We dressed up our fountain by using Ipe hardwood and wrapping the reservoir with a sheet of copper. You can use the ideas we share here to build a modified version to fit your favorite relaxation spot.

WHAT IT TAKES

TIME	COST	SKILL LEVEL
2 days	$400	Intermediate

TOOLS
Table saw, circular saw, miter saw, jigsaw, 18-gauge nail gun, basic woodworking tools

MEET THE BUILDER

MIKE BERNER
ENJOYS CREATING PROJECTS FOR EVERY LEVEL OF DIYER.

1 FRAME THE RESERVOIR

Cut the reservoir frame sides (A) and ends (B) from 2x2 lumber and fasten the bottom piece of marine plywood (C) to form the base of the reservoir.

Align the reservoir sides (D) with the ends of the base and fasten them to the 2x2s. Fasten the reservoir ends (E) to the 2x2s at the bottom with construction screws. Drive trim screws into the edges of the plywood toward the top.

2 PLACE THE LINER

Two options for lining the reservoir are available. Flat pond liners found at home centers are an inexpensive option, but require a bit of origami to fit properly.

We ordered a custom heavy-duty box welded liner from *everything-ponds.com* that fit the reservoir perfectly. At about $200, it was more expensive, but it was well made, strong and easier to install.

3 FASTEN THE LINER

Rip the termination bar (F) down to ¼ in., then cut it to fit inside the reservoir. Drill countersunk pilot holes every several inches, then clamp the termination bar and liner to the top of the reservoir and fasten them with 1-in. screws. This prevents the liner from sliding down.

IPE DECKING

We constructed the water curtain arm from Ipe decking. It's a rot-resistant species that will do well outside for years with little maintenance.

4 LAYER THE WATER CURTAIN ARM

At the table saw, rip off the rounded edges of the Ipe decking, leaving the boards about 5 in. wide. Then cut the horizontal (G) and vertical (H) outer arm parts to length with 15-degree angles on the ends. We cut each pair at the same time to ensure they were the same length and angle. Rip another piece of decking in half for the spine of the arm, and cut two pieces for each of the horizontal (J) and vertical (K) spine parts with the same 15-degree angles. Lay the parts on a flat surface; glue the pieces together, overlapping the spine.

5 FASTEN PLUMBING CLIPS

Before gluing and nailing the final layer of the arm assembly, fasten plumbing clips to hold the CPVC and vinyl tubing along the inside of the spine. Then fasten the final pieces of Ipe to complete the arm.

FIGURE A
WATER FOUNTAIN

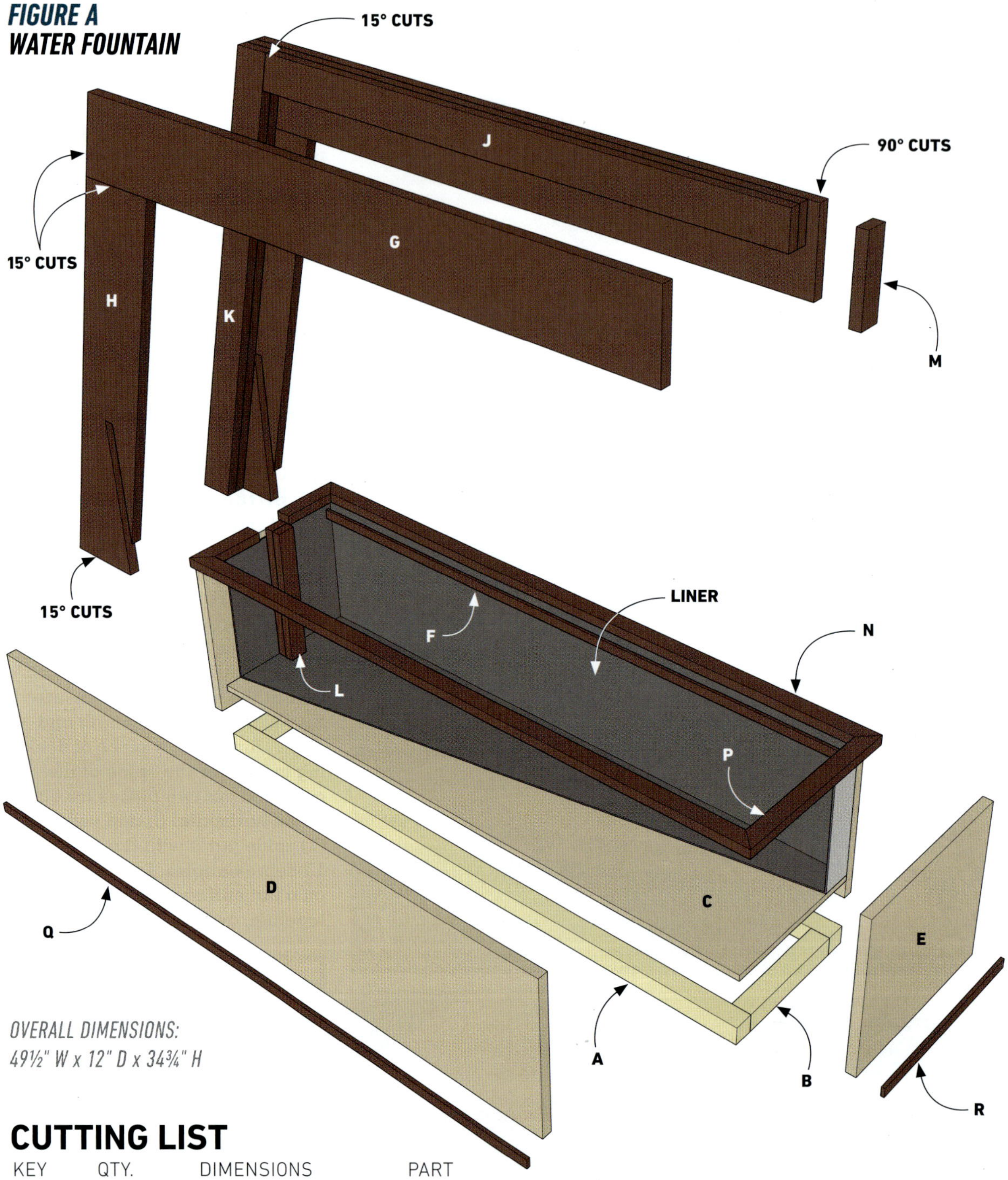

OVERALL DIMENSIONS:
49½" W x 12" D x 34¾" H

CUTTING LIST

KEY	QTY.	DIMENSIONS	PART
A	2	2x2 x 48"	Reservoir frame side
B	2	2x2 x 9"	Reservoir frame end
C	1	¾" x 12" x 48"	Reservoir bottom
D	2	¾" x 12½" x 48"	Reservoir side
E	2	¾" x 12½" x 13½"	Reservoir end
F	2	¼" x ¾" x 47½"	Termination bar
G	2	¾" x 5" x 44⁹⁄₁₆"	Horizontal outer arm
H	2	¾" x 5" x 30⁵⁄₁₆"	Vertical outer arm
J	2	¾" x 2½" x 40⁷⁄₁₆"	Horizontal spine
K	2	¾" x 2½" x 3'	Vertical spine
L	2	¾" x 2½" x 9"	Arm support block
M	1	¾" x 1½" x 5"	Fountain arm cap
N	2	¾" x 2" x 50"	Top side trim
P	2	¾" x 2" x 14³⁄₁₆"	Top end trim
Q	2	¾" x ¼" x 49½"	Lower side trim
R	2	¾" x ¼" x 14"	Lower end trim

MATERIALS LIST

ITEM	QTY.
2x2 x 8'	3
¾" x 4' x 8' marine-grade plywood	1
2" construction screws	1 lb.
Pond liner	
12" copper coil	12'
¾" x 5½" x 8' Ipe (or other rot-resistant or treated hardwood)	4
¾" CPVC pipe	4'
1" vinyl tubing	4'
Fountain pump	
Plumbing fittings	

6 NOTCH THE ARM

Using a Speed square indexed against the bottom of the arm, lay out a 12-in.-tall by ⅞-in.-wide vertical notch to fit over the end of the reservoir. Transfer the mark to both sides of the arm, and cut the notch using a circular saw and jigsaw.

7 WRAP THE RESERVOIR

We decided to wrap the plywood with copper rather than stain or paint it. To apply the copper, roll contact cement on the outside of the reservoir and onto the copper coil. Then carefully place the reservoir onto the copper. Apply one side at a time, folding the copper around the corners with a wood block. We planned for the seam of the copper to be hidden later by the water curtain arm. Once the copper is applied, press it firmly in place with a J-roller.

8 ATTACH THE ARM

Glue two Ipe offcuts together to make the arm support block (L). Position this block on the inside of the reservoir to keep the arm in place. Fasten the block using screws from the outside, and seal it with silicone (8A). Slide the arm over the reservoir edge and fit the plumbing channel over the block (8B).

6

7

8A

8B

9 MARK A LINE

The CPVC pipe that makes the water curtain needs many holes drilled in a straight line. To get them all to line up, scribe a line across the pipe by clamping it down and dragging a marker flat along your work surface.

10 DRILL THE HOLES

Mark the hole locations along the line 1 in. apart. Fasten a pair of plumbing clips to a board to hold the pipe in place while you drill the holes, then clamp the board to the table to keep it in position. Slide the pipe through the clips and drill all the holes.

11 CONNECT THE FITTINGS

We spent a while in the plumbing department at our local home center piecing together the fittings needed to plumb the water curtain to the pump. We ended up using a ¾-in. PVC end cap, a ¾-in. push-to-connect x FIP brass adapter and a ¾-in. MIP x barb brass adapter. After fitting these parts together, we pushed a length of 1-in.-dia. vinyl tube over the barb fitting and used a hose clamp to hold it in place.

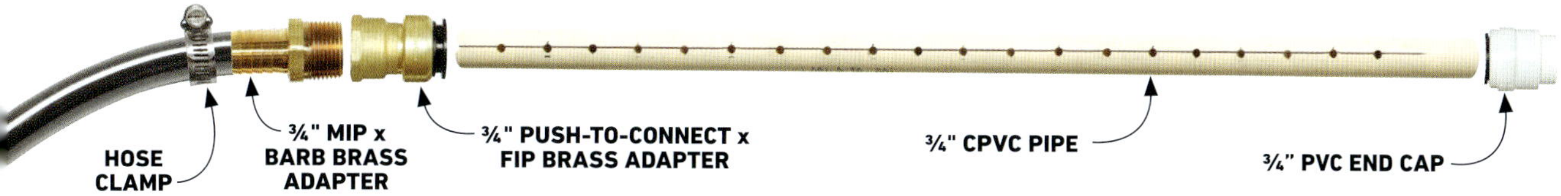

12 CONNECT THE PUMP

Snap the water curtain pipe into the plumbing clips, then cut the vinyl tubing long enough to connect to the pump. Slip the tubing onto a barb fitting on the pump and tighten the nut that connects the tubing to the pump. With the plumbing in place, we used an offcut of Ipe to make the fountain arm cap (M).

13 ADD TRIM TO THE BOTTOM AND TOP

Measure and cut miters on 2-in.-wide pieces of Ipe to make the top side (N) and end (P) trim pieces, and fasten them with a bead of silicone and brad nails. Rip ¼-in. Ipe strips for the lower side (Q) and end (R) trim, and fasten them around the bottom of the reservoir to cover the edges of the copper coil.

PEBBLE MOSAIC STEPPINGSTONES

COLLECT SOME RIVER ROCK AND MAKE YOUR OWN UNIQUE STEPPINGSTONE PATH

BY JEFF GORTON

Alice Medley loves to create works of art from the pebbles she collects. She was generous enough to invite us into her garage workshop to show us how to make these beautiful pebble mosaic steppingstones. She uses a "dry-set" technique that makes it easy to change or adjust the pattern as you go without having to dig stones out of wet mortar.

Medley also shared the plans for an ingenious reusable wooden mold that she purchased from a North Woods carpenter. The initial investment for this project—about $80—covers the plywood, a bag of mortar, the pigment and the muriatic acid. That's enough to make about seven or eight steppingstones. After that each one will cost you less than a dollar.

BUILD THE MOLD

A small sheet of ¾-in. plywood and some 1¼-in. screws are all you'll need to build the mold. Cut out the pieces according to the Cutting List. Figure A shows how the parts go together. When you're done, brush linseed or vegetable oil on the mold to protect it from moisture.

COLLECT THE STONES

Medley collects her stones in northern Minnesota. You'll find similar stones in most parts of the country. Look for them in river and creek beds, or along lakeshores. Wherever you find them, make sure you have permission and that it is legal to collect them. Another possible source is your local landscape supplier or wherever landscaping stones are sold.

Medley likes to sort them by color. She's got buckets and cans full of red, gray, white, brown and speckled stones. Keeping them sorted makes it a lot easier for her to find the right ones as she creates a pattern.

MEET THE EXPERT

ALICE MEDLEY STARTED OUT USING MORE TRADITIONAL MOSAIC MATERIALS LIKE GLASS AND TILE FOR HER OUTDOOR ART PROJECTS. THEN SHE DISCOVERED SHE COULD MARRY HER LOVE OF STONES WITH HER LOVE OF MOSAICS.

MATERIALS LIST

ITEM	QTY.
Collection of small stones	
Bag of Type S mortar mix	1
2' x 2' square piece of 6-mil poly	1
48" x 48" x ¾" plywood	1
1¼" corrosion-resistant screws	40

Optional items: Mortar pigment or colored grout, muriatic acid and stone sealer

CUTTING LIST

KEY	QTY.	DIMENSIONS	PART
A	1	18" x 18" x ¾"	Subbase
B	1	12" x 12" x ¾"	Base
C	12	2¼" x 15¾" x ¾"	Frame
D	4	3¼" x 12¾" x ¾"	Sides

FIGURE A STEPPINGSTONE MOLD

FORMS 12" SQUARE STEPPINGSTONES

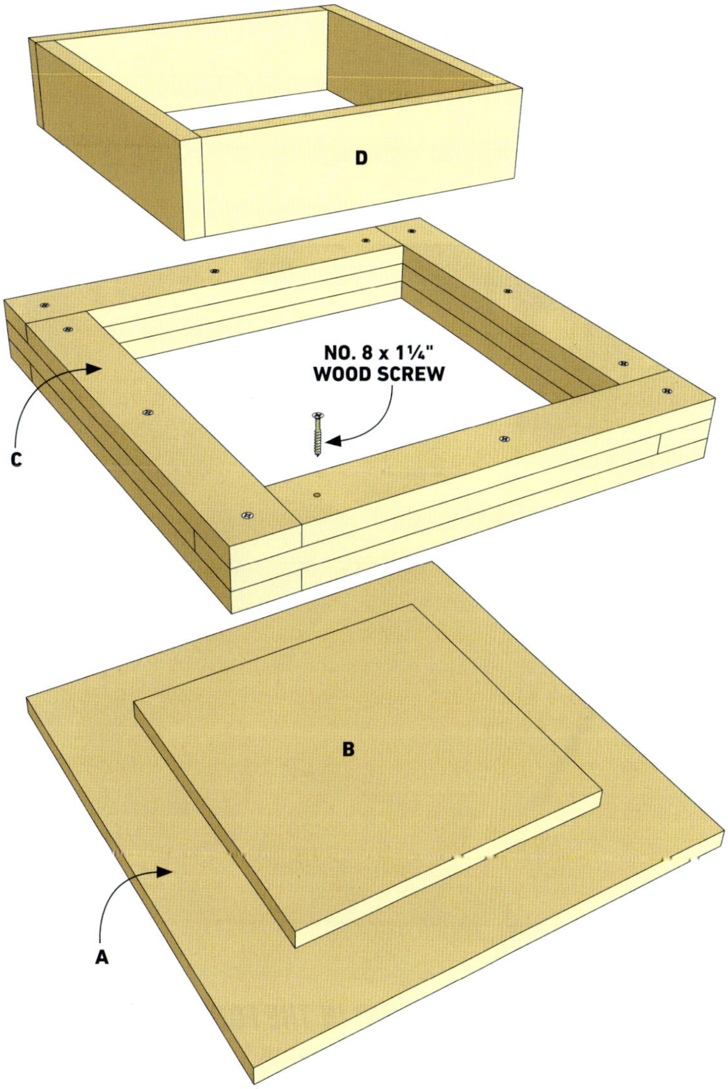

ASSEMBLE THE STEPPINGSTONE

Photos 1-4 show the assembly steps. Medley likes to add a little brown pigment to the dry Type S mortar mix to give the steppingstones a mellower look. You'll find cement pigments and Type S mortar at home centers and masonry suppliers. Or, you can cheat as Medley does and just mix in a little colored ceramic tile grout. Make sure to wear rubber gloves to protect your skin from the mortar, which can cause skin burns.

You don't have to plan your pattern ahead of time. Medley says she has a design in mind and just starts arranging the stones. It's easier to start along the edges or in a corner and work toward the center, though. You'll have less fitting to do as you fill in the last few stones. Keep the stones close together and oriented with the long axis up and down.

While it's tempting, Medley cautions against laying a stone flat. She says it doesn't look as good as you think it will and is more likely to pop out later. When you're done tamping the stones into the dry mortar, inspect the spaces between the stones to see if there are spots that require more mortar. The stones should be buried at least halfway. Fill sparse areas with more mortar. Dust any dry mortar off the stones with a small brush.

The trickiest part of the process is wetting the mortar (Photo 5). We can't tell you exactly how much water to add, but it is better to sprinkle on several small doses

1 ASSEMBLE THE MOLD
This plywood mold goes together quickly and comes apart easily after the mortar hardens. You can use it again and again.

2 SPREAD DRY MORTAR IN THE FORM
Fill plastic-lined form to about ¾ in. from the top edge with dry Type S mortar. Level it with your gloved hand. It doesn't have to be perfectly flat.

3 ARRANGE THE STONES IN A PATTERN
The only rule is to keep the stones close together, so they touch and stand up and are not laid flat.

4 TAMP THE STONES TO LEVEL THE TOPS

Lay a board across the stones and pound on it with a rubber mallet to embed the stones in the dry mortar and set the tops level with each other.

5 SPRINKLE THE STONE

Adjust your spray wand or sprayer to the finest spray setting and sprinkle water over the completed steppingstone to wet the mortar.

6 TAP ON THE FORM

Tap on the form with the mallet to remove air and help the water penetrate. Continue sprinkling and tapping until it seems as though no more water will be absorbed by the mortar.

7 PULL OFF THE MOLD

Allow the steppingstone to harden and cure for at least two days. Then carefully flip it over and remove the mold. Clean it with water and then acid if needed.

than to get impatient and risk adding too much. Medley says the key is to alternate between wetting the top and tapping on the mold with the rubber mallet until it seems as if the water is no longer being absorbed and bubbles quit appearing (Photo 6). Expect to spend about 45 minutes sprinkling and tapping the mold.

When the mortar is thoroughly dampened, set the completed steppingstone in a shady spot and cover it with a damp cloth and plastic. Wait at least 48 hours before removing the mold.

After you remove the mold from the steppingstone (Photo 7), brush the stone off to remove any loose mortar and rinse it with clear water. If the embedded stones have a film of mortar on them after drying, clean them off with muriatic acid diluted according to the instructions on the container. Remember, always add acid to water, not the other way around, and wear rubber gloves and safety glasses.

To enhance the color of the stones, coat them with stone sealer, which is available at home centers and online, or at masonry, landscape and tile suppliers.

FIRST AID FOR YOUR LAWN: WHAT TO DO ABOUT THATCH

If your grass feels soft and spongy when you walk on it, your lawn may have a thatch buildup. Thatch is a fibrous mat of dead stalks and roots that settles between the lawn's green leaves and the soil. When this mat becomes greater than ¾ in. thick, it can cause your lawn to suffer from heat and drought. Affected lawns will rapidly wilt and turn blue-green, indicating they're hot and dry.

Thatch is typically caused by cutting off too much at each mowing (letting the grass get too long) and cutting the lawn too low. Both will produce more dead grass tissue than microbes and earthworms can recycle. Thatch can develop in any soil but is most often associated with high clay content. Other causes are overfertilization and frequent, light watering—both encourage a shallow root system.

So what's the fix? Slice open a section of your lawn (Photo 1). If your grass shows ¾ in. or more of thatch, it's time to rent an aerator (about $110 per day). An aerator is a heavy machine that opens the soil by pulling up finger-sized soil cores. The lawn will absorb more oxygen and water, which will then encourage healthy microbe growth and give worms wiggle room.

Cool-season grasses should be aerated in late summer or early fall. Spring is best for warm-season types. (If you're not sure what type you have, take a sample to an expert at a local garden center.)

Aerate when the grass is growing but the weather is not so hot that it stresses the plants (Photo 2). If the machine isn't pulling plugs, your lawn may be too dry. To avoid this, water thoroughly the day before you aerate. You can also rake in some topsoil (Photo 3) to increase the healthy microorganisms that aid thatch's natural decomposition. Topsoil is available at any garden center.

As for the recovery time, you can expect the thatch layer to decrease by about ¼ in. per year, about the same rate at which it forms.

RENTING A LAWN AERATOR

Gas-powered aerators are available at most tool rental stores. They're slow-moving but powerful machines, so ask the clerk for handling directions. An aerator weighs about 200 lbs., so be prepared for heavy lifting or ask for a ramp to get it into a truck bed or van.

A rented power rake isn't a good substitute for an aerator. Power raking typically removes less than 15% of thatch and may damage the healthy grass as well.

AN OUNCE OF PREVENTION:

1. Mow often and cut no more than a third of the grass height.
2. Water your lawn less often but for longer periods to prevent shallow root systems.
3. Reduce the amount of fertilizer you spread at any one time.
4. Reduce the use of pesticides to help keep the worm and micro-organism populations healthy.
5. Aerate at least once every year if your lawn is prone to thatch.

Before you aerate, go to *call811.com* (or call 811) to arrange to have your underground utility lines marked.

1 Slice the turf grass with a shovel and pry it back. If the thatch depth measures more than ¾ in., aerate at least 3 in. deep.

2 Make two or three passes with an aerator until you've made 3-in.-deep holes 2 in. apart throughout your yard.

3 Spread ¼ in. of topsoil on the yard's most thatchy areas and then rake vigorously to fill the holes with loose soil.

LUCIE B. AMUNDSEN *CONTRIBUTING WRITER*

EARTH-FRIENDLY WEED KILLERS

CHOOSE HEALTHIER PRODUCTS FOR HUMANS AND THE ENVIRONMENT

BY ETHAN O'DONNELL

Unless you have been living under a rock, you are bound to have come across one of the many reports outlining both the toxic chemicals that are used in herbicides and their long-term effects on human beings and the environment. As a result, environmentally friendly products with active ingredients such as vinegar, salt, soap and essential oils have gained popularity.

As more earth-friendly weed killers hit the market every growing season, we chatted with an expert about what these products are and how they work.

MEET THE EXPERT

HEATHER JOHNSON IS THE LEAD HORTICULTURALIST AT BACHMAN'S FLORAL & GARDEN.

CHOOSING THE RIGHT HERBICIDE

CRABGRASS

CREEPING CHARLIE OR GROUND IVY

DANDELION

Whatever the time of year or conditions, you can use environmentally friendly ways to get rid of unwanted weeds or grass—from preemergent to post-emergent, as well as selective and nonselective varieties.

Here are several important notes about products with environmentally friendly active ingredients. First, "A lot of the organic options are burn-down herbicides," Johnson explains, "meaning the roots will remain intact and be able to regrow new shoots later."

Second, Johnson stresses, "Salt and vinegar can remain in the soil after killing the intended weeds, which can affect the growth of wanted plants in the area later."

To choose what's best for your lawn or garden, Johnson advises to start by answering these three questions:

WHAT TYPE OF WEEDS ARE YOU TRYING TO REMOVE?

Common weeds Johnson sees most homeowners struggling to control are dandelions, creeping Charlie and crabgrass. Both dandelions and creeping Charlie are broadleaf weeds. "If your lawn is overrun with these, it's more likely that the health of the lawn is being impacted, and lawn care besides just weed removal needs to be done," Johnson says.

The crabgrass problem is so widespread that companies have developed entire lines of herbicides to eliminate it. These toxic herbicides can be very effective when used correctly. However, Johnson says, "Same as with other weeds, if your lawn is overrun with crabgrass, then there are other health issues that need to be addressed."

HOW MANY WEEDS ARE YOU TARGETING?

In cases where weeds do not appear in large clusters or overtake the lawn, Johnson prefers hand-weeding. "It allows me to dig up the entire weed without the potential of damaging the lawn," she explains.

On the other hand, if the whole lawn is overrun with weeds, she suggests "reseeding along with testing the soil to understand the health of the grass and what nutrients may be needed to amend it."

WHEN ARE YOU APPLYING THE WEED KILLER?

"Some weeds are best handled preemergence, and some are best handled post-emergence," says Johnson. "Crabgrass can be handled pre- or post-emergence, with the most effective time being preemergence, in April or May, to avoid harming the lawn." Broadleaf weeds are best handled post-emergence, but "before they flower and spread."

EARTH-FRIENDLY PRODUCTS WORTH CHECKING OUT

ESPOMA ORGANIC WEED PREVENTER PLUS LAWN FOOD

Espoma Organic Weed Preventer Plus Lawn Food is the best environmentally friendly weed care product for established lawns. This product is made of pure corn gluten meal, making it a safe product for children and pets to play on even immediately after application. In addition to inhibiting weed growth, the product also feeds the lawn, ensuring it stays green and healthy.

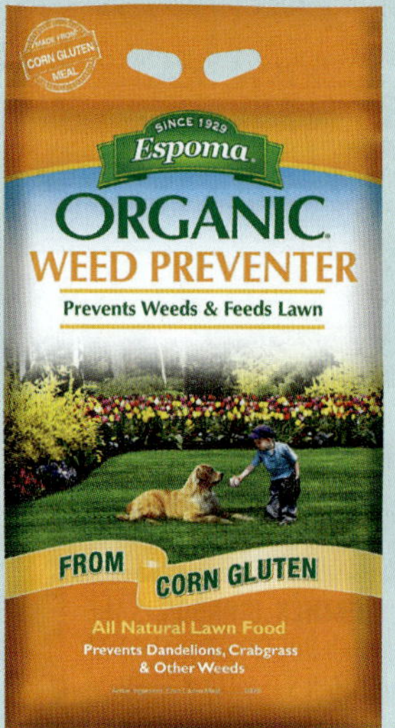

Johnson says organic and preemergent lawn products are "typically a fertilizer or germination inhibitor that won't kill already established grass but will prevent any new plants from germinating."

In order to get the best results, you need to apply the Espoma Organic Weed Preventer twice a year: once in early spring and again in early fall. A 25-lb. bag costs about $60.

A.D.I.O.S. ECO-FRIENDLY WEED CONTROL

A.D.I.O.S. is becoming increasingly popular in parts of the United States where conventional herbicides are restricted. Salt, its active ingredient, is a selective herbicide that can be used against broadleaf weeds such as dandelions, creeping Charlie and thistles. A.D.I.O.S. meets all USDA organic standards and has been approved for use in commercial organic farming. But use sparingly, because the overuse of salt-based products can negatively affect the quality of soil in the long run, says Johnson. A 36-oz. spray bottle costs about $45 at *natural-alternative.com*.

MAKE YOUR OWN EARTH-FRIENDLY WEED KILLER

A mixture of vinegar, salt and dish soap can be used as a spot treatment for weeds, according to Johnson. Concentrated vinegar is a good choice because it's stronger than the household variety, usually near 20% acetic acid. The salt and acetic acid present in vinegar cause the unwanted plants to dehydrate and wither, while dish soap enhances the effectiveness by breaking down the plant's outer layer (cuticle).

DIY WEED KILLER

- *1 gal. of vinegar*
- *1 oz. dish soap*
- *1 cup of salt*

To use this weed killer, mix the ingredients in a plastic spray bottle and spray directly on weeds. Apply the mixture on a sunny day when there is no wind. Because vinegar-based products are nonselective weed killers, they will harm all plants they are sprayed on. "If used in small amounts, this shouldn't affect the soil long term," Johnson says.

GREEN GOBBLER 20% VINEGAR WEED KILLER

Green Gobbler 20% Vinegar Weed Killer is a potent, nonselective vinegar-based weed and grass killer. It is made from ethanol distilled from corn grain and concentrated vinegar containing four times the acetic acid of traditional household vinegar. A gallon costs about $30.

Biodegradable and nontoxic, the OMRI-certified formula will safely remove all types of weeds from driveways, sidewalks and mulch beds.

Most environmentally friendly weed killers need to be sprayed directly on a growing weed so that the active ingredients can be taken up and distributed throughout the weed. So Johnson suggests using "nonselective sprays such as this in an isolated area, where it's easy to target individual weeds."

ELIMINATING WEEDS WITHOUT THE USE OF WEED KILLERS

If you're still feeling uneasy about using any sort of weed killer, environmentally friendly or not, other means are available to eliminate unwanted weeds and grasses.

Pouring boiling water on sidewalk, driveway or patio weeds is an effective method. The boiling water scalds the unwanted weed, and any water runoff will cool on the impervious surface before it reaches other plants.

To eradicate weeds from nonflammable areas such as cracks in sidewalks and gravel driveways, a propane torch is another effective alternative. Weeds growing on dry or combustible materials should never be torched, nor should poison ivy or other poisonous plants because their smoke can cause serious allergic reactions.

For large areas of your yard or between rows of vegetables in your planter boxes where no vegetation is wanted, consider solarizing or smothering the soil.

- To solarize, place a transparent plastic tarp over the soil. The tarp prevents the soil from absorbing water, while at the same time heating the soil and ultimately killing all vegetation.
- To smother weeds, place items such as layers of newspaper or old shower curtains on the soil to block both the sun and moisture.

One of the most effective ways to maintain a weed-free lawn is to follow a lawn care schedule. Johnson recommends using a lawn calendar that outlines when to do each lawn care maintenance task such as mowing, fertilizing and thatching. "Following those tips and hand-removing weeds when they are present is a good way to mitigate weeds without the use of any chemicals," she adds.

If your lawn is more than 50% weeds, Johnson says it's best to reseed the whole lawn.

BUILD A VERTICAL GARDEN

TIME TO GROW UP

WHAT IT TAKES

TIME	COST	SKILL LEVEL
2 days	$1,200	Beginner

TOOLS
Table saw, circular saw, jigsaw, cordless drill, basic carpentry tools

MEET THE BUILDER

JAY CORK MISSES HAVING A HOBBY FARM, BUT THIS VERTICAL GARDEN PROVIDES HIM WITH PLENTY OF VEGGIES—WITHOUT ALL THE COYOTES.

BY JAY CORK

Interested in starting your own vegetable garden but have limited space? This vertical garden—a simple, attractive design built with cedar boards—has a small footprint and vertical "acreage" that'll make the most of any urban backyard. And you will appreciate being able to garden with a lot less bending!

CHOOSING WOOD

Although pressure-treated lumber no longer contains arsenic, we avoid using treated lumber where we're growing food. Decay-resistant woods such as redwood and red cedar look great and last for years.

1 MAKE THE FIRST LEG

Following Figure A, mark the cutting lines on a 2x6 cedar leg blank. Cut the stair steps and angled ends using any method you are comfortable with. We used a jigsaw and a miter saw.

FIGURE A LEG DIAGRAM

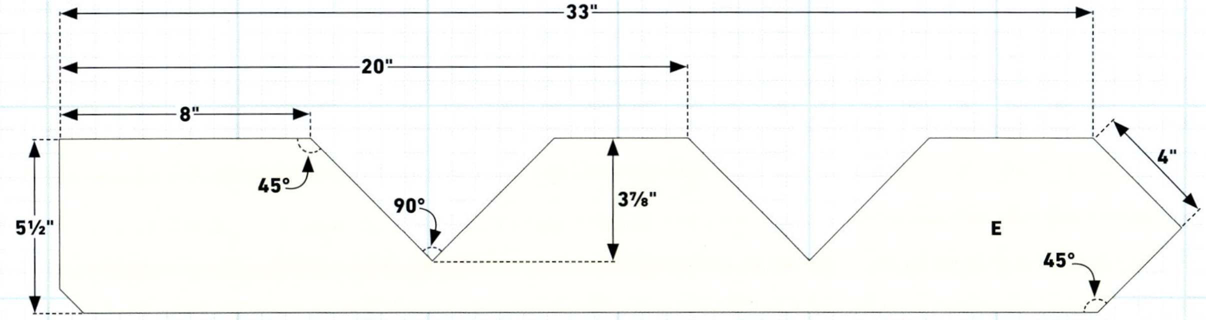

FIGURE B SAW GUIDE

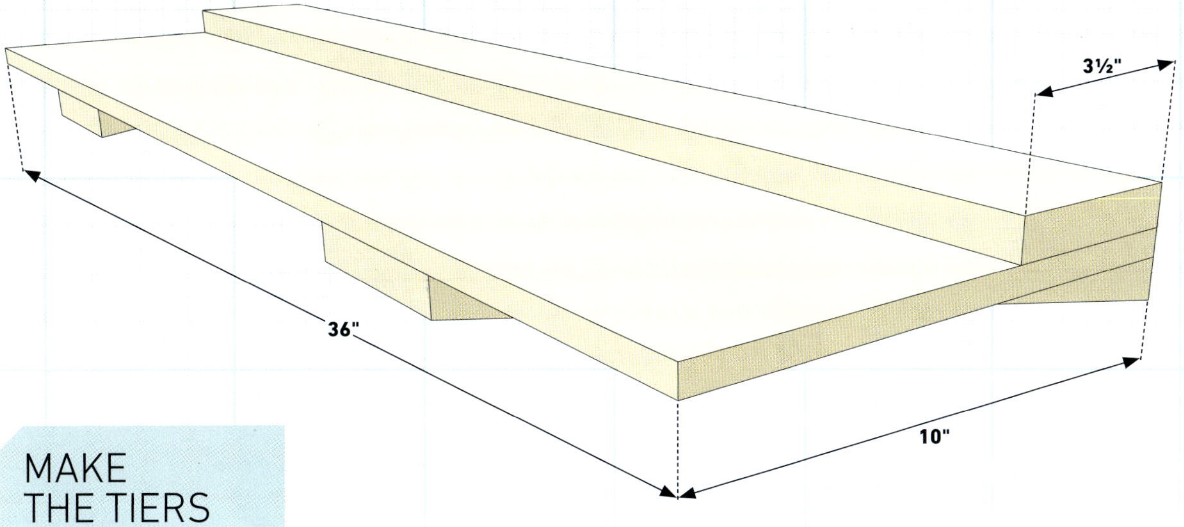

MAKE THE TIERS

Our favorite aspect of this project is its simplicity—it assembles with butt joints and requires only one setup on the saw. We designed the guide (Figure B) so that any circular saw can be used to make these compound miter cuts.

FIGURE C SAW GUIDE BOTTOM

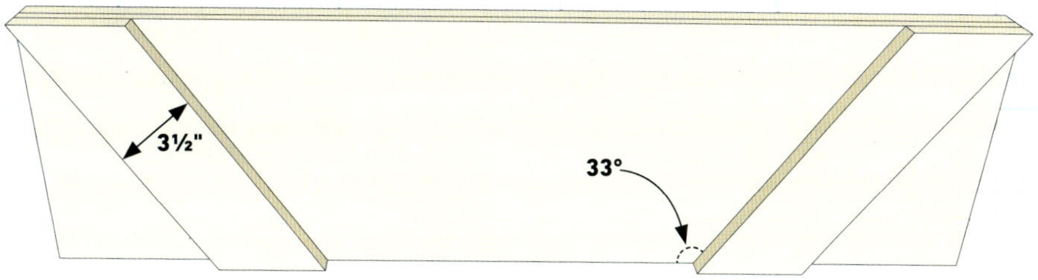

CUTTING LIST

KEY	QTY.	DIMENSIONS	PART
A	3	62½" x 11¼" x 1½"	Tier 1 sides
B	3	48½" x 11¼" x 1½"	Tier 2 sides
C	3	34½" x 11¼" x 1½"	Tier 3 sides
D	3	20½" x 11¼" x 1½"	Tier 4 sides
E	3	33" x 5½" x 1½"	Stand legs
F	1	36" x 1½"	Dowel

MATERIALS LIST

ITEM	QTY.
2x12 x 8' cedar boards	12
2x6 x 8' cedar boards	3
1½" dowel	1
2½" trim screws	Box

2 CUT THE REMAINING LEGS

Use the first leg as a template to lay out the other two. Cut them as you did the first one.

3 ASSEMBLE THE TRIPOD

Make a mark every 1½ in. around the circumference of the center support dowel to indicate the spacing for the legs. Drill pilot holes through the dowel, and use 2½-in. screws to attach the legs.

4 CUT THE TIER SIDES

Clamp the saw guide to the 2x12 cedar and make one angled cut across the cedar board. Make the mark for the opposing cut from the top corner, and then flip the guide around and make the second cut. Make three sides for each tier level.

SET UP THE SAW GUIDE

Tilt the blade on the saw to 16 degrees and make a cut on the saw guide. This will make the zero-clearance base for your saw. Now you can line up all your cuts to the cut edge at the bottom of the guide.

FIGURE D **TIER PARTS**

OVERALL DIMENSIONS:
64½" W x 36" H x 64½" D

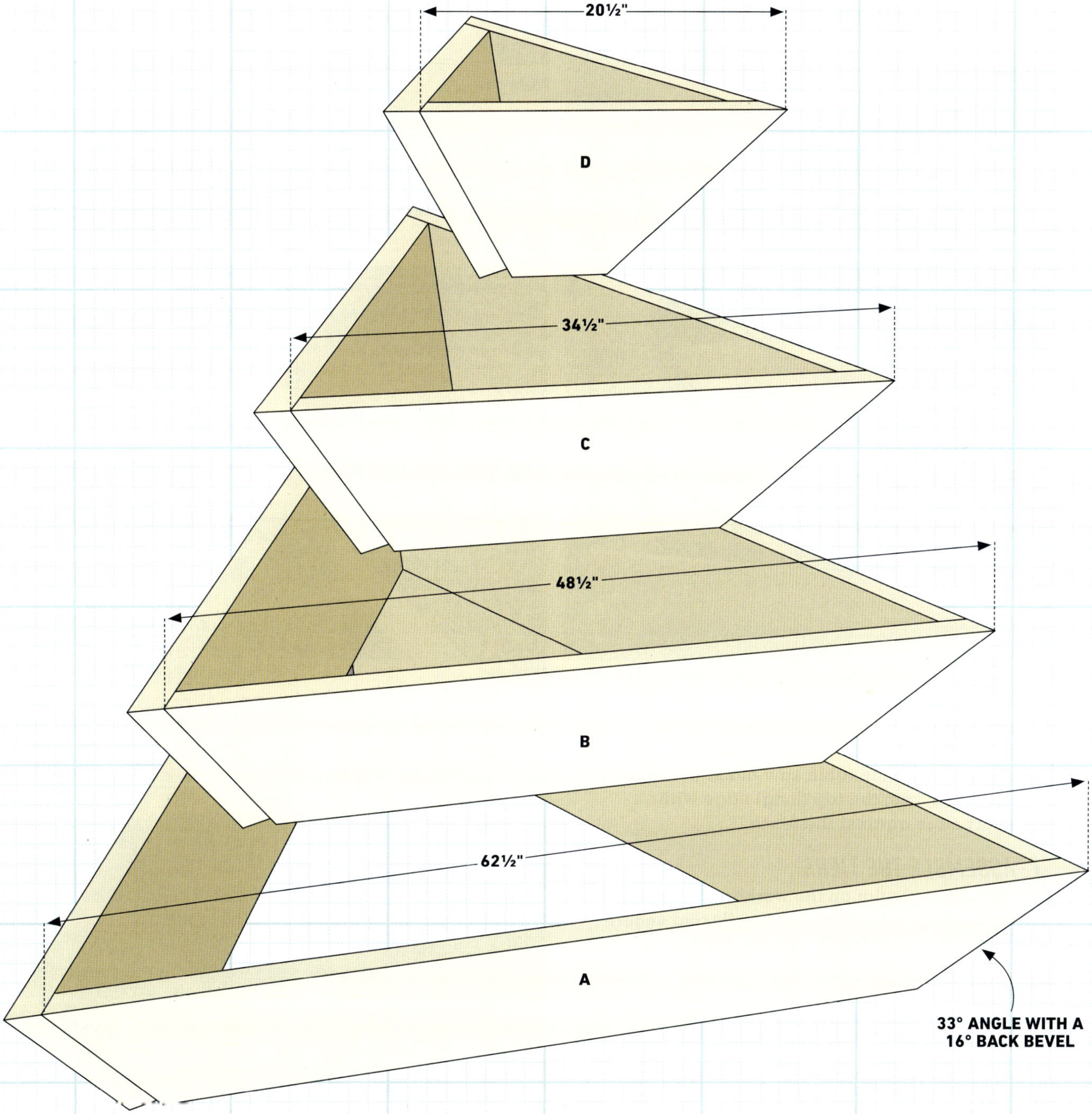

5 BEVEL THE TOP EDGES

Before assembly, bevel the top edges of the tier boards so they appear level when assembled. With the table saw blade set to 22½ degrees, trim the top (long) edge with the short edge against the fence.

6 ASSEMBLE THE TIERS

With one side flat on the workbench, tack the next side in place with brad nails and secure it with trim screws. Finish with the third side.

7 FIND LEVEL GROUND

Find or create a level area where the lower tier and legs can sit. It doesn't have to be perfectly level; just make sure it's not tilting too much. Set the lower tier with the leg stand centered inside. Set the second tier and start filling with soil.

8 PLANT AND ENJOY

Fill the garden with soil as you stack the tiers. Now you're ready to start growing! This vertical garden is perfect for herbs and small greens. Even carrots would do well! And be sure to check out "Grow Mini Vegetables" on the next page.

GROW MINI VEGETABLES

TINY VARIETIES FOR TINY SPACES

BY CAROL J. MICHEL

If your current vegetable garden exists within a 1-ft.-wide strip of soil between your patio and a fence, perhaps you do your best to squeeze some green beans and a few tomato plants into that little area. Here we'll show you how you can grow dozens of mini vegetable varieties in that same limited space.

WHAT ARE MINI VEGETABLES?

Mini vegetables, also referred to as dwarf or compact vegetables, are vegetable plants that are much smaller than their standard counterparts. According to Josh Kirschenbaum, PanAmerican Seed vegetable accounts manager, no parameters are set for what defines a dwarf vegetable, but they are notably smaller than a standard-size vegetable and can perform well in a container.

Like full-size vegetable plants, dwarf or mini vegetable plants usually require full sun. When they're grown in containers, you'll also need to water them more frequently—as often as once or twice a day during the hottest days of summer, depending on the size of the container. You'll also need to fertilize them more often because frequent watering quickly leaches out the nutrients the vegetables need to thrive.

A LITTLE HISTORY

As Jen McGuinness noted in her book *Micro Food Gardening: Project Plans and Plants for Growing Fruits and Veggies in Tiny Spaces*, people are moving to cities, and by 2050, well over half of us will live in an urban environment. Fortunately, the plant industry recognizes this, and plant breeders at companies such as PanAmerican Seed started breeding dwarf vegetable varieties about 15 years ago with a focus on those that grow well in both containers and hydroponic systems, such as the AeroGarden.

WHY GROW MINIS?

You won't harvest bushels of produce when you grow mini vegetables or fruits, but there are still many good reasons to grow them.

ENJOY HOMEGROWN TASTE. You'll discover that homegrown vegetables, even small ones, often taste better than varieties you buy in grocery stores. Plus, you can't get fresher vegetables than those you pick and eat right away. If you grow dwarf vegetables using an indoor hydroponic system, you can also get that fresh taste year-round.

SPEND LESS TIME AND EFFORT. Planting mini vegetables in containers takes less time and overall effort than planting a vegetable garden in the ground.

TEACH KIDS ABOUT FOOD. When kids see dwarf vegetables growing up close, they learn where their vegetables come from.

GAIN EXPERIENCE TO GROW FULL-SIZE VEGETABLES. Many people are timid about planting a large vegetable garden, even when they have the space for it. After having success with dwarf vegetables, you may have the desire to grow regular-size vegetable plants.

THE CHALLENGES

Growing dwarf vegetables isn't completely trouble-free. They can still be attacked by the same insect pests and diseases found in in-ground vegetable gardens.

You'll also need to spend time caring for them. This often means daily watering and weekly fertilizing with plant fertilizer labeled for use with vegetables. Lastly, the containers, potting soil or hydroponic system can cost quite a bit initially. Fortunately, most containers can be reused for years.

KATARINA CABBAGE

TABLETOP VEGETABLES

If your only growing space is a sunny windowsill or a small table outdoors, "tabletop vegetables" may be your best option. Kitchen Minis from PanAmerican Seed were bred to be grown in small containers. You buy the potted vegetable plant and enjoy picking fresh vegetables for a few weeks.

Once they have stopped producing, you can compost the plants and recycle the containers. Several varieties of sweet peppers, hot peppers and cherry tomatoes, and a cucumber called Quick Snack, are available. Find out more at *kitchenminis.com*.

CHOOSING YOUR VEGETABLES

Deciding which mini vegetables to grow is the same as deciding which vegetables to grow in a regular garden.

- Choose vegetables you already love to eat. Maybe try one or two you don't like and see if you like the homegrown version.
- How big will the plant get at maturity? *Dwarf, mini, compact* and *ultra-compact* are all terms used to describe smaller vegetable plants. Read the label to determine the mature size so you won't be surprised.
- How big will the harvested vegetables be? Some dwarf plants also produce much smaller vegetables, while others grow vegetables that are almost full size.
- Don't limit yourself to just vegetable plants labeled as dwarf, compact, mini, etc. Also look for full-size varieties—which may be naturally smaller plants to begin with—that are described as growing well in containers.
- Finally, choose a few varieties that you can eat as you pick them. Nothing is better than a fresh sun-warmed cherry tomato right off the vine.

HERE ARE 12 OF OUR FAVORITES

1 GREEN BEAN: MASCOTTE

This is another vegetable that tastes its best when freshly picked. If you don't have room for a big row of beans, try Mascotte (*burpee.com*), a dwarf plant that produces beans up to 5 in. long. It was named an All-America Selections winner in 2014.

If you keep picking the beans as they mature, which takes about 50 days from sowing, the plants should keep flowering and produce more beans for several weeks.

- Sow seeds directly in containers when the possibility of frost has passed, spacing the seeds according to the instructions on the packet.
- Seeds should germinate in a few days.

2 CABBAGE: KATARINA

It's surprising how big a cabbage plant can get and how much better homegrown cabbage tastes. Try Katarina (*territorialseed.com*), which produces a small, tasty head of cabbage and grows well in larger containers. This cabbage tolerates light frosts, so you can get an early start by putting it outside a few weeks before your last frost.

You should have mature cabbage heads ready to harvest in about six weeks. This cabbage variety was named an All-America Selections winner in 2016.

- Sow seeds indoors four to six weeks before transplanting outdoors or buy transplants in early spring.
- To keep cabbage butterfly larvae from eating the leaves, you may need to cover them with a light horticultural cloth.

3 CUCUMBER: PATIO SNACKER

Cucumber Patio Snacker (*territorialseed.com*) is a dwarf vegetable variety you can grow in a large container. Cucumber plants are vines, so add a small trellis to give the vines something to climb up.

The big surprise is that this plant, although smaller than most cucumber plants, produces larger cucumbers, up to 7 to 8 in. long, in 50 days or so.

Keep picking the cucumbers to encourage the vine to keep flowering. Also, encourage bees to visit your plant by planting flowers nearby. Cucumbers produce separate male and female flowers and need bees to pollinate them.

- Sow seeds directly outside in a large container.
- Thin to one or two seedlings by carefully pulling out the other seedlings.

5 TOMATO: LIZZANO

If you are looking for the classic cherry tomato to grow in a container on your patio, try Lizzano (*territorialseed.com*). It was an All-America Selections winner from 2011.

This variety produces fruit over a long period and is resistant to late blight. In a container on the ground, it will need a cage or other support; it does well in a large hanging basket, where it can hang down from the edges.

- Start seeds indoors six to eight weeks before your first frost-free date or purchase plants in late spring.
- Harden off seedlings by placing them outside in shade for a few hours a day when temperatures are above 60 degrees.
- Plant seedlings in their permanent container once there is no risk of frost.

6 TOMATO: PATIO CHOICE YELLOW

Cherry tomatoes may be small, but that's not true of all cherry tomato plants. Patio Choice Yellow F1 (*trueleafmarket.com*) was an All-America Selections winner from 2017. It's a smaller plant that does well on a patio in a container.

To keep your tomatoes (and all mini vegetables in containers) healthy and growing, fertilize them regularly with a liquid

4 WATERMELON: CAL SWEET BUSH

You may think there is no way you can grow a watermelon in a container, but you can! Cal Sweet Bush is a compact bush-type plant with short vines that grows well in containers. An All-America Selections winner in 2019, it's available at *trueleafmarket.com*.

Let it grow all summer and in about 90 days, you'll have your own homegrown watermelon. Just remember to grow it in full sun and keep it watered throughout the summer.

- Sow seeds directly outside in a large container.
- Thin to one seedling, the strongest, by carefully pulling out the other seedlings.
- One seedling should produce one watermelon.

PATIO CHOICE YELLOW TOMATO

fertilizer because nutrients can quickly leach out of the soil with regular watering.

- Start seeds indoors six to eight weeks before your first frost-free date or purchase plants in late spring.
- Harden off seedlings by placing them outside in shade for a few hours a day when temperatures are above 60 degrees.
- Plant seedlings in their permanent container once there is no risk of frost.

7 PEPPER: QUICKFIRE

You can round out your mini vegetable collection of peppers with a hot Thai-type pepper called Quickfire (*parkseed.com*). An All-America Selections winner from 2022, it produces hot peppers on smaller plants, perfect for containers. The hot peppers show above the foliage, so they are easy to harvest when you need one to spice up a favorite dish.

Some gardeners wonder if hot peppers grown next to sweet peppers make the sweet peppers hot too. They don't. Growing them near each other won't affect the taste of either one.

- Start seeds indoors six to eight weeks before your first frost-free date or purchase plants in late spring.
- Harden off seedlings by placing them outside in shade for a few hours a day when temperatures are above 60.
- Plant seedlings in their permanent container once there is no risk of frost.

8 TOMATO: LITTLE NAPOLI

Not all dwarf tomato plants produce cherry tomatoes. Little Napoli (from *burpee.com*) is a mini plant that produces a Roma-type tomato, the type used to make tomato paste and sauce.

Little Napoli grows best in a large container with some support in the form of a small tomato cage or sturdy stakes. Tie the vines loosely to the stakes or gently guide them to grow up through the cage. This helps the plant grow upright, which ensures good fruiting. It needs full sun, and in a container may need daily watering.

- Start seeds indoors six to eight weeks before your first frost-free date or purchase plants in late spring.
- Harden off seedlings by placing them outside in shade for a few hours a day when temperatures are above 60.
- Plant seedlings in their permanent container once there is no risk of frost.

9 EGGPLANT: PATIO BABY

Even if you don't like eggplant, grow this dwarf variety, Patio Baby (*burpee .com*), and try cooking the small eggplants it produces. Because the plants top out at less than 2 ft. tall, they do well in large containers in full sun.

A unique feature of this eggplant variety, an All-America Selections winner in 2014, is that it doesn't have thorns on the leaves or calyxes (that green cap where the eggplant attaches to the plant itself) like other eggplants. This is a big plus at harvest time.

- Start seeds indoors six to eight weeks before your first frost-free date or purchase plants in late spring.
- Harden off seedlings by placing them outside in shade for a few hours a day when temperatures are above 60.
- Plant seedlings in their permanent container once there is no risk of frost.

10 PEPPER: JUST SWEET

When it comes to mini peppers, there are many varieties to choose from, including Just Sweet (*parkseed.com*). An All-America Selections winner in 2019, these pepper plants can grow up to 3 ft. tall but don't need to be staked.

The peppers are sweet and good for snacking. When mature, they turn yellowish orange. Keep picking the peppers and the plant should keep flowering and producing more throughout the growing season.

- Start seeds indoors six to eight weeks before your first frost-free date or purchase plants in late spring.
- Harden off seedlings by placing them outside in shade for a few hours a day when temperatures are above 60.
- Plant seedlings in their permanent container once there is no risk of frost.

11 BASIL: EMERALD TOWERS

Emerald Towers from *burpee.com* is a tall basil plant that grows almost straight up, making it a good accent plant in a container with other edible plants. Plus, it's slow to produce flowers, which allows you to harvest leaves from it for most of the growing season. These plants don't need a large container to grow but should be watered regularly.

- Start seeds indoors four to five weeks before your first frost-free date or purchase plants in late spring.
- Harden off seedlings by placing them outside in shade for a few hours a day when temperatures are above 60.
- Plant seedlings in their permanent container once there is no risk of frost. You can also direct-sow seeds in containers outdoors after your garden is frost-free.

LOVE FRESH PEAS?

You can grow Peas-in-a-Pot on your patio too. Bred for containers and small space gardens, it's a 10-in. plant with a good yield. Check it out at *burpee.com*.

12 PEPPER: POT-A-PENO

Pot-a-Peno was an All-America Selections winner in 2021. This jalapeno-type pepper from *burpee.com* grows well in a container or a hanging basket where it will cascade down the sides.

You can pick the peppers while green or let them ripen to red. Not only will the color change, but the flavor will too. Try them both ways!

- Start seeds indoors six to eight weeks before your first frost-free date or purchase plants in late spring.
- Harden off seedlings by placing them outside in shade for a few hours a day when temperatures are above 60.
- Plant seedlings in their permanent container once the risk of frost has passed.

MEET THE EXPERT

CAROL J. MICHEL, AN AWARD-WINNING AUTHOR, ALSO HAS A BLOG CALLED *MAY DREAMS GARDENS*.

DIY HYDROPONIC GARDEN

FRESH VEGETABLES AT YOUR FINGERTIPS

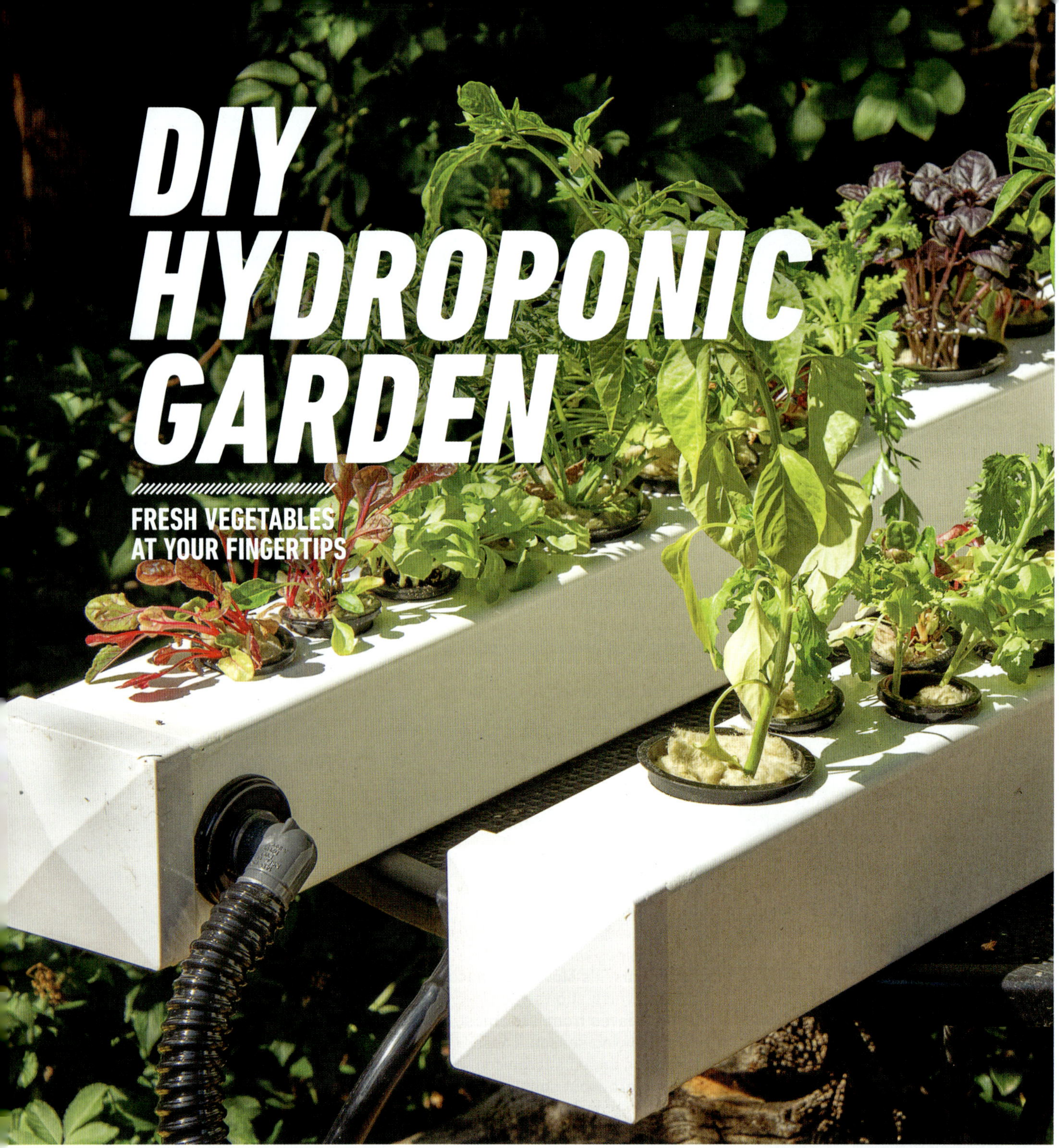

BY KARUNA EBERL

You may think hydroponic gardening is a complex science that is out of your reach. But it's just PVC parts, a pump and some water. Building this type of garden is actually faster and easier than preparing a soil garden bed. Plus, it produces faster-growing vegetables with a fraction of the water. We made a system compact enough to sit on a table in a small house or apartment, but still large enough for nightly salads. It can even be moved outdoors for summer and inside for winter.

FIGURE A
HYDROPONIC GARDEN

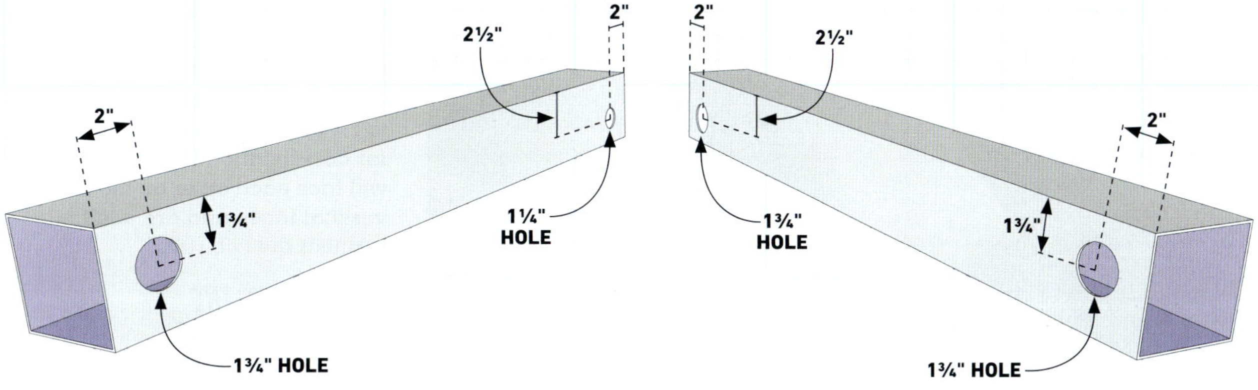

MATERIALS LIST

ITEM	QTY.
1' length of 1" PVC Schedule 40 pipe	1
10-piece package of 3" net cups for hydroponics	1
10.2 oz. clear aquarium silicone sealant	1
27-gal. tough storage bin with lid (should not be translucent)	1
4 oz. Gorilla Clear PVC PrimaGlue	1
4" square PVC fence post, 6' long	1
50-piece package of black plastic slotted mesh net plant cups for hydroponics	1
Boshart 1" insert x 1" D MPT Polypropylene 90-degree elbow	1
Boshart ½" insert x ½" D MPT Polypropylene 90-degree elbow	1
Kedsum 660 gph submersible Ultra Quiet water pump with 6' lift height	1
Lifegard Aquatics ½" double-threaded bulkhead	1
Package of TotalPond vinyl tubing: ½" diameter	1
Package of plant nutrients	1
1" Schedule 40 PVC union	1
Sealproof 1" diameter corrugated pond tubing: 20' length	1
Sheet of 120-grit sandpaper	1
Sheet of 28 small plugs: 1½" Rockwool starter plugs for hydroponics	1
Charlotte Pipe 1" Schedule 40 MPT x S male adapter	2
Lifegard Aquatics 1" double-threaded bulkheads	3
4" white vinyl pyramid-style fence post caps	4
90-degree elbow: 1" barbed x NPT male	1

1 CUT YOUR FENCE POSTS

Cut the 6-ft. PVC fence post into two 36-in. pieces. Cut the ends as straight as possible so the end caps seal properly. Also cut two 2½-in. pieces of 1-in. Schedule 40 pipe.

MEET THE EXPERTS

KARUNA EBERL AND STEVE ALBERTS ARE ON THE FINAL STRETCH OF RENOVATING AN ABANDONED HOUSE IN A NEAR-GHOST TOWN IN RURAL COLORADO.

WHAT IT TAKES

TIME	COST	SKILL LEVEL
1 day	$300	Beginner

TOOLS

¾" paddle bit, handsaw, measuring tape, miter saw, permanent marker, drill/driver, hole saws: 1¼", 1½", 1¾" and 2½"

2 DRILL THE CONNECTION HOLES

Drill the connection holes in your 4-in. PVC fence post sections. Three of the holes are 1¾ in. diameter and one hole is 1¼ in. diameter. (See Figure A for hole locations.) These holes will face each other on the inside vertical faces and are used to connect the two rails.

3 LAY OUT THE CUP PATTERN

Use a permanent marker to indicate the center for each hole. Leave at least 3 in. of space at each end so you don't interfere with the fittings to be installed later.

4 DRILL THE CUP HOLES

Drill cup holes on the top faces of the rails. Drill 1½-in. holes for small cups and 2½-in. holes for large cups. After drilling the holes, use sandpaper to smooth the edges of the holes.

PRO TIP

Small net cups are good for shorter-term plants like lettuce. Large net cups are good for longer-term plants such as peppers and strawberries.

5 GLUE THE RAIL CONNECTION FITTINGS

Assemble the fittings and 1-in. PVC lengths in the order shown in Photo 5B. Apply the PVC glue to the inside of the receiving fitting and the outside of the inserting fitting (Photo 5A). Push the pieces together while giving them a slight twist, about a quarter turn. Hold pressure for 30 to 45 seconds or until the fittings don't pull apart.

6 INSERT THE BULKHEAD FITTINGS

Insert the fittings in the connection holes you drilled in Step 2. The threads go inside the square post, and the gasket seals go on the outside. Tighten the nuts onto the threads until the fittings are tight.

5B

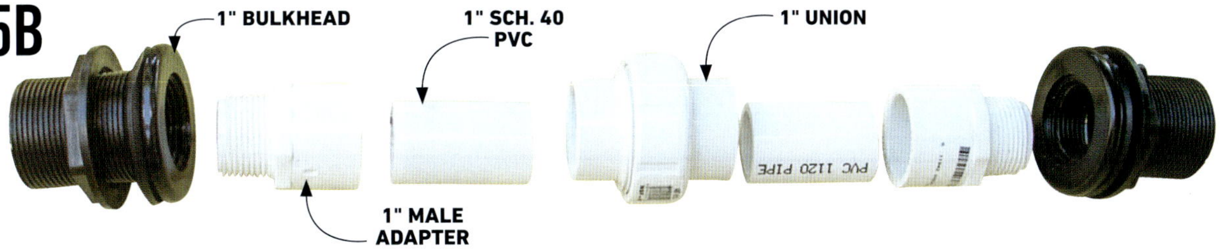

7 ADD THE FITTINGS

Attach the PVC fittings on the matching post ends. Insert the ½-in. elbow into the ½-in. bulkhead fitting (Photo 7B). Insert the 1-in. elbow into the 1-in. bulkhead fitting (7A) directly across from ½-in. fitting. Angle elbows downward 45 degrees to connect to the water reservoir.

8 SEAL AND GLUE END CAPS

Apply silicone to the inside of each end cap, with a bit extra in the corners. Then apply PVC glue along the inside edge of the cap, adjacent to the silicone. Apply glue to the outside of the post. Push the end cap in place and hold for 30 to 45 seconds. Fill any gaps in the corners with silicone.

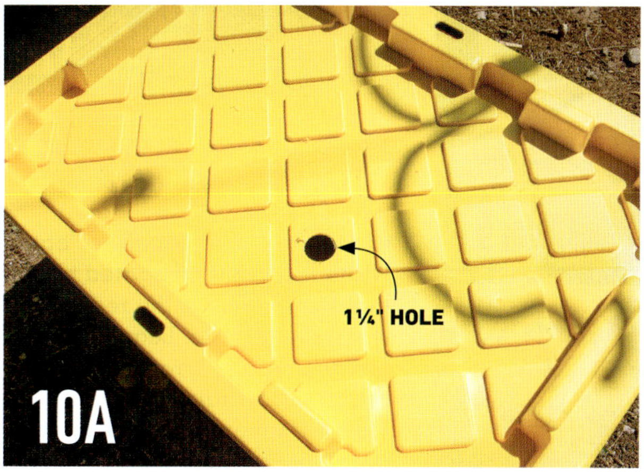

9 CONNECT THE RAILS

Place your rails next to each other with the union fittings aligning with the other halves. Tighten the union fittings as much as you can by hand.

10 PREPARE THE WATER RESERVOIR

Drill a 1¼-in. hole through the bin lid for the outflow tubing (Photo 10A). Drill a ¾-in. hole through the side of the reservoir near the top of the sidewall for the inflow waterline that will connect to the water pump (10B). Drill another ¾-in. hole next to the inflow waterline for the cord to pass through. Place the water pump in the center of the reservoir and route the cord through the ¾-in. hole next to the inflow tubing hole (10C).

11 ATTACH INFLOW AND OUTFLOW TUBING

Push the corrugated tubing onto the 1-in. elbow barb. Route the 1-in. corrugated tubing through the top of the reservoir in the $1\frac{1}{4}$-in. hole. Leave about 8 in. tubing in the reservoir and cut off the remaining length. Push the inflow $\frac{1}{2}$-in. tubing onto the elbow barb, route it through the $\frac{3}{4}$-in. hole in the side next to the cord and cut it to appropriate length. Push the inflow tubing onto the pump barb until it is fully seated. Fill the water reservoir three-quarters full and add any necessary nutrients.

12 PREPARE NET CUPS

You can use seeds, seedlings or starter plants from a nursery. If your plants come in soil, remove as much of it as you can from the roots before inserting them in the Rockwool starter plugs.

13 FINISH IT UP

Plug in the pump, and insert the plant cups into the holes in the rails. Don't leave any holes empty. Open holes let sunlight into the system, which promotes algae growth.

GREAT GOOFS®

LAUGHS AND LESSONS FROM OUR READERS

WITH FRIENDS LIKE THESE...

All winter long, whenever it snowed, our next-door neighbor Ron came out with his snowblower and cleared off our 225-ft. driveway. He even did it at night! So when spring arrived and his grass had reached an unprecedented height and was almost ready to drop its seed, I thought I'd return his kindness and surprise him by mowing his yard while he was at work. Several other neighbors stopped by to encourage me as I gamely pushed the mower through the knee-high grass. Ron, returning home from work, came running across the yard with tears in his eyes. Turns out he had been waiting for the grass to reseed itself.

ALEX JONES

TOTALLY HOSED

When we first moved into our new house, most of our stuff hadn't been delivered yet, but we did have our water bed and decided to set it up. When it was ready to be filled, I realized we didn't have our garden hoses. Luckily, the previous owner had left one behind, so I ran it out the window and went outside to hook it up to the outdoor faucet.

I turned on the faucet and paused for a few minutes to meet my new neighbor. When I finally went inside, I discovered I had watered my new bedroom with a soaker hose!

JOSHUA KOCH

7 MISCELLANEOUS ODDS & ENDS

THE ART OF BLADESMITHING

FORGE SOMETHING NEW FROM SOMETHING OLD

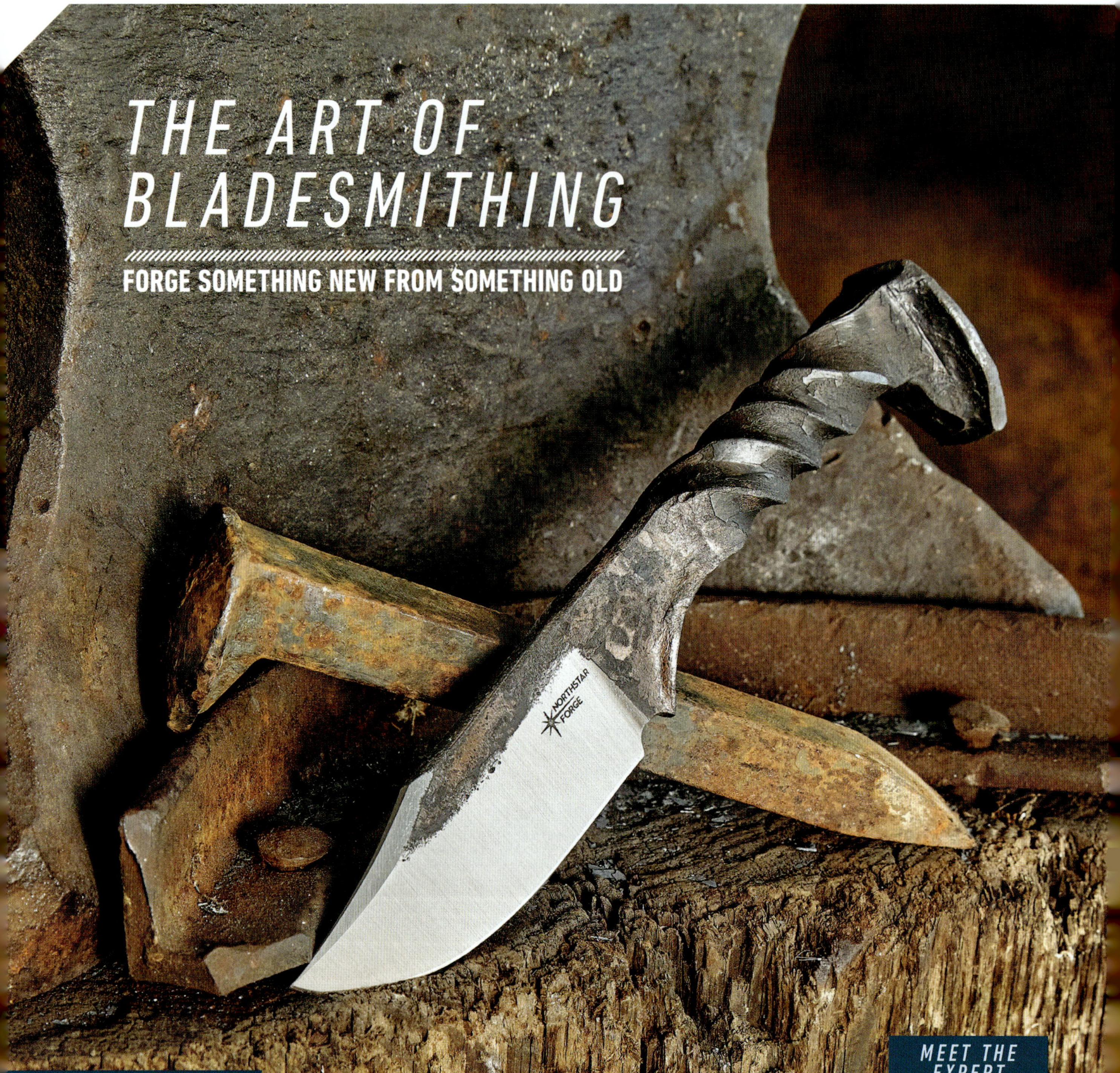

BY JAY CORK

An art form that has spanned millennia, bladesmithing is currently seeing a surge in popularity. DIYers need to be careful, though—you just might find yourself with a new hobby or profession.

For Jason Kraus, that's exactly what happened. Now he's made swords, daggers and axes for more than a decade. Here he's going to show us how to make a beautiful knife from an ugly railroad spike.

MEET THE EXPERT

A FULL-TIME BLADESMITH FOR OVER 10 YEARS, **JASON KRAUS** HAS APPEARED ON THE HIT SHOWS *FORGED IN FIRE* AND *MASTER OF ARMS*. HE OPERATES NORTHSTAR FORGE IN CARVER, MINNESOTA.

THE GAS FORGE

A gas forge is by far the most reliable and controllable type of forge to operate. Coal forges may have old-world charm, but they come with a steep learning curve.

If you want to get up to speed quickly, start with gas. Such a forge is simple—a propane tank feeds a burner that's placed in an insulated chamber. Find a gas forge online by searching for "gas forge for knife making."

1 BRING UP THE HEAT

After the forge has come up to temperature, it's time to get the steel up to working temperature. Jason secures the railroad spike in a set of tongs and places it in the forge until it's glowing bright orange—about 1,500 degrees.

2 FORM THE HANDLE

One of Jason's favorite handle shapes is the simple twist. Once the railroad spike is glowing orange, he puts it in a vise and twists it 360 degrees.

3 DRAW OUT THE BLADE

Now that the handle has been defined, Jason draws out material on the anvil. He's not aiming for a specific shape, just a uniform thickness of ¼ in.

4 HAMMER THE BLADE PROFILE

Once Jason draws out the blade material, he defines the curved profile of the blade edge. He does this by forging the shape with a hammer on the anvil.

5 REFINE THE BLADE SHAPE

Using a grinding wheel, Jason refines the shape by putting a curve in the top of the blade. It's easier to do this before the heat-treating process.

6 NORMALIZE THE STEEL

Subjecting the steel to multiple heat cycles "normalizes" the particles, providing a uniform grain structure. Jason heats the blade in the forge and lets it air-cool a total of five times.

GRAIN STRUCTURE: GOOD VS. BAD

These two cross sections of steel show results of the normalization process. The steel on the left is perfectly normalized; the steel on the right, from a broken knife blade, is poorly normalized.

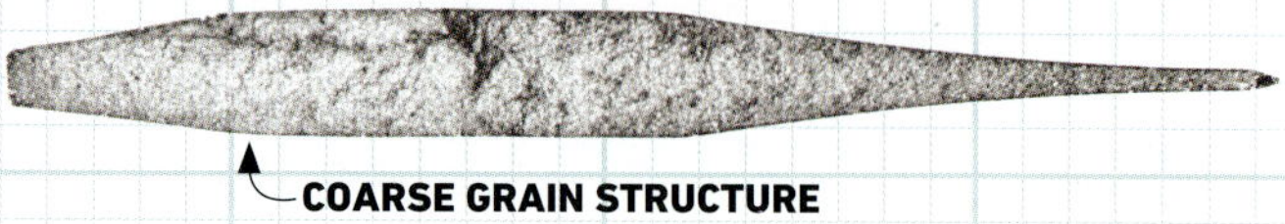

7 QUENCH THE BLADE

Once the blade has been normalized, Jason sets the knife back in the forge. He brings the temp up to 1,600 degrees—he can tell by the steel's bright orange color—and quickly submerges the blade in quenching oil. This thoroughly hardens the steel.

8 TEMPER THE STEEL

The final step in the heat treatment process, "tempering" softens the steel slightly to produce a blade edge that is hard but not brittle. For railroad spike knives, Jason uses a torch to bring the temperature to 375 degrees and lets the blade air-cool.

9 GRIND A FINAL TIME

After the steel has been tempered, Jason grinds the blade profile down to a fine edge with his belt grinder. To protect his fingers, he holds the blade against the platen with a push stick. The blade looks sharp, but it's not quite there.

10 SHARPEN THE KNIFE

Jason develops a strong razor-sharp edge by holding the knife to the belt between the wheels—a process called slack-belt sharpening. With light, even pressure, he draws the blade across a progression of belts, each one finer than the last—starting at 320 grit and stopping at 3,000 grit.

JASON'S TOOLS

Bladesmithing calls for safety goggles, a leather apron and these heavy-duty tools.

ANVIL

This anvil is over 100 years old and came from Sweden. A bladesmith uses an anvil and a hammer to draw out the steel, and to form the curves of the blade.

TONGS

Much like clamps in a wood shop, a forge can't have too many tongs.

TORCH

Jason used a MAPP gas torch to temper our railroad spike knife. For everything else, he uses an industrial oven.

ROUNDING HAMMER

Jason forged this 3-lb. hammer himself, and it's one of his favorites. One side is rounded and the other is flat.

THE FLAT SIDE HELPS REMOVE HAMMER MARKS AND FLATTEN THE STEEL

THE ROUNDED HEAD IS USED TO DRAW OUT THE STEEL

THE TWIST-O-MATIC 3000

Jason made this tool himself by welding an adjustable wrench to a monkey wrench. He uses it to twist the railroad spike while it's held in a vise.

WIRE BRUSH

Jason uses a wire brush to remove scale while he works the steel.

7 BICYCLE MAINTENANCE TIPS

KEEP YOUR BIKE IN TIPTOP SHAPE AND RIDE SAFE!

BY JAY CORK

Riding a bike is great fun, but owning one requires regular upkeep. If you want to avoid running to the bike shop every time something comes up, you will need at least a basic understanding of bicycle maintenance.

Joe Blegen hasn't owned a car in more than a decade, relying solely on two wheels for his daily commutes. We caught up with Joe in his classroom, where he teaches high school students valuable lessons on bicycle maintenance.

MEET THE EXPERT

JOE BLEGEN TEACHES BICYCLE MAINTENANCE AT OPEN WORLD LEARNING COMMUNITY IN ST. PAUL, MINNESOTA.

PRERIDE CHECKLIST, OR "ABC"

Before every ride, go through this ABC checklist.

A - Air. Check the air pressure in your tires and adjust it as needed. Check it with a hand-held gauge or use the gauge on a floor pump.

B - Brakes. With the bike tires on the ground, roll the bike forward and squeeze both brake levers—first the front and then the rear. There should be no slipping or squeaking. The brake lever should feel firm and responsive.

C - Chain. With the rear tire off the ground, check that the derailleur operates both up and down the gears and the chain is running smoothly.

CHECK THE CHAIN FOR WEAR

Depending on the riding conditions, a typical multispeed chain needs to be replaced every 1,000 to 1,500 miles. A chain-wear measuring tool is inexpensive and useful for keeping track of your chain's condition.

LUBRICATE YOUR CHAIN

Wipe off any dirt and debris, and drip the chain lube onto the links. Joe uses Finish Line Wet Lube in the classroom and on his own bikes. Don't use aerosol lubricants such as WD-40; they're not designed for bicycle lubrication. They evaporate quickly and won't provide long-term lubrication.

KEEP YOUR TIRES HEALTHY

Keep your tires inflated within the suggested psi range. This protects the inner tube and keeps the tires in good shape. When storing a bike for long periods of time, hang it up. Keep in mind that tires and tubes lose air over time. Check them regularly.

SET THE SEAT HEIGHT

Make sure your seat is adjusted to fit your body on the bike. With the pedal crank at its lowest position, your leg should have about a 10-degree bend.

CHANGE THE INNER TUBE

Removing the inner tube for repair or replacement is relatively straightforward, but here's a trick to avoid damaging it or your tire. Pry the tire bead away from the rim bead with your fingers. It might take some effort, but do this around the entire circumference of the wheel. It's tempting to use a screwdriver or pry bar for this step, but don't! One small slip, and you've got another hole to patch.

Once the old inner tube is out, tuck the new tube into the rim, starting at the stem. Seat the tire bead to the rim and inflate the tire slowly.

ADJUST THE DERAILLEUR

Before adjusting the derailleur, ensure the cable is firmly seated. Adjust the action of the derailleur by loosening or tightening the cable barrel adjustment. Sometimes this is just a matter of trial and error—make an adjustment and try all the gears until the derailleur operates smoothly, both up and down the gear cassette.

CHECK YOUR BRAKE PADS

Before you make any adjustments to your brakes, double-check that the wheel is firmly seated in the frame dropouts.

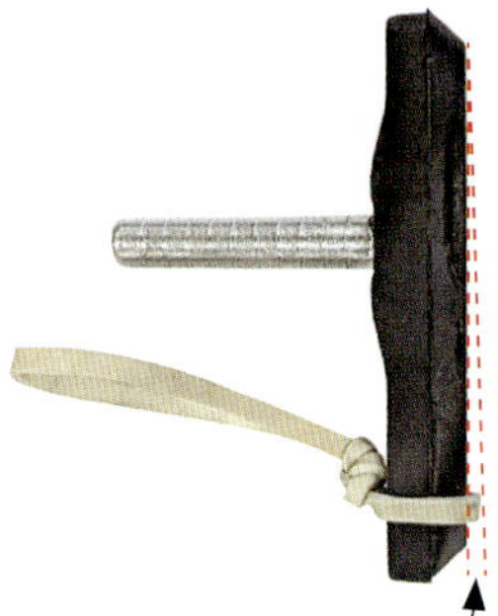

GAP CREATED BY RUBBER BAND

RIM BRAKES

Rim brake pads apply stopping force to the wheel rim and are the most common. Misaligned pads will wear at an angle (as shown) and require replacement sooner—they will also suffer in performance. In order to wear evenly, rim brake pads must be set at a slight angle to the rim. Joe uses a rubber band to help achieve this. He loops it around the leading end of the brake pad as he sets it in place. This creates just the right angle so that when the pad is engaged, it will flatten out against the rim and wear evenly.

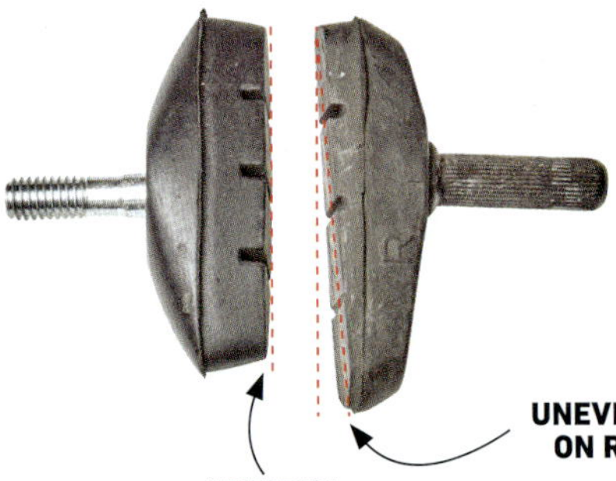

NEW RIM PAD

UNEVEN WEAR ON RIM PAD

WORN DISC BRAKE PAD

NEW DISC BRAKE PAD

DISC BRAKES

Disc brakes are becoming more popular and offer a step up in performance. Unlike rim brakes, they are located at the center of the wheel and are less affected by mud and water. But like all brake pads, they wear down. Replace them once they get to about 1 mm thick. Each type and manufacturer of disc brakes has a specific procedure for replacement. Consult your user's manual or talk to an expert at your local bike shop to learn what is required for yours.

JOE'S TOOLS

Here are Joe's essential tools for bike maintenance. You can buy them individually, but most are part of the Advanced Mechanic Tool Kit at parktool.com.

12" ADJUSTABLE WRENCH (included in kit)

METRIC HEX WRENCH SET (included in kit)

PHILLIPS AND FLAT-HEAD SCREWDRIVERS (included in kit)

FRAME PUMP For easy tire pressure adjustments on the go, get this pump online for about $25.

TAPE MEASURE (included in kit)

CABLE CUTTER (included in kit). This is used to cut brake and derailleur cables.

CONE WRENCHES (included in kit). These wrenches allow for easy adjustment of hub bearings.
ROTOR TRUING TOOL (included in kit). Joe uses this to straighten bent or damaged disc rotors.
PARK TOOL DUMMY HUB (included in kit). This holds the chain for cleaning when the wheel is not in the frame.
CHAIN-WEAR INDICATOR (included in kit). It helps you determine when your chain is due for replacement.
TIRE LEVERS (included in kit). These are used for tire removal and installation.
COMBO TOOL This chain whip (for removing cassettes) with 15 mm pedal wrench is included in the kit.
PARK CHAIN TOOL (included in kit). This tool is used to remove chain rivets on chains without a master link.
SHIMANO/SRAM CASSETTE LOCKRING REMOVER AND FREEWHEEL REMOVER Find it online for about $10.
PARK MASTER LINK PLIERS (included in kit). This lets you easily remove chain master links.
VALVE CORE TOOL (included in kit). This is used to remove or install tire valves.
SPOKE WRENCH (included in kit). This is used for truing wheels and adjusting spoke tension.
TORX AND HEX THREE-WAY WRENCHES (included in kit)
PATCH KIT This kit lets you fix a flat on the go. About $15 online.
CHAIN CLEANER (included in kit). This allows you to thoroughly clean the chain without removing it.
MULTITOOL Bicycle multitools can handle many basic fixes when you're on the road.

9 ALTERNATIVE USES FOR SAWDUST

Every fully stocked wood shop has a table saw. And under it you can usually find a pile of sawdust, even if the saw is used only occasionally. If a shop has a belt sander or band saw, there's probably another pile of finer sawdust under that. It seems even people without stationary tools have sawdust accumulation on their workbenches.

Sawdust recycling may not be the first thing on the minds of DIY woodworkers, but it's a priority in large industrial shops. Because it's the main ingredient in particleboard, medium-density fiberboard (MDF) and composite wood products, sawdust is a valuable resource to be carefully collected and sold. Small-scale woodworkers may not produce enough sawdust to sell, but that doesn't mean they should throw it away.

Of course, virgin sawdust from solid, untreated wood is the most valuable and versatile. It comes in handy in the shop, in the garden or around the house. Sawdust from engineered wood products such as plywood, oriented strand board (OSB), MDF, particleboard or pressure-treated wood is toxic and shouldn't be used around plants or animals, but that doesn't make it useless.

Next time you sweep the shop floor or dust off your workbench, save that pile of sawdust. Here are some of the things you can do with it.

1. PREVENT SLIPS IN THE WINTER

Sawdust is a safe, noncorrosive salt alternative you can spread on icy walkways or driveways to provide traction. If there is vegetation nearby, use only nontoxic sawdust from non-engineered wood to avoid poisoning plants. When winter is over, the sawdust will decompose readily in higher temperatures.

2. KILL WEEDS

If you have any black walnut, you've got the makings of an effective weed killer. Spread black walnut sawdust on cracks in your walkways or driveway, and let the natural oils from the wood soak in. It'll kill the weeds. Don't use black walnut sawdust anywhere else in your garden, however; it will do the same thing to your plants.

3. DISPOSE OF OLD PAINT

Can't figure out what to do with those old paint cans with only a little paint left in them? It's illegal to throw them in the trash as they are, but if you pour in enough sawdust—treated or untreated—it will soak up the paint and harden. You can then chip or scrape out the paint/sawdust mixture, safely throw it into the trash and reuse the can.

4. CONSIDER RECYCLING SAWDUST AS COMPOST

Sawdust has a high carbon-to-nitrogen ratio, making it a good substitute for dry leaves or whatever "brown" matter you toss in with your leafy greens to provide a good compost mixture.

Chemically treated sawdust shouldn't be put in a compost tumbler. But if you have a pile in the yard, you can leach the chemicals out of the mixture by dousing the pile with water a few times during the summer. Untreated sawdust is also an inexpensive, effective additive for composting toilets.

5. USE IT FOR YOUR PETS

Nontoxic sawdust from nonengineered wood is fragrant and absorbent. Use it in several ways to make life easier for your pets. Not all woods are safe for every animal, so check with your veterinarian.

- Substitute sawdust for cat litter. It isn't flushable, but you can bury used sawdust litter in the ground without hurting the environment.
- Spread it as a bed for your pet guinea pigs or rabbits. Use it for bedding for chicken coops and horse stalls.

6. STORE ROOT CROPS

In the days before refrigeration, people stored carrots, potatoes, parsnips and other root crops in cold soil. Untreated sawdust can make a lightweight substitute.

Spread a layer of sawdust on the bottom of a wooden or cardboard box. Arrange the vegetables so they aren't touching one another, then fill the box with sawdust and store it in a cool place.

7. CLEAN UP SPILLS AND DUST

Here's another great use for chemically treated sawdust: Spread it on the floor to soak up spills. Wood fibers effectively absorb oil or paint spills in the garage, and also soak up pet urine and vomit. If you add some baking soda, the mixture will also deodorize. To clean a dirty or dusty floor, moisten some sawdust, spread it, then sweep it up.

8. MAKE YOUR OWN FIRE-STARTING BRICKS

You could also compress nontoxic sawdust into bricks, then throw them into the wood stove or fireplace as kindling. Mix the sawdust with water, compress it into a brick mold and let the bricks dry in the sun.

Another way: Moisten the sawdust, let it stiffen overnight, then form it into balls and dry them in the sun. Add a little melted paraffin or candle wax and lint from the dryer to make the bricks or balls easier to light.

9. CREATE WOOD FILLER

Mix the fine dust that collects in the bag of an orbital or belt sander with shellac to make wood filler. Avoid the common mistake of adding white carpenter's glue—that will turn the mixture into gray mush. Using shellac allows the filler to take stain and polyurethane. Wood glue doesn't allow this, so the filler ends up a different color when finished.

One advantage of wood filler made from sawdust: It has wood's natural color. To preserve that, apply a clear resin-like lacquer or polyurethane. For a super-strong filler, go with epoxy.

CHRIS DEZIEL CONTRIBUTING WRITER

HOW LONG DOES STORED PAINT STAY USABLE?

BY SAM ROSENMAYER

Most homeowners have at least a few leftover cans of used paint. All paint eventually goes bad, and sometimes it can be difficult to tell if it's still good or needs to be pitched. We reached out to Tyler Wehr, a Sherwin-Williams paint store manager, to shed some light on the subject.

Wehr said that how we store paint makes the greatest impact on its life span. Do not store your paint in locations that dramatically fluctuate in temperature, such as a garage where it drops to freezing in the winter and becomes hot in the summer. Storing paint at room temperature (60 to 80 degrees) in a dark, dry space is the best option.

A simple way to check if your paint is still good is to stir it and check for sour odors that could indicate mold growth. Also make sure the paint has a smooth texture and is free of lumps.

The proper way to store a paint can after it's been opened is to clean around the lid and rim so you achieve an airtight seal. Dried-up paint in the can's recessed groove may allow the paint to be exposed to air. The exposed paint will dry up and sometimes harbor bacteria growth, making it unusable.

The storage container that you use for your leftover paint should not have a lot of airspace. For example, if you have little paint left, the original 1-gal. paint can wouldn't be appropriate. Some people prefer to use an airtight glass jar. Make sure to label your paint with the date, what you used it for and the paint color.

The estimated life span of properly stored water-based paints (latex, acrylic) and oil-based paints (enamel) is eight to 10 years.

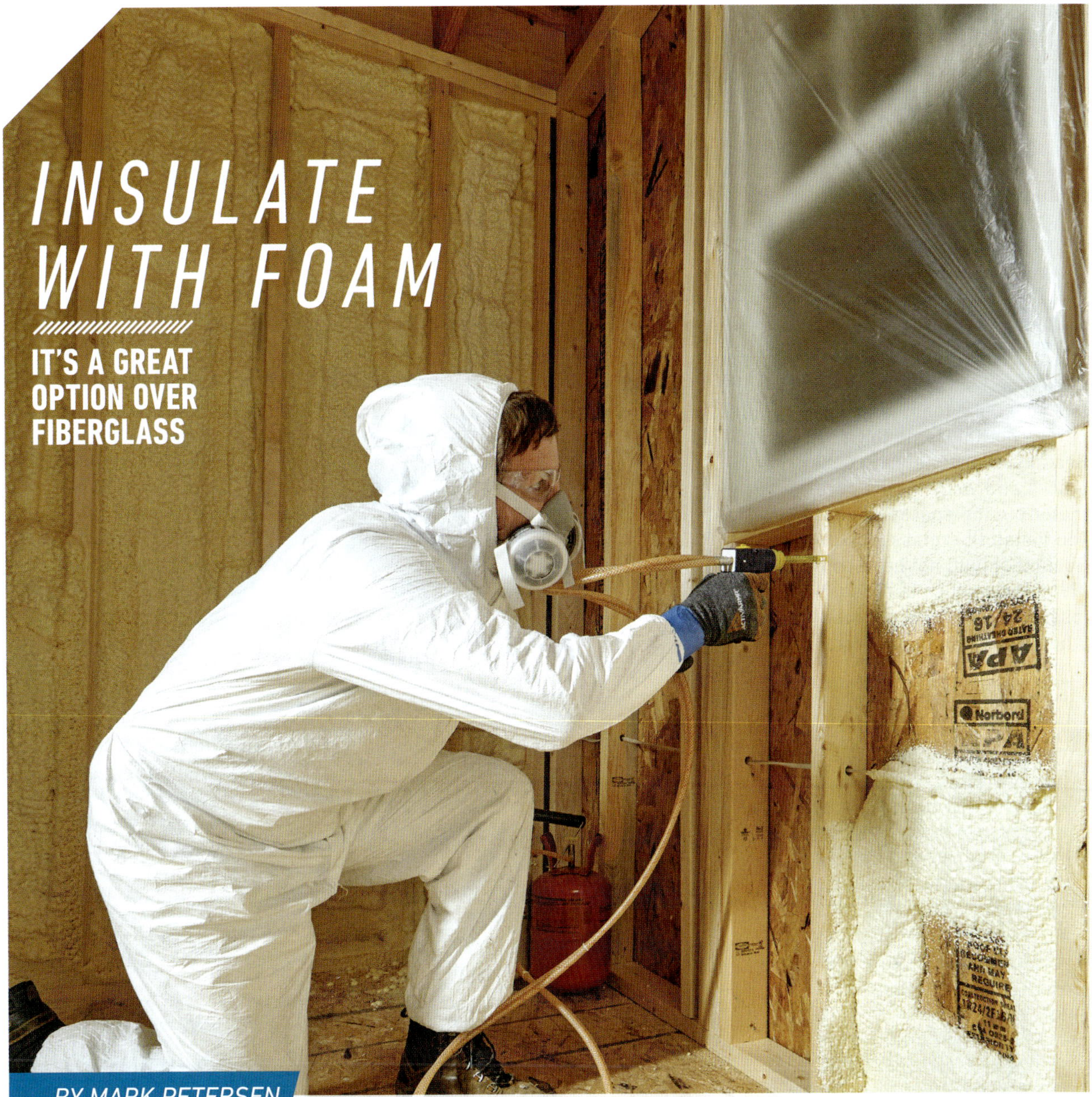

INSULATE WITH FOAM

IT'S A GREAT OPTION OVER FIBERGLASS

BY MARK PETERSEN

Closed-cell polyurethane spray foam has some outstanding qualities—it has a high R-value (see p. 265 for what this means), expands into hard-to-reach areas, and is resistant to water, mold and insects. It can even add structural support.

However, it is expensive, so we spoke with a couple of manufacturers and some pro insulators about where and when to use it, when to call in a pro with a truck-mounted unit and when a DIY kit is the best option. We also assembled some great installation tips to help you spray safely and get the best value for your investment.

We used the Froth-Pak Insulation 210 two-component, low-pressure kit. It has an R-value of 6 per inch.

MEET THE EXPERT

BOB TEMPLIN WORKS FOR CITYWIDE INSULATION IN SHAKOPEE, MINNESOTA. IN THE INSULATION BUSINESS FOR OVER 35 YEARS, HE STARTED LONG BEFORE SPRAY FOAM INSULATION BECAME MAINSTREAM.

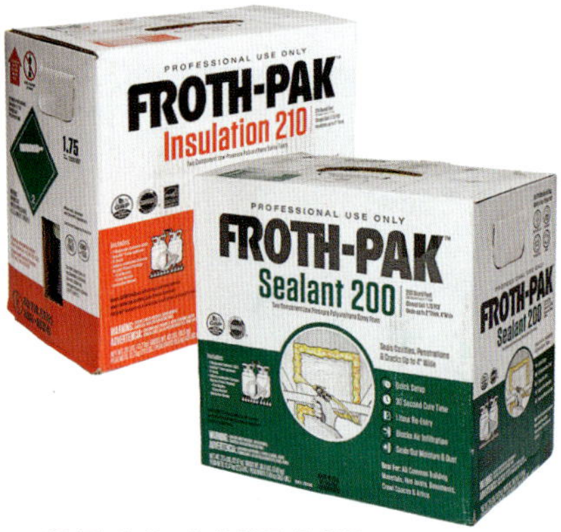

KNOW HOW FOAM IS MEASURED

Most two-part spray foam kits have a number assigned to them: 120, 200, 210, 600, etc. That number usually indicates how many board feet the foam will cover. So, a 200 kit will cover 200 sq. ft. at 1 in. thick.

SEALANT VS. INSULATION

Closed-cell spray foam sealant looks just like foam insulation, but it's not the same thing. Sealant is formulated to seal cracks and voids, or the perimeter of stud spaces before you install fiberglass insulation. Sealant should not be used to fill larger cavities because it loses its fire-retardant properties when applied in thick layers.

OPEN-CELL VS. CLOSED-CELL FOAM

Two kinds of spray foam are available: open and closed. Closed-cell foam costs more than open-cell, but the properties of closed-cell make it more popular. It's more resistant to water and can provide an air and vapor barrier (depending on the thickness). It also provides nearly double the R-value per inch over open-cell.

Open-cell insulation has one superior property over closed-cell foam—it works great as a sound barrier. It's often used under stairs and between walls and floors for that reason.

WEAR THE PROPER GEAR

Protect your lungs with a respirator and be sure to wear a full protective suit, chemical-resistant gloves and wraparound goggles. Tape your gloves to your sleeves and wear your junkiest shoes. Acetone will dissolve fresh foam right away, but the foam must be scraped off once it cures. If you don't want something covered with foam spatter, cover it or keep it away from the action.

TRUCK VS. KIT

Most insulating pros with truck-mounted units have a minimum charge that can be in the thousands, so buying a spray foam kit makes sense for small jobs and for when you need to insulate in stages over the course of a few days or weeks. Kits are also handy for insulating jobs in remote locations far from a spray foam company. You can buy kits that produce foam with the same R-value as the foam sprayed from truck-mounted units (just under R-7).

For large jobs, it makes sense to hire a pro because the cost will be considerably less than if you use a kit yourself. You'll also want to call in a pro if the weather is cold. Truck-mounted units have built-in heaters, which can spray foam at close to freezing temperatures. Kits require ambient and surface temps to be 65 degrees.

Keep in mind that a house will have to be vacated for up to 24 hours if a truck is called in, but many of the kit products allow you to inhabit the house immediately after spraying.

MAKE A PLAN BEFORE YOU PULL THE TRIGGER

Long before you don your safety gear, plan your work: (1) Clear the room of everything that could get in the way. (2) Mask everything else. (3) Decide which areas you'll spray first. (4) Place ladders or step stools where you will need them. (5) Set up a fan or two to vent the fumes outdoors.

Before you start, shake the cans to mix the contents and then shake them every few minutes after that. You'll have to install a new tip every time you stop spraying for more than 30 seconds—the foam sets inside the nozzle and clogs it. Spray foam kits come with extra tips, but it's a good idea to purchase more.

MASK WINDOWS AND DOORS

Use a hammer tacker to staple plastic to the framing around windows and door frames. Don't worry about covering gaps between the windows and the framing because you'll want to fill those with low-expanding canned foam specifically designed for windows. Cover all the switch and outlet boxes with masking tape so they don't fill with foam.

PRO TIP: When you insulate exterior walls with foam, you don't need to use gasketed electrical boxes as you would if you were insulating with fiberglass—the foam will air-seal around the boxes.

CONSIDER SMALLER KITS

Three 200 kits will cost more than one 600 kit, but the 600 kit will have larger tanks that require two hands to be moved around—not easy to do if you're working alone!

CHARGE THE LINE

Before installing the first tip/mixing nozzle, point the gun into a garbage bag or empty box. Pull the trigger until both chemicals are flowing evenly.

LUBE THE GUN WITH EVERY TIP CHANGE

The end of the gun needs to be lubricated before the first tip is installed and again before the tanks are stored after use. Many pros prefer to lube the tip of the gun every time they install a new tip. Kits will come with petroleum jelly lubricant. Always follow the manufacturer's instructions on operation, tip changes, storage and disposal.

PICTURE-FRAME FIRST

Before filling the wall cavity, spray the perimeter with a ½-in. layer, which will expand to a 1-in. layer. These layers are called lifts. This will ensure that the foam penetrates any voids where the studs meet the sheathing and reduce the risk of bulging. If foam is sprayed into a large gap between the stud and the sheathing and then immediately covered by a thick layer, the pressure of the expanding foam can cause sheathing that isn't securely fastened to bulge out. Wait a few minutes after picture-framing the cavity before you go back and lay down the first layer in the center of the wall.

NEVER SPRAY A WET SURFACE

Never spray foam on a surface with a moisture level of more than 20%—the foam won't stick. If you're patching a wall that recently sustained water damage or was recently assembled with new wet lumber, test the moisture level before you spray. You can get a basic moisture meter at some home centers or online for less than $40.

SPRAY THE RIM AND THE BOTTOM PLATE

A foam sill sealer is needed between the bottom plate and the concrete foundation wall. Voids in the wood and concrete or tears in the sill sealer can create gaps where air and insects can penetrate. While you're sealing the rim board, cover the bottom plate and top off the concrete as well. There's no need to picture-frame the joist spaces before filling them, but don't spray a lift more than 2 in. thick.

SPRAY 2-IN. LIFTS AND WAIT

The two most common spray foam installation mistakes are failing to wait for lifts to cure and spraying lifts that are too thick. Always wait a few minutes before spraying additional lifts, and never spray a lift more than 2 in. thick. The foam needs time to cure before being covered with another lift. Uncured foam results in reduced R-values. The allowable thickness of lifts varies by manufacturer, so do your homework.

DON'T LEAVE FOAM INSULATION EXPOSED IN LIVING AREAS

To comply with building codes, spray foam insulation cannot be left exposed in living areas. It needs to be protected by a thermal barrier such as drywall. Rim joist cavities are one exception. They can be sprayed with foam and left exposed if the foam is less than 2 in. with a Class A fire rating.

Foam can be left exposed in nonliving areas such as attics and crawl spaces that are not used for storage, but the foam must either have a Class A rating or be covered by an ignition barrier such as drywall, mineral fiber insulation or a special spray-on coating. Fire and smoke specs differ among manufacturers, so always consult your local building official to confirm which foam you can use and where.

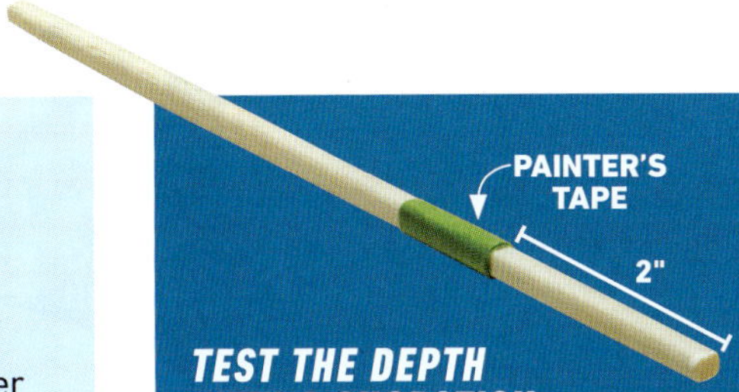

TEST THE DEPTH WITH A CHOPSTICK

It's important to know how thick the foam is, but it can be difficult to judge, especially in rim joist spaces. You could buy a fancy pin depth gauge (not shown), or you could wrap a piece of tape around a chopstick at your desired depth and use it for testing.

START AND STOP AT CABLES AND PIPES

Don't blast over pipes and cables on the first lift. Instead, shoot some foam underneath them at the same time you're picture-framing the stud cavities. This will ensure that the foam doesn't wrap over the cables and leave an uninsulated void behind the pipes or cables.

SCRAPE OVERSPRAY WITH A CURRY COMB

Run a straightedge along the outside of the studs and scrape down any high spots with a curry comb. Remove large chunks of foam with a handsaw. Curry combs are designed to groom horses and are available online or at farm supply stores for less than $20.

COMBINE FOAM WITH FIBERGLASS

Fiberglass insulation can be used in conjunction with spray foam. The process is called "flash and batt." Just picture-frame the wall cavities and lay down one lift. Then fill the rest of the cavity with fiberglass insulation. This is a popular way to save money but still takes advantage of the outstanding air-sealing properties of closed-cell foam.

For 2x4 stud walls, the fiberglass insulation will have to be split to fit. In this case, we sprayed just under 2 in. of foam (R-10.8) and split 3½-in. R-13 batts in half (R-6.5) to achieve an R-17.3 insulation value. Never cram oversize batts into a wall cavity because fiberglass insulation loses R-value when it's compressed.

CORK
SHEEP'S WOOL
DENIM
MINERAL WOOL

BETTER HOME INSULATION

IMPROVE THE ENERGY EFFICIENCY OF YOUR HOME—AND PROTECT THE ENVIRONMENT TOO

BY SAMUEL ROSENMAYER

Most homeowners know insulation affects a house's energy efficiency and sound barriers, but insulation also affects our environment and health. You may want to evaluate your insulation if your home doesn't maintain temperatures well or feels drafty, if sounds are amplified or if your energy bill is extremely high. A home that isn't well insulated will release more greenhouse gases because the HVAC system will work much harder to keep the house at desired temperatures.

To learn about the best insulation options, we talked with Tony Leiner, who is the owner of Whole House Insulation Inc. in Milwaukee, Wisconsin, and has been in the industry for over 40 years. His advice to homeowners: "Do your homework on different insulations, and know what chemicals you're exposing yourself and others to."

The good news is that we have come a long way with insulation. We are not stuck with products that are packed with toxic and carcinogenic fumes. Without compromising efficiency, here are some sustainable insulation options that are safe and good for the environment, and do an exceptional job of insulating.

Your insulation needs depend on the climate you live in and the R-value insulation levels required by local building codes.

***R-value** refers to the resistance (hence the "R") of heat transfer from hot air to cold air, or how well an insulation material resists this heat transfer. The higher the number, the more thermal-resistant the material is and the more effectively it insulates.*

CELLULOSE INSULATION

A green product derived from recycled materials, cellulose insulation comes in a loose-fill or blow-in form. It is treated with boric acid to repel mold and pests, is safer to install than fiberglass because it doesn't contain carcinogens or gases, and is noncombustible. Cellulose provides a good sound barrier, and it costs about the same as fiberglass. Cellulose is Leiner's preference. "This insulation provides thermal protection, and our customers are happy with the product," he says. "New construction is beginning to use cellulose insulation because it is better for the environment and is the best product to install." For every inch of thickness of cellulose insulation, there is an R-value of 3.5.

MINERAL WOOL INSULATION

Also known by the brand name Rockwool, mineral wool insulation is manufactured by melting basalt rock with slag—a byproduct of the copper and steel industry—and spinning the resulting material into fibers. The fibers are then woven into batts, which are about the same size as fiberglass batts, but denser.

Mineral wool also repels water, so mold can't grow on these batts. The batts' extra bulk also provides better soundproofing. Mineral wool batts are about 25% more expensive than fiberglass, however. Mineral wool has an R-value of 4 per inch.

DENIM INSULATION

Did you ever think your old jeans could someday become insulation for someone's home? Denim insulation, also known as UltraTouch Insulation, is composed of 80% recycled denim jeans. It's flame retardant and treated with boric acid, which helps prevent bacteria growth and repels bugs.

Denim has properties that can reduce the transfer of heat, which makes it a good barrier and a competitor of traditional fiberglass insulation. You can purchase denim insulation in batts so it is very easy to install in walls, attic floors and ceilings. This has a good R-value of 3.5 per inch, but the downside is that this tends to be 10% more expensive than fiberglass insulation.

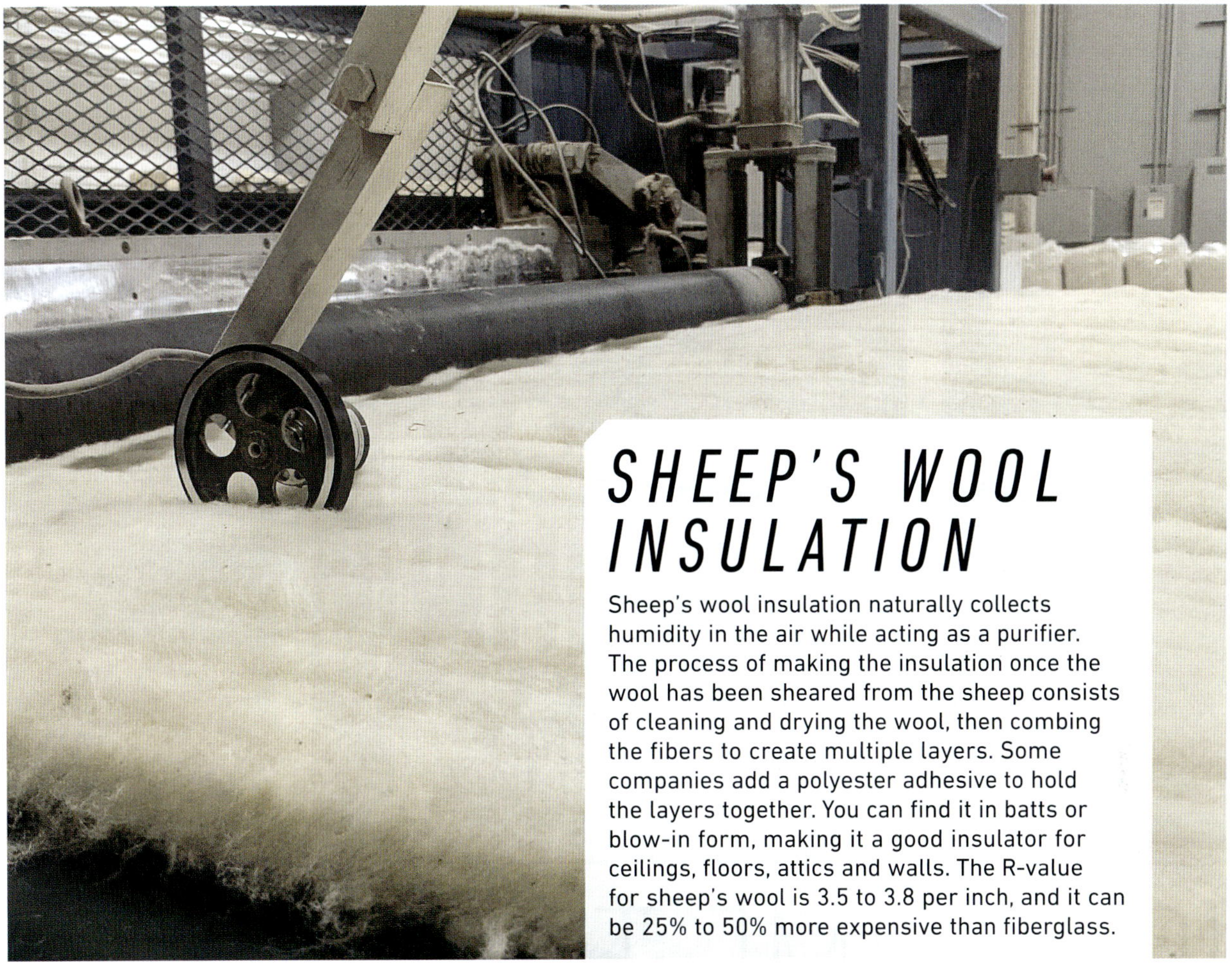

SHEEP'S WOOL INSULATION

Sheep's wool insulation naturally collects humidity in the air while acting as a purifier. The process of making the insulation once the wool has been sheared from the sheep consists of cleaning and drying the wool, then combing the fibers to create multiple layers. Some companies add a polyester adhesive to hold the layers together. You can find it in batts or blow-in form, making it a good insulator for ceilings, floors, attics and walls. The R-value for sheep's wool is 3.5 to 3.8 per inch, and it can be 25% to 50% more expensive than fiberglass.

CORK INSULATION

Cork is derived from the external bark on a specific type of oak tree from the Mediterranean and North African region. Cork is unique in that it regenerates itself after it has been harvested. Cork naturally has antifungal, fire-resistant and antimicrobial properties, so additional chemicals aren't needed for it to be an effective insulator in homes.

Cork insulation comes in the form of corkboards and can be used for roof or wall insulation. It has an R-value of 3.6 to 4.2 per inch and is one of the most sustainable insulations, but it can be expensive. Depending on the thickness of the corkboard, it will cost about $4 to $12 per square foot, which is significantly more than the 40¢ to $2 per square foot for fiberglass.

MEET THE EXPERT

TONY LEINER IS THE OWNER OF WHOLE HOUSE INSULATION INC.

BY MIKE BERNER

IS IT TIME TO UPDATE YOUR WIRING?

EXPERT RECOMMENDS UPGRADES FOR COMFORT, CONVENIENCE AND SAFETY

If you live in a house that is 20 years old or older, its electrical system likely could use an update. Even as wireless technology rapidly advances, we will still need safe and reliable wiring systems in our homes for the foreseeable future to supply power for appliances, fixtures, heating, cooling and much more. If the wiring in your home is outdated, it could be time to do some rewiring—at least in certain areas. An upgrade will be a game changer, especially if you've been struggling with insufficient power, fuses or, worse yet, knob-and-tube wiring.

MEET THE EXPERT

JOHN WILLIAMSON IS A LICENSED MASTER ELECTRICIAN & RETIRED MINNESOTA CHIEF ELECTRICAL INSPECTOR.

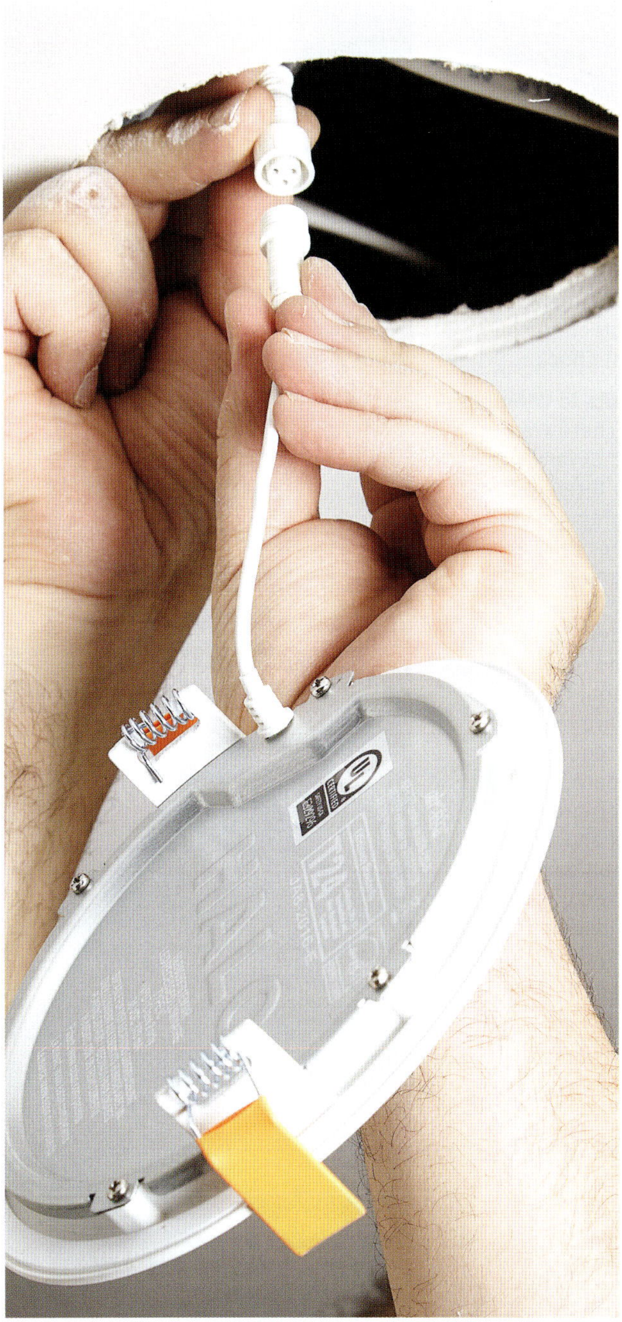

UPDATES FOR COMFORT AND CONVENIENCE

Not all wiring updates require a complete do-over. If your home has a more modern system with breakers that were installed in the '90s or later, there are updates that will simply make day-to-day living better.

■ **Upgrade or add lighting, inside and out.** The lighting in older homes is sparse and often not where you need it. Today, we recognize that good lighting in a home is important for health and safety. Typical updates are to add overhead can lights where there were none or convert existing can lights to low-voltage, longer-lasting LED replacements. Updating your outside fixtures with worn finishes or adding a motion-sensing flood light for safety are good ideas.

■ **Add receptacle outlets to meet the current electrical code.** Older homes simply don't have enough outlets. Homeowners often resort to extension cords and power strips to compensate, which aren't a substitute for permanent wiring and can be hazards if used improperly.

■ **Install ceiling fans in bedrooms and/or living spaces.** Besides being popular and stylish, they can be adjusted to spin in both directions to help with indoor air quality. In winter, they can be set to recirculate warm air that rises to the ceiling. In summer, of course, you have to readjust them so the air blows downward to provide a cooling effect.

■ **Reconfigure switches to operate overhead lights.** It was common for electricians to install switches to one-half of an outlet, allowing the homeowner to turn on lamps when entering a room. To reconfigure the switches to power the ceiling lights, the switched outlets need to be replaced and new wiring installed.

COMPLETE OVERHAULS

A full restart of your electrical system would be necessary for only a few reasons, and they all come down to a home that has not been maintained properly or has been neglected.

■ **Replace antiquated knob-and-tube wiring.** At this point, it's rare. Insurance companies haven't been insuring homes with knob-and-tube for quite some time.

■ **Have a plan for aluminum wiring.** In the 1970s and '80s, some electricians used aluminum wire instead of copper. This wiring can begin to corrode over time and cause loose connections, leading to higher resistance and heat that can increase the risk of fire. Aluminum wire doesn't need to be replaced. Contractors can use several approved devices, connectors and methods to make aluminum connections safe without rewiring.

■ **Be aware that fire, flood and rodents can certainly ruin an electrical system.** Following a fire or flood, a contractor will assess the situation and replace damaged components. If a rodent infestation occurs, it may not be as obvious. Squirrels, rats, mice, raccoons and other rodents can chew through wires, causing loose connections and shorts, increasing the risk of fire.

IMPROVEMENTS FOR SAFETY

These safety updates can be large or small projects. They range from a DIY project that can be done in under an hour to a major overhaul that can take a contractor weeks to complete.

■ **Upgrade the service panel.** Older homes may have only 30- or 60-ampere service—certainly not enough capacity to supply all appliances, equipment and conveniences in a modern home. The service panels in houses through the 1940s may use fuses, which means you can't take advantage of the latest GFCI and AFCI circuit breaker technologies for maximum safety. If your home doesn't have at least a 100-ampere service, it should be upgraded.

■ **Replace any two-prong receptacle outlets with properly grounded three-prong receptacle outlets.** This will probably mean replacing boxes in the wall as well. Most older boxes are likely too small for modern three-prong duplex receptacle outlets.

■ **Change to tamper-resistant receptacles.** Tamper-resistant outlets have become mandatory in new construction and remodels. They are designed to keep out foreign objects, protecting children from electrical shock.

■ **Add branch circuits to comply with today's code.** There was a time when the old 60-ampere fuse panel had only three to five general-purpose lighting and receptacle circuits for the entire house, and maybe one or two 240-volt circuits for an electric range or water heater. But today's homes typically need much more than that. The National Electrical Code outlines the bare minimum rules only. Today it requires at least two 20-ampere small-appliance circuits for kitchen counter receptacles and at least one 20-ampere circuit each for laundry, bathroom and garage receptacles. All are dedicated circuits too, meaning they can't be used for lighting or additional outlets. So you'll likely also need more general-purpose circuits.

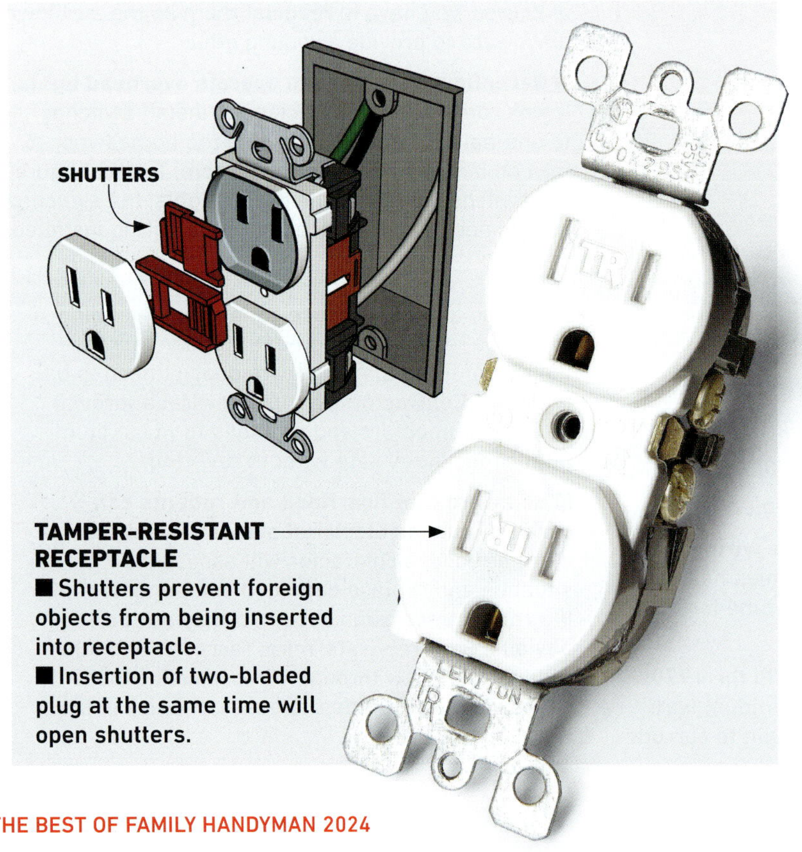

ADDITIONAL WARNING SIGNS

Not all electrical problems are immediately noticeable. If your lights and outlets work, everything should be in good shape. But if you experience any of these warning signs, you might have a problem. Call an electrician to diagnose, fix or update your system.

■ Circuit breakers tripping frequently: This might signal an overloaded circuit.

■ No GFCI outlets: GFCI receptacles are required to protect circuits near water sources, such as those in your kitchen, bathrooms and laundry room.

■ A tingling sensation or vibration when touching an outlet, appliance or switch.

■ Outlets that are discolored or charred.

■ Dimming lights or flickering lights.

If you are worried you might need some major updates to your electrical system, we advise hiring an electrician. A large rewiring project in an existing home is not a DIY project unless you have advanced or professional-level experience and knowledge, not to mention an enormous amount of spare time.

GREAT GOOFS®

LAUGHS AND LESSONS FROM OUR READERS

ARE YOU SMARTER THAN A SECOND GRADE KID?

Our neighbors were moving and offered to sell me their snowblower at an attractive price. My neighbor admitted that the engine hadn't been started in a couple of years, but I was confident I could make it run. Armed with starting fluid and fresh gasoline, I went at it, but an hour later I was completely exhausted. I had pulled on the rope countless times, sprayed starting fluid into the carburetor and checked the spark plug, but I hadn't been able to fire up the engine.

As I sat trying to catch my breath, my 7-year-old son, Seth, walked in to see what was going on. I explained the situation as best as I could (without using my "adult" words). He calmly reached over, turned the key and said, "Try it now, Dad." It started on the next pull.

CHRIS HAROLDSON

DUMPSTER DIVING

During a major remodel, I hauled a pickup load of rotted boards to the landfill. The dumping area had huge trash containers, each about the size of a railroad boxcar, set down in a pit.

I backed up to a container that was empty except for a pile of cardboard. I thought the boards would slide off the pickup easily since they were wet and slippery, but they didn't budge. So I gave a mighty pull—they all came loose, and I went flying over backward into the trash along with them! I wasn't hurt, but I was embarrassed. I stacked up cardboard to help me climb out before anybody recognized me.

JOSEPH KEHOE